Principle of Petri Nets

Chongyi Yuan

Principle of Petri Nets

Springer

Chongyi Yuan
Peking University
Beijing, China

ISBN 978-981-97-7335-0 ISBN 978-981-97-7336-7 (eBook)
https://doi.org/10.1007/978-981-97-7336-7

Computer Science
Theory of Computation

Editorial Contact: Kamesh Senthilkumar

This Springer imprint is published by the registered company Springer Nature Singapore Pte Ltd.
The registered company address is: 152 Beach Road, #21-01/04 Gateway East, Singapore 189721, Singapore

In memorial of Prof. Carl Adam Petri; it will be his 100 years' birthday in 2026.

Preface

I had four books on Petri nets published before this writing. All four books were in Chinese.

One book would be sufficient, why four?

The first book, *Petri Nets*, was published by Southeast University Press in the year 1989. Petri nets were new in China at that time and I had just returned from visiting Petri's institute in Bonn. It was Prof. Gu Guanqun, president of Southeast University, who invited me to give a talk on Petri nets in his lab, and then there was the first book.

The second book, *Principles of Petri Nets*, was published by Publishing House of Electronics Industry in 1998. A national plan to publish a set of textbooks on computer science and technology was just in progress. It was Prof. Yang Wenlong who recommended me. There was the second book.

The first book contains definitions of basic concepts and analysis methods. The second book is just an enrichment of the first one with examples given at my classes on Petri nets for master students at School of Computer Science and Technology, Peking University.

Seven years later in 2005, after teaching practice, the set of textbooks on computer science and technology had its second version. There was the third book *Principles and Applications of Petri Nets*. This book puts its emphasis on applications. A solution to the N-lift problem was proposed and the three-layer model of business process management made a big difference from the most widely accepted BPM model at that time, i.e., WF-net by Prof. Aalst from Holland. With local determination principle, the complexity of N-lift problem was reduced from (M, N,2) to (1,1,1), i.e., M-floor, N-lift, and up-and-down directions to one floor, one lift and one direction. The three-layer model distinguishes management from business itself and distinguishes process model for all cases from process model for individual cases.

A BPM model for individual cases requires, in addition to tokens for control flow, variables for message passing. Unfortunately, places in Petri nets are not qualified as a complete integer type, let along other data types. The only operations on places are plus and minus on positive integers.

C-net and C-net systems were proposed to amend the lack of variables in Petri nets. Without C-net systems, the business process model for individual cases, called case semantics, would not be possible. Different values of the same variable(s) carry different information to require different traveling routes.

In the year 2010, beloved Carl Adam Petri left us. To pay my last respect to him, I started the writing of the fourth book, *Petri Nets Application*. "Without application, there is no reason for nets to exist" was his words in my heart. For personal reasons, the writing lasted a long time, and the book was published in 2013.

My sincere thanks to all friends mentioned above. In addition, two of my students, Yan Xiongliang and Shen Xiaoming had helped me a lot to format my draft. Thanks to them. Mr. Zhang Hang, a master student at that time, had done all figures in the book *Principle of Petri Nets*, from which many figures in this book are taken. Thanks to him.

Thanks to Mr. Zhu Wei and thanks to Springer, it is their kind help, I had this chance to write this book on Petri nets in English. Thanks to Yan Xiongliang for his help. It was him who made my draft comply with the requirement of Springer. I must admit that tiny detailed revision is annoying in deed.

This book contains my contributions to Petri nets. This is a good opportunity for me to listen to criticisms from foreign friends.

Beijing, China Yuan Chongyi

Contents

Chapter 1
Introduction

Abstract As a member in the family of system madels, Petri nets is different from all others. This chapter tells what makes Petri nets different.

Prof. Carl Adam Petri had left us for 15 years. His smile and his words are still vivid in my mind. He talked about fishing with his hand. A hand worked like a net.

Petri nets, as a graphical system model, have been widely used for long. It is a system model suitable for asynchronous concurrent systems. It consists of two parts: special net theory and general net theory. Special net theory defines various systems in a hierarchy with net as their shared structure, while general net theory introduces natural laws explored by net systems.

Prof. Carl Adam Petri used to say that without general net theory, there is no need to have special net theory, and without application, there is no need to have nets ("nets" is Prof. Petri's word for Petri nets). In other words, nets is system + theory + application. This book tries to give readers a 3-in-1 overall picture of nets.

Different from internet, Petri net is a system model, supported by theory, for system design and system analysis. More importantly, a net system is comparable to a blueprint: A net on paper can be implemented in reality (see attachment: Prof. Petri's preface *Status Report on net Theory* for my Chinese book on nets in 1989).

The author had spent almost 4 years visiting the institute in Bonn, Fed. Rep. Germany at that time, of which Prof. Petri was the director. For many work-days in those years, from 10.00 a.m. to 15.00 p.m. (by the way, Prof. Petri used to take no lunch) I listened to him in his office, talking about his ideas. What listed in Part 1 is my understanding of his words. Readers may skip it for the first reading at your own will.

In what follows, "Nets" (instead of nets) is used as synonym of Petri nets.

C. Yuan, *Principle of Petri Nets*, https://doi.org/10.1007/978-981-97-7336-7_1

1.1 What Makes Nets Special

Some concepts on Nets in the literature were invented just for paper writings. They appear only in research papers and/or books. What listed below may help to figure out such concepts.

1. Observation

   Objective observation is the basis for Nets. By "objective" we mean that the observed changes (causes and effects) must be independent of the observer, the time and place to observe and any other factors in relation. Besides, the observation concerns of neither physics nor chemistry, i.e., what Nets care is not the academic reasons behind changes. Instead, observable changes, including quantities and properties, are the focus of Nets. Such a change is called a transition.
2. Global state and local determination

   There exists a changing global state for every system that is often used, by many, as a means for system analysis and system control. But, existence is one thing and being observable is another. When system size is great enough, it becomes impossible to observe the instant global state. For example, there is no way to count the world human population, even if the population is frozen at a given time point. Thus, Nets do not make use of global state for system analysis or system control. In Nets, every transition has its own extension that would decide whether it is enabled to occur, and if it occurs, the effect would be limited within this extension. The existense of extension is a natrual law, i.e. the local determination law, as given by the lemma below. It is of course possible that the extension of a single change contains too many elements to observe. Such changes are not considered as transitions, i.e., not suitable for Nets to describe. For example, the broken of glass, from a tea cup into pieces, is not a transition.

   Lemma: There exists an extension for every transition that decides whether it may occur and what is the exact effect if it occurs.
3. Time and global time

   Time appears as real numbers in some disciplines of sciences, and as such, it is not only global, full ordered, but also continuous, evenly distributed, etc. Petri Nets do not consider to have such a pure theoretical concept of time for application.

   Global time by clock, as a concept in applications, is often used for system control. For example, time-tables for trains and flights are based on clock.

   Though global time by clock is already well accepted in daily life, and its inaccuracy is also well tolerated, but, global time is just a virtual existence. TV programs may tell you a "standard time" by astronomical clock, but the voice would be heard only when it reaches you, i.e., some seconds (milliseconds?) later. Furthermore, you may hear the same voice more than once if you switch, from station to station, quick enough. So, astronomical clock does not yield an accurate time. Very often is the case that different clocks may tell different time a bit later after time calibration.

Real "global" time exists only for systems in which a single timer is shared. Such a time is better called system time, rather than global time. In case a timer has to be used, users must be aware that there is nothing to be precisely punctual. A physical timer may stop running, and its error may accumulate to demand correction. Besides, time is not a decisive factor: trains and flights may be delayed or even canceled for various reasons. School classes are scheduled by minutes, but "on time" is only a good wish.

Petri Nets do not take global time as a consisting feature on the one hand, and on the other hand, they allow a real timer (clock, watch, or any other means for timing) to appear in a net application.

Instead of time, Nets make use of casual dependence to keep trace of happenings. Casual dependence is of branching nature. When a system is turned on, every object has its own route to travel. Things on one route are naturally ordered while things on different routes are concurrent. In case two things meet with each other, then they are "at the same time" at this crossing point.

The concepts of time/timed Petri Nets exist in the literature, in which time plays a decisive role. As said above, time could not be a decisive factor. So, time/timed Petri Nets are not included in this book.

4. Global control

   Global control relies on global states or global time, and as thus it is not a consisting feature of Nets. The concept of logic time was proposed for global control. But, such a never-stop and error-free logic time exists only in research papers.

5. Probability

   The concept of probability tells regularity displayed in repetitive activities. As such, it is not a means to predict what to occur next, or whether something is to occur. Probability once was used by CCTV for rain forecast as an improvement, but such "improved" forecast didn't last long.

   To say "the rain probability for tomorrow is 0.7" is the same as to say "for 100 days like tomorrow, there would be 70 rain days." It said a lot, but not even one word about rain or not tomorrow.

   Probability belongs to statistics, does not belong to Nets.

6. Continuity and discrete

   The concept of continuity in mathematics is always connected to real numbers.

   Our body consists of cells. No matter how great the number of cells is, it is finite. Does that mean our body is not continuous?

   A rabbit tries to catch a turtle that is x_0 meters ahead. The turtle is x_1 meters ahead when the rabbit completes x_0 meters, the turtle is x_2 meters ahead when the rabbit completes x_1 meters, and so on and so forth. Mathematics concludes that the rabbit will catch the turtle since $x_0 + x_1 + x_2 + \cdots$ is a convergence sequence, i.e., $\sum_{i=0}^{\infty} x_i < \infty$. Isn't it nice? But the reality is, the rabbit will catch the turtle when x_i is smaller than the jump distance of the rabbit.

Both the body cells and the rabbit and turtle story tells a truth that pure math is sometimes just approximation of reality.

Net topology will define the concept of continuity so that a finite set becomes a continuous space, and a mapping between two finite Nets becomes continuous. The merit of a continuous mapping will be introduced in the chapter on net topology.

7. Measurement

   A ruler is for measuring the length (or height) of something. A mark on a ruler is just a point, occupying no length. Different observer may read a ruler differently for the same object, since, often is the case that no mark on the ruler matches the object length precisely. Instead of a ruler, Nets take a "rope" (to be defined) as measuring means. Intuitively, a rope is twisted from more than one line. A rope uses a tiny range as a "mark" in the way that boundary point between two neighboring ranges on this line is covered by a tiny range on that line, so that a length falls into one unique range to give a unique measure.

8. Infinity

   Nets respect the fact that quantities of all resources in reality are finite while a net is allowed to have infinitely many nodes. For example, the alternating of four seasons has neither a start, nor an end. As such, the net to record alternating occurrences of seasons is infinite in size. A net may have its element set with cardinality $\aleph_0$ (the number of integers), or even $\aleph$ (the number of real numbers).

9. Concurrency and sequence

   These two concepts refer to two transitions and one state in a system. Two transitions may be found being concurrent or being ordered at a given system state. Two transitions are concurrent at a state if both of them are enabled at that state and their occurrences do not interfere with each other. Two transitions are ordered at a state if they have to occur one after another. Concurrent transitions used to be understood and even defined as "to occur at the same time." This is not a correct understanding. Concurrent transitions may be observed to occur at the same time this moment, but may also be observed to occur one after another some other time. Besides, at the same time by clock is transitive while concurrency is not. This in-transitivity fact will be explained later in this book.

10. Stochastic Petri Nets

    Stochastic Petri Nets might be useful in reality, and it has already been included in Terminology of Computer Science and Technology. The author understand this as a trade-off: a way is better than no way. But, stochastic Petri Nets do not belong to Petri Nets since time is a decisive factor for it while the concept of time does not belong to Petri Nets.

    From theory to practice, trade-off seems unavoidable. We cannot live without a timer on the one hand, and on the other hand, when time is up, the expected may disappoint you. This is similar to a computer. A computer has become a must for our work and in our daily life ever since long. But, where there is a computer, there may exist a software bug. We have to live with it.

Part I
Special Net Theory: System Hierarchy

This part defines the hierarchy of net systems and introduces their properties and analysis methods. Chapter 2 presents formal definitions of concepts shared by net systems to prepare for detailed presentations in separate chapters that follow.

Chapter 2
Concepts Shared by Net Systems

Abstract A net consists of three kinds of elements,namely transitions, places and arrows. resources are represented with tokens that reside in places to give a resourse distruibusion on net. These concepts are shared by all net systems.

2.1 Net

2.1.1 What Is Around Us: Nets

There are two kinds of elements around us, static elements and dynamic elements. These elements relate with each other to form invisible nets and to make our surroundings alive. Petri nets are an abstraction of reality in which static elements are called tokens and dynamic elements are called transitions. Tokens are classified according to the roles they play and reside in places they belong to. Here "place" is a term in Nets, irrelevant to geographic position. Transitions and places are connected by arrows along which tokens flow from place to place when a transition fires (occurs). Thus, arrows are called a flow relation. Tokens may be consumed (to vanish) or produced (to appear) in the course of transition firings.

It must be made clear that a transition in Nets is of an atomic nature. It either occurs completely or does not occur at all. In other words, once it starts, it would not be interrupted, unless the system crashes.

Before approaching to formal definition, let's have an example first. Figure 2.1 below is a graphically presented directed net N_1 and a net system with N_1 as its underlying structure.

The transition set of N_1 is $T(N_1)$, or simply T,

$$T = \{t_1, t_2, t_3, t_4, t_5\}$$

The place set of N_1 is $S(N_1)$, or simply S,

C. Yuan, *Principle of Petri Nets*, https://doi.org/10.1007/978-981-97-7336-7_2

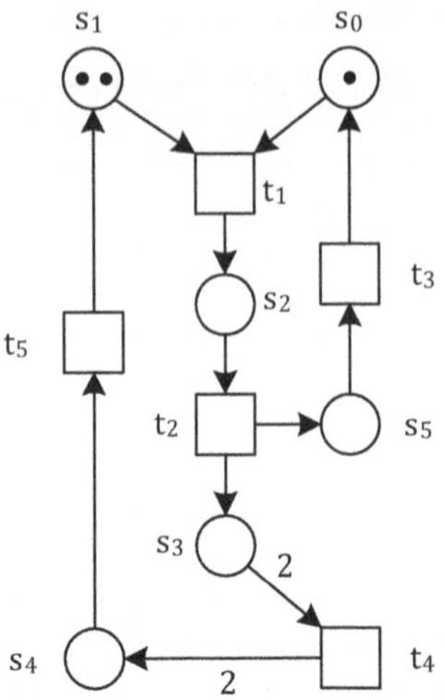

Fig. 2.1 A system and its underlying directed net N_1

$$S = \{s_0, s_1, s_2, s_3, s_4, s_5\}$$

The flow relation $F(N_1)$ is the set of arrows, or simply F,

$$F = \Big\{(s_0, t_1), (s_1, t_1), (t_1, s_2), (s_2, t_2), (t_2, s_3), (t_2, s_5), (s_5, t_3), (t_3, s_0), (s_3, t_4),$$
$$(t_4, s_4), (s_4, t_5), (t_5, s_1)\Big\}.$$

$(S, T; F)$ is called a directed net since tokens must flow along arrows in F. An arrow is also called an arc.

As indicated by the above example, directed net is a triple constructed from a place set and a transition set. The semicolon before F indicates that F is defined from S and T.

Every place s_i in S has a capacity to hold a certain number of tokens. The function to map a place to its capacity is called capacity function and denoted with K, $K: S \to I$ where $I = \{1, 2, \ldots\}$ is the set of non-zero positive integers. In case the capacity $K(s_i)$ allows it to receive tokens freely, then the capacity of s_i is ω (infinite), i.e., $K(s_i) = \omega$. For directed net N_1 in Fig. 2.1, capacities of all places are ω, and ω is the default value for capacity function. All arc weights (numbers of tokens to be consumed or produced by transition firings) are 1 by default, except $w(s_3, t_4) = w(t_4, s_4) = 2$. $W: F \to I$ is the weight function on F.

The initial token distribution M_0 on S is given by $M_0(s_0) = 1$, $M_0(s_1) = 2$, and $M_0(s_i) = 0$ for all places s_i other than s_0, s_1.

Note that a token distribution is called a marking on S. A marking is a global state, based on which transition rules (dynamics of a net system) will be defined.

What are the definitions based on global states? Does this contradict the claims given in Part 1 above? Readers may doubt it since it seems inconsistent with the local determination lemma.

The extension of a transition is a part of a marking. Transition rules are just referring to the extension of a transition via marking. A transition may be enabled by an incomplete marking as long as the given part of this marking includes its extension.

2.1.2 Formal Definitions and Basic Terms

Definition 2.1 Directed Net A triple $(S, T; F)$ is called a directed net if

$$S \cup T \neq \varnothing$$
$$\wedge S \cap T = \varnothing$$
$$\wedge F \subseteq (S \times T) \cup (T \times S)$$
$$\wedge dom(F) \cup cod(F) = S \cup T$$

An S-element is called a "place" and a T-element is called a "transition."

This is not a pure formal definition. Pure formal definitions serve the need of automatic treatment. A pure formal version of the above definition may be given with predicate $dnet(S, T; F)$ defined as below.

$$dnet(S, T; F) \equiv S \cup T \neq \varnothing \wedge S \cap T = \varnothing$$
$$\wedge F \subseteq (S \times T) \cup (T \times S)$$
$$\wedge dom(F) \cup cod(F) = S \cup T$$

$dnet(S, T; F)$ is equal to "$(S, T; F)$ is a directed net." The weak point of pure formal definitions is a bit harder for some readers to understand.

What this definition tells is:

$S \cup T \neq \varnothing$: a net contains at least one element, non-empty.
$S \cap T = \varnothing$: S-elements and T-elements are different.

$F \subseteq (S \times T) \cup (T \times S)$:

F is a binary relation defined on S and T. It is asymmetric: (s, t) and (t, s) are different elements in F.
$dom(F) \cup cod(F) = S \cup T$: No isolated element in $(S, T; F)$.

Note F is constructed from S and T with $dom(F)$ as its domain and $cod(F)$ as its co-domain:

$dom(F) = \{x| (x, y) \in F\}$, the starting elements of pairs in F, and $cod(F) = \{y| (x, y) \in F\}$, the end elements of pairs in F. So, $dom(F) \cup cod(F) = S \cup T$ requires all elements to be either a starting element and/or an end element.

As conventional graphical presentation, a circle is used for a place, a box for a transition, and for $(x, y) \in F$, a pair in F, (x, y) is an arrow from x to y. An arrow is also called an arc.

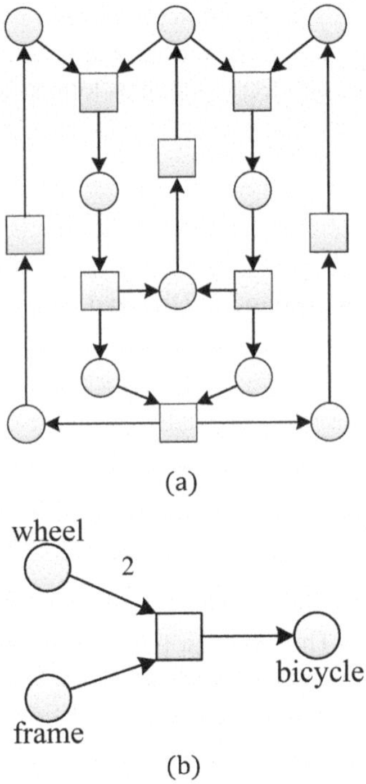

Fig. 2.2 (**a**) A directed net. (**b**) Bicycle assembly

Table 2.1 Possible explanations of net elements

S-elements	T-elements	S-elements	T-elements
States	Change	Resources	Resource production
Place	Transition	Open set	Close set
Condition	Event	Role	Activity
Language	Translator	Chemicals	Chemical reaction
Structure	Construction	Country	Board
Logic statement	Calculus, prove, relate	Condition	Facts
Unit data	Managing unit data		

In Fig. 2.2 below, (a) is an example of directed nets presented graphically with unnamed elements. Figure 2.2b presents a bicycle assembling transition in which elements are named as they are called in daily life.

Figure 2.2b may also be explained as a chemical reaction. Two atoms of hydrogen and one atom of oxygen are combined to form a water molecule.

As Fig. 2.2b suggests, a net may be understood differently in different areas. Thus, as a common practice, net elements are named with meaningless identifiers. Net elements must be connected to physical objects only for real applications. It is in this sense that net is said to be an unexplained system model. Possible explanations of S-elements and T-elements are as shown in Table 2.1 below.

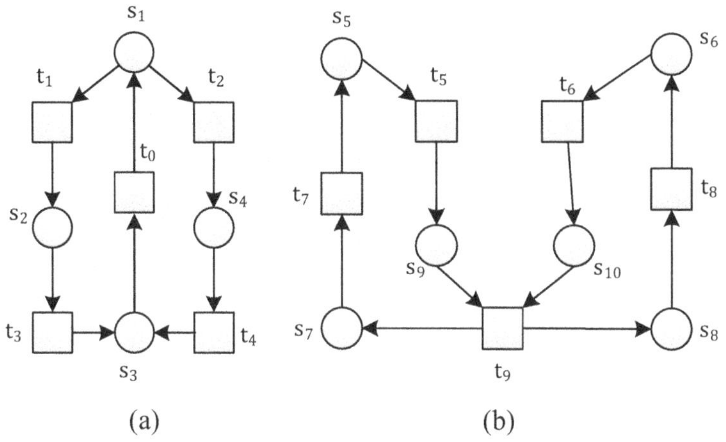

Fig. 2.3 A disconnected net $N =$ (a) + (b)

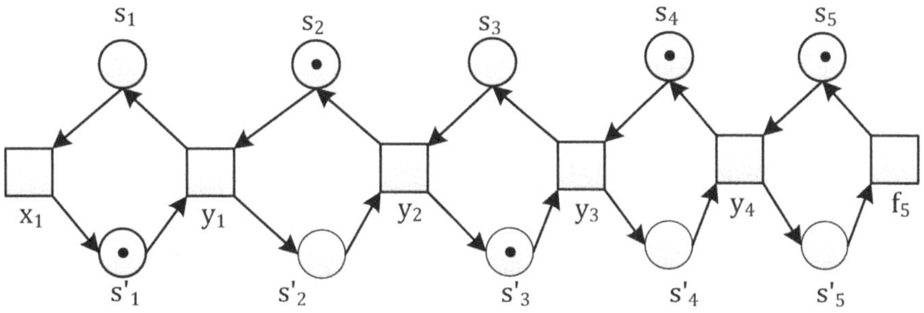

Fig. 2.4 A line to transfer water buckets

Items in this table may be understood differently. Anyway, it is just for readers' reference.

System design is a purposeful task. A net with freely named elements may gain generality, i.e., to be applied in different areas.

Definition 2.1 contains only necessary requirements for a triple to be a directed net. As a tradition, fundamental concepts are always defined as simple as possible to leave room for later enrichment. For example, a net is not necessary to be connected as shown in Fig. 2.3 below, in which (a), (b) and $N =$ (a) + (b) are all directed nets by definition. Elements of N are named with meaningless symbols, since N is not connected with reality.

People may line up to transfer water buckets to fight a fire. In the course of doing so, some weak or aged persons may become too tired to continue. A net modelling such a scene has a variable size since people may quit or join. The net in Fig. 2.4 below describes such a line consisting of 5 persons. Place s_i and s_i' are states of the i_{th} person to hold a full bucket or an empty bucket, depending on where the token is.

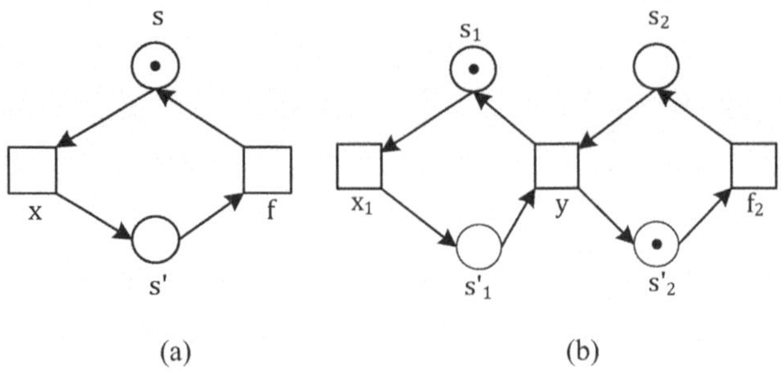

Fig. 2.5 Join and quit

Figure 2.5a consists of two transitions participated by s_i while (Fig. 2.5b) presents how s_i and s_{i+1} exchange bucket. Another way to read Fig. 2.5 is: from (a) to (b), a new face has joined the line, while from (b) to (a), a weak or aged one quits.

Figure 2.6 is an occurrence net describing happenings in a duration of time. It is clear that occurrence nets are capable of self-healing.

Definition 2.2 Basic Terms For directed net $N = (S, T : F)$ and $t \in T$, $s \in S$,

${}^{\bullet}t = \{s | (s, t) \in F\}$: the set of input places of t,

$t^{\bullet} = \{s | (t, s) \in F\}$: the set of output places of t,

${}^{\bullet}t$ is called the preset of t, and $t^{\bullet}$ is the post-set of t,

${}^{\bullet}t \cup t^{\bullet}$ is called the extension of transition t,

${}^{\bullet}s = \{t | (t, s) \in F\}$: the set of input transitions of s,

$s^{\bullet} = \{t | (s, t) \in F\}$: the set of output transitions of s,

${}^{\bullet}s \cup s^{\bullet}$ is called the scope of place s.

Based on this definition, for a subset A of $S \cup T$,

${}^{\bullet}A = \{x | \exists y \in A : (x, y) \in F\}$, the preset of A,

$A^{\bullet} = \{y | \exists x \in A : (x, y) \in F\}$, the post set of A.

A transition has a fixed extension; this is the certainty of nets. Certainty and atomicity are the very fundamental properties of Nets. These are good points as well as weak points. The good point is, a net system as defined below has a fixed underlying structure and stable properties. The weak point is, it leads to less flexibility and too detailed descriptions. Example 2.1 below explains this.

Example 2.1 A Bag and* n *Balls To represent, in terms of Petri nets, how to take out, with just one grasp, all n balls from a bag, regardless of what the concrete value of n is. It is easy to do so in reality for human beings, as long as balls are not too many to hold. For nets, it seems that a single transition with n as the weight on its input arc will do. But n is an unknown integer and the arc weight of a transition must be a constant; a single transition is not feasible. There must be many transitions to fulfil the request of that input arc; its weights are from 1 to m, where m is an integer no less than n. Among these m transitions, there must be one that matches n, since the concrete value of n is in the set $\{1, 2, \cdots, m\}$. Human hands are flexible enough for

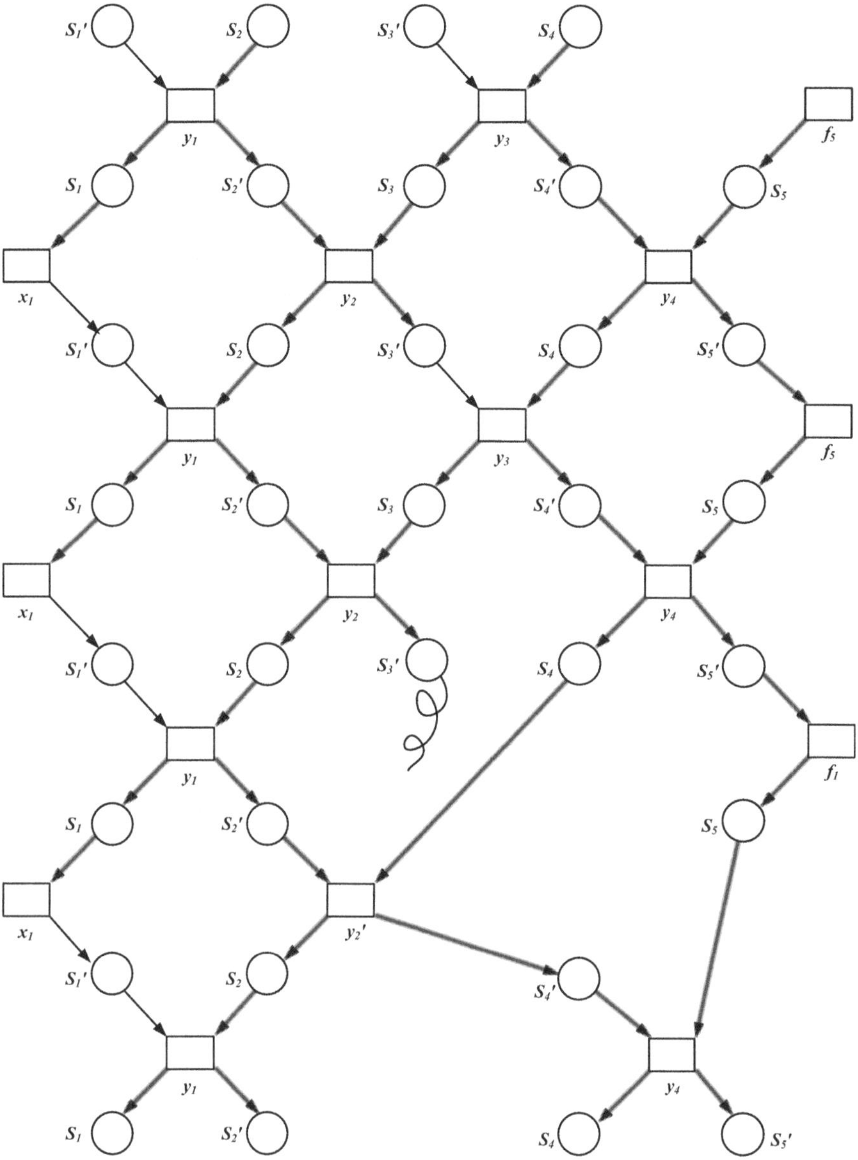

Fig. 2.6 A recording of the firefighting line

balls of an unknown number, but nets are not so. This is shown in Fig. 2.7a below where $n = 3$ is assumed for simplicity.

For no more than three balls, three transitions with input weights 1, 2, 3 respectively are sufficient. All three transitions in Fig. 2.7a are enabled and in conflict.

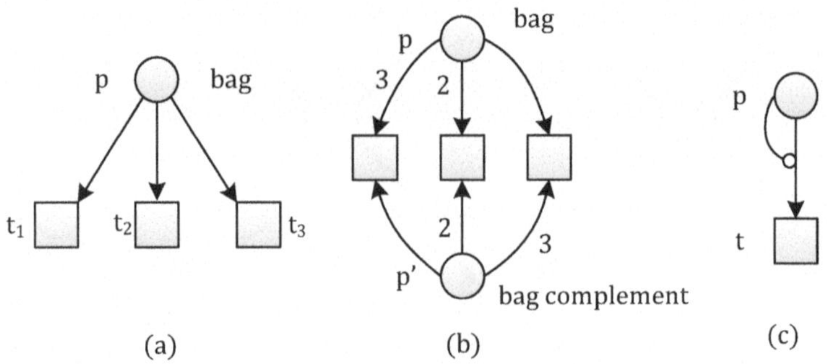

Fig. 2.7 To take out balls from a bag

Since 3 is not given, it is not known which one of the three transitions would take out all balls.

Fig. 2.7b is a net solution for no more than 3 balls in which place p' contains $3 + 1 = 4$ tokens. Only one of the three transitions in (Fig. 2.7b) is enabled, and its firing will take out all balls in place p.

The complexity in this ball-out problem comes from fixed arc weights. This inflexibility is improved by self-control nets as shown in Fig. 2.7c in which $W(p, t)$ is p, the name of a place. $W(p, t) = M(p)$ when transition t fires at marking M. Different markings give different weights. Graphically, there are two ways to represent $W(p, t)$ is p. One way is to connect the place (to be taken as arc weight) to the arc as shown in (Fig. 2.7c); another way is to write the name of the place (to be taken as arc weight) on the arc.

To apply Petri net with success, the first thing is to correctly recognize T-elements and S-elements. On the one hand, you are forced to do so, on the other hand, you would better understand things by doing so.

Two pupils, sitting at the same desk, would like to draw a line in the middle of the desk to claim their respective "territories." What would happen if they argue about whom the line segment in the middle belongs to? No matter which one of the two the segment belongs to, this question suggests that this segment is a resource, or a token. But, with the help of Petri nets, you would think differently. If your elbow moves across the middle line, its state changes from "at home" to "visiting neighbor." So, the middle line is a transition, a transition with one input arc from "at home" and an output arc to "neighbor's home."

Example 2.2 File Transfer on Internet This example illustrates further how to distinguish T-elements and S-elements.

Fig. 2.8 below contains two tables: the one on top shows 5 network nodes and their respective power of parallel transfer; the one below gives the start nodes and the target nodes for each of the files to be transferred. In addition, the duration of time needed by each of the files is also included.

Node	v_1	v_2	v_3	v_4	v_5
power of parallel transfer	1	1	2	1	3

file	e_1	e_2	e_3	e_4	e_5	e_6	e_7
start and target node	v_1, v_3	v_1, v_2	v_2, v_3	v_3, v_4	v_3, v_5	v_4, v_5	v_2, v_5
duration	5	3	2	2	6	4	3

Fig. 2.8 Network nodes and files to be transferred

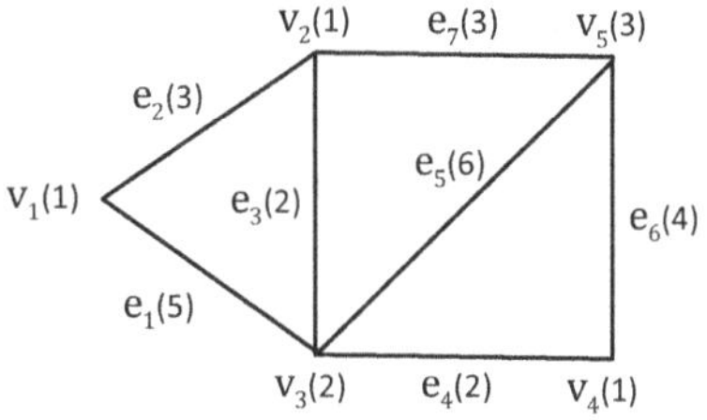

Fig. 2.9 Files and network nodes: a graph

Without careful thinking, people would draw a graph, as shown in Fig. 2.9 in which file names are written on indirected arcs. The fact that the i_{th} file consumes n unit time for transfer is denoted with $e_i(n)$.

To build a net for file transfer, what is the transition: network nodes or files? Normally, a node would be considered as a transition since it is nodes that carry out the transfer, while files are what are to be transferred.

On the contrary, it is a file that requires two nodes to have it transferred. Thus, nodes are resources and files are transitions. Readers are suggested to think about it and keep it in mind. For a better understanding, this problem will be discussed again later when place/transition systems are presented.

2.2 Net Systems

A given initial state, a capacity function on S, and a weight function on arcs in F are needed for a net to become a system.

Definition 2.3 Capacity and Marking on S $K : S \rightarrow \{1, 2, \cdots\}$ is called a capacity function on S, where $\{1, 2, \cdots\}$ is the set of non-zero positive integers.

$M : S \rightarrow \{0, 1, 2, \cdots\}$ is called a marking on S, if $\forall s \in S : M(s) \leq K(s)$.

$K(s)$ is the maximum number of tokens place s may hold, while $M(s)$ is the number of tokens place s is holding at marking M. So, “marking” is synonymous with “state.” A given marking serves as initial state. Graphically, $M(s) = n$ is represented with n black dots inside circle s, i.e., tokens are represented by black dots. $K(s) = m$ will be written beside circle s, if necessary. The default capacity is ω.

$K(s) = \omega$ is not allowed by definition since the capacity of place s is bound to be finite by nature. But, $K(s) = \omega$ may appear, by default, in a graphically presented system. This means that the real value of $K(s)$ is not known and it is for sure that the real load on place s would never exceed the unknown $K(s)$.

Definition 2.4 Weight Function $W : F \rightarrow \{1, 2, \cdots\}$ is called a weight function on F.

For $(x, y) \in F$, $W(x, y)$ is the weight on arc (x, y), indicating the number of tokens to be consumed/produced in case the transition (y or x) fires.

As graphical representation, $w(x, y)$ would be written on arc (x, y). The default weight is 1. Note that $W(s, t) \leq K(s)$ is not required. In case $W(s, t) > K(s)$, transition t is “dead” (can never be enabled for firing) as per the transition rule given below. The concept of dead transitions plays an important role in a general net theory (GNT for short). In fact, it leads to Enlogy, a branch of GNT for logical reasoning. A dead transition is not meaningless, but rather, it is a property of the net system. It is just like the activities prohibited by law in a society that is supposed to reflect people’s moral trend.

Definition 2.5 Net System $\sum = (S, T; F, K, W, M_0)$ is a net system if

$(S, T; F)$ is a directed net,

K, W are respectively a capacity function on S and a weight function on F,

M_0 is the initial marking on S.

Figure 2.10 contains two graphically represented net systems that share the same structure given in Fig. 2.2a, with the only difference being weights on arcs (t_1, s_3) and (s_3, t_3). As we will see, when system dynamics are defined later, Figs. 2.10a, b share the same set of transition sequences, i.e., their behaviors are equivalent, though (a) is a P/T system and (b) is an EN-system as defined later in Chap. 3.

A net may be unconnected, but a net system must be connected, since separation leads to independent behavior.

2.3 Transition Rules

Transition rules given below define dynamics of $\sum = (S, T; F, K, W, M_0)$, i.e., what would enable a transition to fire (to occur), and what would be the effect when it fires (occurs).

“$M[t>$” is a binary predicate defined on marking set and transition set; $M[t>$ is true if t is enabled to fire by M.

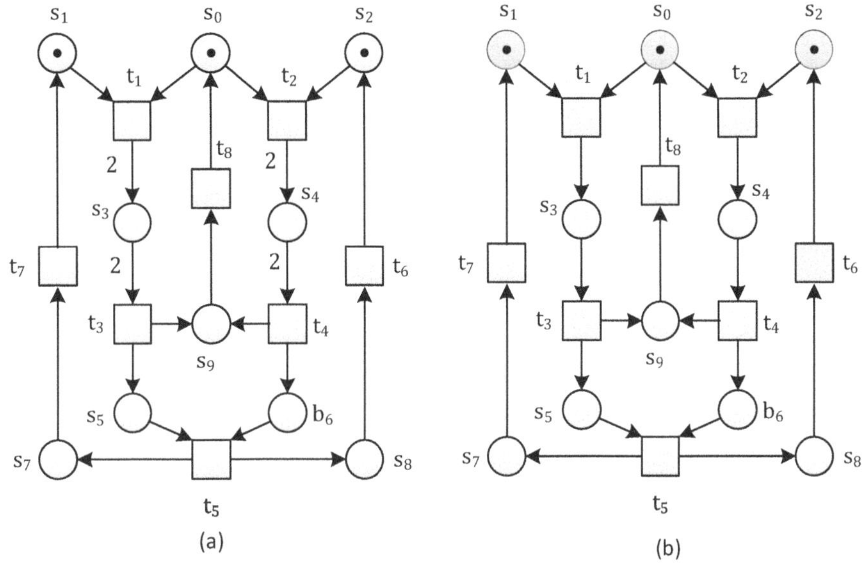

Fig. 2.10 Net systems (**a**) and (**b**)

Definition 2.6 Enabled Transition

$$M[t> \equiv \forall s \in {}^{\bullet}t : M(s) \geq W(s,t) \wedge \forall s \in t^{\bullet} : W(t,s) + M(s) \leq K(s)$$

The formula in this definition tells the following:

$\forall s \in {}^{\bullet}t : M(s) \geq W(s, t)$: there are enough tokens to be consumed in all input places of t,

$\forall s \in t^{\bullet} : W(t, s) + M(s) \leq K(s)$: there is enough room for every s in $t^{\bullet}$ to receive tokens produced by t.

The definition of $M[t>$ requires $W(t, s) + M(s) \leq K(s)$ for $s \in {}^{\bullet}t \cap t^{\bullet}$, though the token number is $M(s) + (W(t, s) - W(s, t))$ after the firing of t. There is no reason to assume any order between "+ $W(t, s)$" and "− $W(t, s)$."

It is not assumed that ${}^{\bullet}t \cap t^{\bullet} = \emptyset$. A shared tool must be released after use. A catalyst remains unconsumed after a chemical reaction, etc. The formula ${}^{\bullet}t \cap t^{\bullet} \neq \emptyset$ captures the function of a tool and a catalyst.

Similar to ${}^{\bullet}t \cap t^{\bullet} \neq \emptyset$ or ${}^{\bullet}t \cap t^{\bullet} = \emptyset$, there are other structure properties. In the definition below, *dnet*$(S, T; F)$, a triple predicate, is assumed true. *dnet*$(S, T; F)$ is synonymous with "being a directed net."

Definition 2.7 Structure Properties

(a) $N = (S, T; F)$ is said to be pure if $\forall t \in T : {}^{\bullet}t \cap t^{\bullet} = \emptyset$. N is simple if $\forall x, y \in S \cup T : {}^{\bullet}x = {}^{\bullet}y \wedge x^{\bullet} = y^{\bullet} \rightarrow x = y$.

(b) $N' = (S, T; F^{-1})$ is the reverse net of N, in which $F^{-1} = \{(x, y) | (y, x) \in F\}$.

(c) N is a finite net if $|S \cup T| < \omega$, i.e., $S \cup T$ is a finite set.

(d) Net $N' = (S', T'; F')$ is a sub-net of N if $S' \subseteq S \wedge T' \subseteq T \wedge F' \subseteq F$.

(e) Let $P = \{(x,y) | (x,y) \in F \vee (y,x) \in F\}$ be the set of undirected node pairs obtained from N. $(S \cup T, P)$ is the undirected net corresponding to N. N is a connected net if P is a connected graph.

Above defined are properties of a net as a whole. There are local properties like a siphon or a trap. A set of places $S_1 \subseteq S$ is a siphon if ${}^{\bullet}S_1 \subseteq S_1^{\bullet}$, and for $S_2 \subseteq S$, S_2 is a trap if ${}^{\bullet}S_2 \supseteq S_2^{\bullet}$. Trap and siphon are structure properties. A trap was once called a "deadlock," but deadlock is a semantic property, i.e., two sides in the same system keep waiting for each other. Siphon and trap may find their use, but not yet so far.

By the way, Definition 2.7 is semi-formal, while Definitions 2.6 and 2.8 below are formal. A semi-formal definition serves human readers, while a formal definition is for AI tools. A formal definition requires that which is to be defined is a predicate like *dnet*$(S, T; F)$ in Definition 2.1 above.

Back to enabled transition. If $M[t>$, t may fire to produce a successor marking M', denoted with triple predicate $M[t>M'$.

Definition 2.8 Successor Marking

$$
\begin{aligned}
M[t>M' \equiv\ & M[t> \\
& \wedge \forall s \in {}^{\bullet}t - t^{\bullet} : M'(s) = M(s) - W(s,t) \\
& \wedge \forall s \in t^{\bullet} - {}^{\bullet}t : M'(s) = M(s) + W(s,t) \\
& \wedge \forall s \in {}^{\bullet}t \cap t^{\bullet} : M'(s) = M(s) + W(t,s) - W(s,t) \\
& \wedge \forall s \in \left(S - {}^{\bullet}t \cup t^{\bullet}\right) : M'(s) = M(s)
\end{aligned}
$$

It is easy to prove that M' satisfies the definition of marking.

To simplify the above formula, the concept of weight function may be extended.

Definition 2.9 Extended Weight Function $W' : (S \times T) \cup (T \times S) \rightarrow \{0, 1, 2, \cdots\}$ is the weight function extended from W, if

$$W'(x,y) = W(x,y) \text{ if } (x,y) \in F \sim 0 \text{ if } (x,y) \notin F$$

With extended weight function W', the successor marking M' is redefined by Definition 2.10.

Definition 2.10 Successor Marking By Extended Weights

$$M[t> \equiv \forall s \in S : M(s) \geq W'(s,t) \wedge M(s) + W'(s,t) \leq K(s)$$

$$M[t>M' \equiv M[t> \wedge \forall s \in S : M(s) = M(s) + W'(t,s) - W'(s,t)$$

Professor Petri used to call a net system a "token game." The game, to be played by one or more persons, allows tokens to be moved according to transition rules only. There is no restriction on number of tokens to be moved in one step. The goal of this game is not to produce a winner, but just to let players get familiar with transition rules and to find out all possibilities in the course of token move. Interested readers may try it by hand simulation on the system in Fig. 2.2a. Please figure out phenomena between transition firings, including conflict (choice), sequence, and concurrency. Notice that concurrency is not transitive. All these phenomena will be formally defined when EN-system is introduced.

Readers may doubt that a marking is a global state, and it is used here to define the concepts of $M[t>$ and $M[t>M'$. Does this contradict the principle of local determination? The answer is no. The only part of S that plays a role in $M[t>$ and $M[t>M'$ is the extension of t, i.e., $^{\bullet}t \cup t^{\bullet}$. It is just for wording convenience, the whole marking M is mentioned.

For system $\sum = (S, T; F, K, W, M_0)$, the set of reachable markings, denoted by $[M_0 >_{\Sigma}$ or simply by $[M_0>$, consists of all markings obtained by consecutive transition firings, starting from M_0. $[M_0>$ is given constructively by the next definition.

Definition 2.11 $[M_0>$, Set of Reachable Markings $[M_0>$ is the marking set consisting of all markings given by the next two formulas:

$$M_0 \in [M_0 >,$$
$$(M \in [M_0 > \wedge \exists t \in T : M[t > M') \rightarrow M' \in [M_0 >$$

Note that $[M_0>$ "is given by the next two formulas" is different from $[M_0>$ "is the marking set that satisfies the next two conditions." The former is a draft for an algorithm, while the latter is a definition. As a definition, it must be precise. There are more than one marking set that satisfies the above two conditions. For example, the set of all conceivable markings is the biggest one. $[M_0>$ is the smallest.

The above two formulas may serve as the basis of an algorithm to compute $[M_0>$. An algorithm needs operation details and a termination condition. Details will be provided together with termination condition later in Sect. 5.2, Chap. 5. Note that $[M_0>$ may be an infinite set for a finite net system.

By the above two formulas, every reachable marking M corresponds to at least one transition sequence σ, $\sigma = \tau_1\tau_2\cdots\tau_n$, such that the consecutive firings of transitions in σ lead to M, i.e., $M_0[\tau_1 > M_1[\tau_2 > M_2\cdots M_{n-1}[\tau_n>M_n$, and $M_n = M$. This fact is denoted by $M_0[\sigma > M$. From now on, σ is called a transition sequence only if $M_0[\sigma>$. An infinite sequence of transitions is a transition sequence if every prefix of it is a transition sequence.

Note that, for a given marking in $[M_0>$, there might be more than one transition sequence leading to it.

Would Definition 2.11 lead to missing, from $[M_0>$, of markings reachable by concurrent transition firings? The answer is no. All arc weights are constants, so the effect of concurrent transition firings is the same as sequential firings of the same set of transitions.

For net system $\sum = (S, T; F, K, W, M_0)$, several concepts are given below.

Definition 2.12 Live System, Fair System, and Bounded System
1. Transition t is live if $\forall M \in [M_0> \exists\, M' \in [M > : M'[t>$;

Σ is live if all transitions are live.

2. Σ is fair to transitions t and t' if for any infinite transitionsequence σ(if exists), #(t, σ) and #(t', σ) are either both infinite or both finite, where #(t, σ) and #(t', σ) are respectively the number of occurrences of t and t' in σ; Σ is fair if it is fair to all pairs of two transitions of it.
3. If for positive integer k,$\forall M \in [M_0 > \ \forall s \in S : M(s) \leq k$, then Σ is a k-bounded system. In case the concrete value of k is not known while it does exist, then Σ is bounded.

Note that $[M>$ above is the set of markings reachable from marking M.

The concepts of both a live system and a fair system refer to infinity. But infinity for human lives is not reachable at all. If people agree on such concepts of being live or being fair, then all societies in the world, including societies in history, are fair and not live, since nothing would live forever, i.e., #(t, σ) and #(t', σ) are always finite. Is it possible to redefine them without infinity? This question will be discussed when the problem of dining philosophers is discussed.

A net system has been defined as a 6-tuple, and the 6-tuple can be graphically represented for visual study and to make face-to-face discussions easy to go. Besides, it leads to the study of net topology, another branch of General Net Theory. In this topology, the operation "folding" is a continuous mapping between nets as well as net systems. The system hierarchy, to be introduced in Chap. 3, is an example of folding from EN-system to high level systems.

For system analysis, algebraic representation is better if Σ is finite.

Let be $\sum = (S, T; F, K, W, M_0)$, $S = \{s_1, s_2, \cdots, s_m\}$ and $T = \{t_1, t_2, \cdots, t_n\}$. The structure of Σ may be represented with a matrix with S and S as its raw and column index sets respectively.

Definition 2.13 Incidence Matrix The $m \times n$ matrix $A = (a_{ji})$ is the incidence matrix of Σ if

$$a_{ji} = W(t_i, s_j) \text{ if } s_j \in t_i^{\cdot} - {}^{\cdot}t_i \sim$$

$$- \mathrm{W}(s_j, t_i) \text{ if } s_j \in {}^{\cdot}t_i - t_i^{\cdot} \sim$$

$$W(t_i, s_j) - W(s_j, t_i \text{ if } s_j \in t_i^{\cdot} \cap {}^{\cdot}t_i \sim)$$

$$0 \text{ if } s_j \notin t_i^{\cdot} \cup {}^{\cdot}t_i$$

where $\sim$ is the separator. Note that a_{ji} is the number of tokens received/lost by/from place s_j when transition t_i fires once.

With the extended weight function W', the above formula is reduced to:

$$a_{ji} = W'(t_i, s_j) - W'(s_j, t_i)$$

Now, $M_0[\sigma > M$ is equivalent to the equation below:

$$A \cdot \sigma(T) + M_0 = M$$

in which "·" is the operator for matrix multiplication ("·" may be omitted if there is no possibility of confusion), M_0, M are both S-indexed column vectors respectively for the initial marking and the successor marking, while $\sigma(T)$ is a T-indexed column vector, of which the i-th element $\sigma(t_i)$ is the appearing number of t_i in σ.

Example 2.3 Incidence Matrix Below is the incidence matrix of the system in Fig. 2.2a:

$$\begin{array}{c} \\ s_0 \\ s_1 \\ s_2 \\ s_3 \\ s_4 \\ s_5 \\ s_6 \\ s_7 \\ s_8 \\ s_9 \end{array}
\begin{array}{c} \begin{array}{cccccccc} t_0 & t_1 & t_2 & t_3 & t_4 & t_5 & t_6 & t_7 \end{array} \\
\begin{bmatrix}
1 & -1 & -1 & 0 & 0 & 0 & 0 & 0 \\
0 & -1 & 0 & 0 & 0 & 0 & 0 & 1 \\
0 & 0 & -1 & 0 & 0 & 0 & 1 & 0 \\
0 & 2 & 0 & -2 & 0 & 0 & 0 & 0 \\
0 & 0 & 2 & 0 & -2 & 0 & 0 & 0 \\
0 & 0 & 0 & 1 & 0 & -1 & 0 & 0 \\
0 & 0 & 0 & 0 & 1 & -1 & 0 & 0 \\
0 & 0 & 0 & 0 & 0 & 1 & 0 & -1 \\
0 & 0 & 0 & 0 & 0 & 1 & -1 & 0 \\
-1 & 0 & 0 & 1 & 1 & 0 & 0 & 0
\end{bmatrix} \end{array}$$

Let $\sigma(T) = (2, 1, 1, 1, 1, 0, 0, 0)^t$, where letter t at the upright corner denotes a transpose operation. We have

$$A \cdot \sigma(T) = (0, -1, -1, 0, 0, 1, 1, 0, 0, 0)^t.$$

Since $M_0 = (1, 1, 1, 0, 0, 0, 0, 0, 0, 0)^t$,

$$A \cdot \sigma(T) + M_0 = (1, 0, 0, 0, 0, 1, 1, 0, 0, 0)^t.$$

Note that as long as $\sigma(T)$ is a T-indexed column vector with positive integers as its elements, $A \cdot \sigma(T)$ would always compute to a marking, though not necessarily reachable from M_0.

Similarly, let $\delta(S)$ be a S-indexed column vector with positive integers as its elements, then $A^t \cdot \delta(S)$ would always compute to a T-indexed column vector, in which A^t is the transpose matrix of A. The i-th element of this vector is $\Sigma_j a_{ji}\delta(s_j)$, which is the weighted variant of token numbers when t_i occurs, in which $\delta(s_j)$ is the weight of a_{ji}.

Definition 2.14 Invariant $\sigma(T)$ is called a T-invariant if $A \cdot \sigma(T) = \theta_S$, in which θ_S is the S-indexed zero column vector.

$\delta(S)$ is called a S-invariant if $A^t \cdot \delta(S) = \theta_T$, in which θ_T is the T-indexed zero column vector.

Example 2.4 Invariant of the Systems in Fig. 2.10 For the system in Fig. 2.10a, $(2, 1, 1, 1, 1, 1, 1, 1)^t$ is a T-invariant. $(1, 1, 1, 1, 1, 1, 1, 1, 1, 1)^t$ is a S-invariant.

The net in (Fig. 2.10b) shares the above invariants with the net in (Fig. 2.10a).

Note that, both T-invariant and S-invariant are structure properties, having nothing to do with initial marking.

There are semantic invariant as well. For example, the number of tokens held by places s_1, s_3, s_5 and s_7 is a constant for the system in Fig. 2.10b. As given by the initial marking, this constant is 1. This is, in fact, the trace of the bride if the net system is explained as a church wedding. The bride is always in one of these places, and every place has a chance to hold the bride.

Chapter 3
The System Hierarchy

Abstract Net systems form a hierarchy according to the functions S-elements play. At the bottom is EN-system in that a S-element is a condition; above it is P/T-system in that a S-element may hold more than one resource of the same kind, still above are predict/transition systems and color net system, in which a S-element may hold resources of different kind that play the same role. C-net system does not belong to this hierarchy, since it has variables as its consisting feature.

This chapter aims to leave an overall impression on readers about net systems and the way they are related.

3.1 Informal Description

The hierarchy of net systems reflects the process of observation. What is observed first is concrete happenings that consume and produce particular resources, including materials, spaces, and human beings (to be occupied/released). Since a piece of resource (including a parking space) is called a token in Nets, the word "token" will be used next instead of "resource." Occurrence nets are proposed for recording observed concrete happenings (similar to a video recording with irrelevant stuff filtered). To fold different occurrences of the same element into one, a system named elementary system, EN-system for short, is obtained. For example, recording the coming and going of the four seasons in the past years, for which an occurrence net is obtained. Human experience would lead us to extend this occurrence net to the infinite past and the infinite future. Folding all respective occurrences of Spring, Summer, Autumn, and Winter into one place each, a net consisting of 4 places and 4 transitions to describe the alternating seasons is obtained. This is a 4-season system in which the unique token notifies the current season. The alternating season belongs

C. Yuan, *Principle of Petri Nets*, https://doi.org/10.1007/978-981-97-7336-7_3

to nature, and it does not have an initial state. In contrast to abstraction from nature, a man-designed system has an initial state.

By the way, axioms on concurrency will tell you that the above-mentioned occurrence net and the 4-season system do not completely describe the alternating seasons. The General Net Theory will suggest a different 4-season system.

The EN-system describes how individual tokens flow from place to place. Places in an EN-system are in fact conditions since each place may hold a token, or no token, i.e., being true or false.

Above the EN-system in the hierarchy is place/transition system, P/T-system for short, in which a place is a "warehouse" for tokens of the same kind (playing the same role). Thus, a place is obtained by folding conditions if tokens in these conditions belong to the same type. A place has a fixed capacity, i.e., the maximum token allowance. Here, "place" has nothing to do with a geographic position.

The application of P/T-systems is limited by constant arc weights. An improved version called self-modifying net system is proposed that allows arc weight to be a place name, and the number of tokens held by this place at marking M is the instant arc weight at M.

Still above in the hierarchy are high level net systems, including predicate/transition system and color net system. A place in a high-level net system may hold tokens of different kinds. The difference between predicate/transition systems and color net systems is the way how markings and arc weights are represented and how transition rules are specified. Figure 3.1 below shows one system represented respectively with an EN-system, a P/T-system, and a high-level system obtained respectively by folding. The way to do folding is informally illustrated by Fig. 3.1. Note that the folding from the EN-system to the P/T-system is a syntax operation on structure, while the folding from the P/T-system to high-level net systems is an operation related to token semantics. Note that the predicate/transition system, Pr/T-system for short, and the color-system in Fig. 3.1 share the same structure. There is no need to understand the detailed semantics now before these systems are formally defined. Just note that both places and transitions are predicates in Pr/T-systems, while places and transitions in color-systems are dyed with color. For color-systems, a place has a set of token color, while a transition has a set of occurrence color.

The Pr/T-system and the color net system in Fig. 3.1 are informally explained below. They will be formally defined in respective chapters.

In a Pr/T-system, a place is a predicate that specifies an incomplete proposition like "ready (to do something)," "rest (for some action)," etc. The Pr/T-system in Fig. 3.1 explains related concepts in which all tokens are freely named. It may be understood as a church wedding: a wedding host (named $<w>$), and the wedding couple (named $<a>$ and $<b>$). To start with, $<w>$, $<a>$ and $<b>$ are all held by predicate "ready" (for the ceremony), i.e., $M_0(\text{ready}) = <w> + <a> + <b>$. The formula $<w> + <a> + <b>$ is a symbolic sum, another way to write a set. There is a fixed set D of tokens for a Pr/T-system, and the predicates must be complete and mutually exclusive so that each token would belong to exactly one predicate at any marking. So, Pr/T-systems are token conservative. For a system to be conservative, every transition must also be conservative. The weight on an arc is also a symbolic

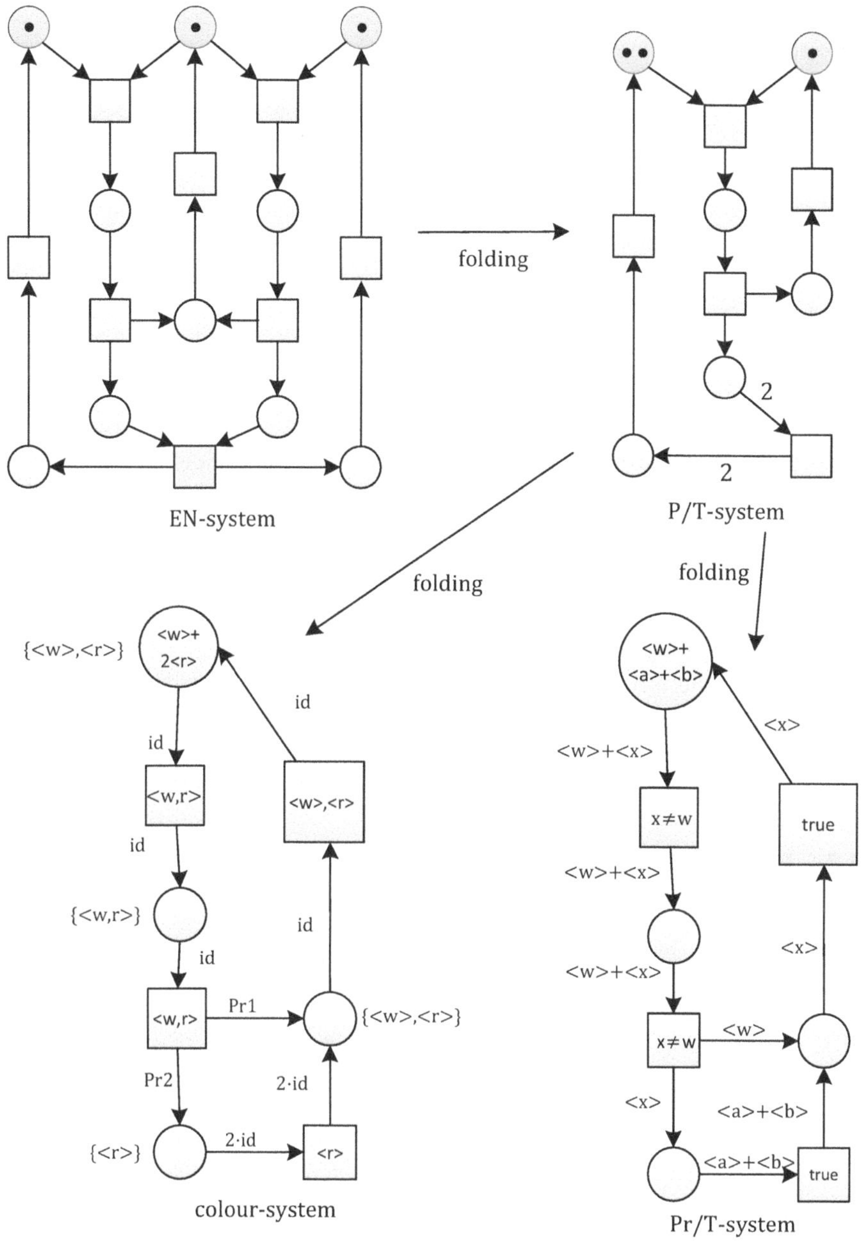

Fig. 3.1 Net system hierarchy by folding

sum in which variable names like *x* or *y* may appear to require a substitution with concrete tokens. A transition may be marked with a static predicate to specify restrictions on variable substitution. Note the scope of a variable like *x* is limited to a single transition: the same variable on the input/output arcs of one transition represents the same token, while the appearances of the same variable on arcs of different transitions have nothing to do with each other. So, *x* doesn't play the role of carrying a value from one transition to another. It is thus not qualified as a math variable, though it is called a "variable" here. In case a transition does not set a restriction on variables (if any) connected to it, it is the 0-ary predicate "true."

In a color net system, all tokens are dyed, one color for one kind. For example, <*w*> is a token dyed "white," and <*w*, *r*> is composed from a white token and a red token. A place is associated with a set of token color. Quantities of tokens are given by positive integers, say 2 <*r*> for two red tokens. In color nets, every transition has also a given set of occurrence color to specify its firing patterns. The weight on an arc between s and *t* is a function to map a given pattern on *t* to the color set of s. The set of token color and the set of occurrence color are written inside transition boxes or aside the related place elements.

The author proposed a different class of net systems called C-net for programming (letter C is the initial of Computing and Communication, that is what a program does). To amend the lack of data types in all net systems, the concept of variables is adopted as a new kind of S-elements. A transition may write and/or read a variable. Graphically, a variable is denoted by a double circle ⍰, a write operation is denoted by "⍰⍰ ⍰," from transition to variable (⍰ is an arrow with small circle as its head), while a read operation is denoted with "⍰ ⍰ ⍰," which is from a variable to a transition. C-net is based on Nets, but no folding operation is involved. Thus, it does not belong to the hierarchy. A brief introduction on C-net here aims to leave a preliminary impression on readers. Its detailed introduction is to be given later in Chap. 9.

3.2 Formal Definitions of the 3-Bottom Layers of the Hierarchy

An occurrence net is itself not a system; it is just a trace left by system activities. It is included here since it is considered as the foundation of the system hierarchy. All systems have inherited a net structure from occurrence net.

Definitions of occurrence nets, EN-systems, and P/T-systems are given next in this section. They are the three low layers of the hierarchy. Properties and analysis methods of net systems in the hierarchy will be introduced in respective chapters for each of them.

Definition 3.1 Occurrence Nets A directed net $(S, T; F)$ is an occurrence net iff

$$\forall s \in S : \left|{}^{\cdot}s\right| \leq 1 \wedge \left|s^{\cdot}\right| \leq 1$$

$$\wedge F^{+} \cap (F^{-})^{+} = \varnothing$$

This definition is based on Definition 1.1: The concept of directed net is enriched:"$\forall s \in S : |{}^{\bullet}s| \leq 1 \wedge |s^{\bullet}| \leq 1$" indicates the fact that a token is produced (if not available initially) and/or consumed by at most one transition, while $F^{+} \cap (F^{-})^{+} = \varnothing$ denotes that there is no loop in $(S, T; F)$, i.e., rebirth of the same token is impossible. Note that

$$F^{+} = F^{1} \cup F^{2} \cup F^{3} \cup F^{4} \cdots$$

$$(F^{-})^{+} = F^{-1} \cup F^{-2} \cup F^{-3} \cup F^{-4} \cdots$$

where

$$F^{1} = F;$$

$$F^{i} = \left\{(x, y) | \exists z : (x, z) \in F^{i-1} \wedge (z, y) \in F\right\} \text{ for } i > 1$$

and

$$F^{-1} = \{(x, y) | (y, x) \in F\};$$

$$F^{-i} = \left\{(x, y) | \exists z : (x, z) \in F^{-(i-1)} \wedge (z, y) \in F^{-1}\right\} \text{ for } i > 1$$

Occurrence nets are means to record processes in a net system and it is in this sense that occurrence nets are said to be the semantics of net systems. It will be mentioned again when system processes are defined. Axioms on concurrency are proposed based on occurrence nets.

Definition 3.2 EN-System Net system $\sum = (S, T; F, K, W, M_0)$ is an EN-system if

$$\forall s \in S : K(s) = 1 \wedge \forall (x, y) \in F : W(x, y) = 1$$

$K(s) = 1$ implies that s is a condition. A transition is called an event if its extension consists of conditions only. Thus, the underlying net for an EN-system is conventionally denoted with $(B, E; F)$ since the German (Prof. Petri's mother tongue) word for condition is "*B*edingung." The initial marking is now a subset c_{in} of B, consisting of conditions that are initially true. Thus, an EN-system is a 4-tuple $(B, E; F, c_{in})$ and capacities and arc weights all are the constant integer 1 by default. An EN-system is the elementary layer in the net system hierarchy.

Definition 3.3 P/T-System Net system $\sum = (S, T; F, K, W, M_0)$ is a P/T-system if

dnet$(S, T; F)$, and K, W, M_0 are respectively a capacity function on S, a weight function on F, and a marking on S.

P/T-system is considered in the literature as the general form of a net system with EN-system being a special kind of it. But to the author, a better understanding is that a P/T-system is folded from an EN-system.

Chapter 4
EN-System

Abstract An EN-system describes how individual resources are consumed and produced.

The EN-system $(B, E; F, c_{in})$ is at the very bottom of the net system hierarchy and describes the individuals' behavior. It is not suitable for real use since its degree of abstraction is low. But on the other hand, it is suitable for studying fundamentals in nature. The net structure for EN-systems is assumed to be pure, i.e., the preset and post-set of every event shares no element.

4.1 Completeness

A man-designed system is complete if it contains all elements necessary for the intended purpose. As part of nature, an EN-system is complete if and only if every element of it has its individuality to distinguish itself from others. Figure 4.1 below explains this.

The alternating of seasons has been mentioned above. As per our understanding of daily life, Fig. 4.1a seems correct. But it is just a rough model in people's mind. The reality is, there exist hot days in Spring and nice days in Summer. People have tolerated such inaccuracy since it well serves the daily needs including farming.

This model is not qualified as a theoretical one. A critical question on Fig. 4.1a is: does the event of a season change take time? If it does, which season that time belongs to? If not, at which moment such a change takes place? There is no answer to these questions based on Fig. 4.1a. Figure 4.1b answers above question well. Instead of a single condition for one season in (Fig. 4.1a), there are three conditions in (Fig. 4.1b), among them, an accompanying condition d_i for every event t_i is observed. The time taken by event t_i may be long or short, its accompanying condition d_i tells that it is in progress. The other two conditions d_{i-1} and d_{i+1}

C. Yuan, *Principle of Petri Nets*, https://doi.org/10.1007/978-981-97-7336-7_4

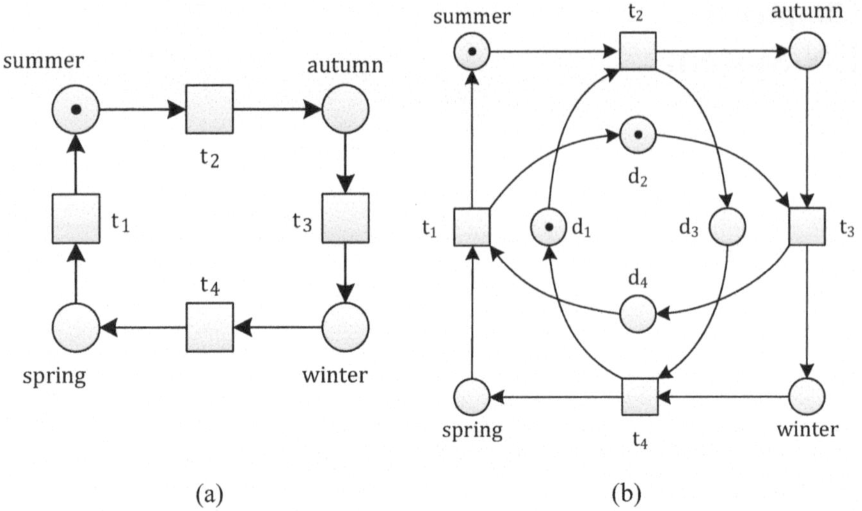

Fig. 4.1 Four seasons

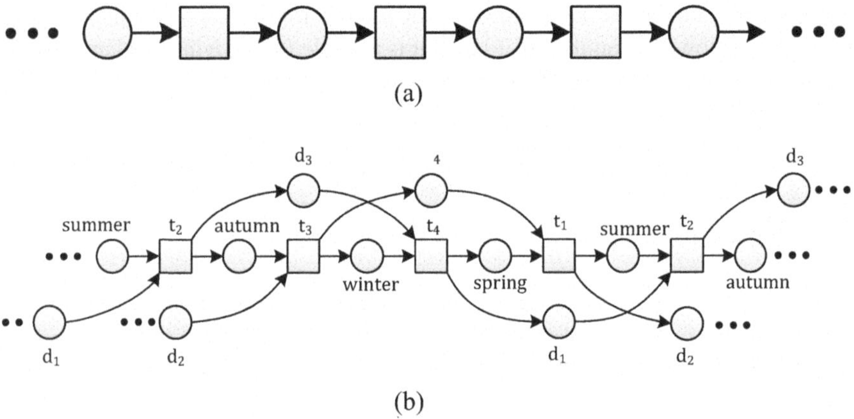

Fig. 4.2 (**a**) A line and (**b**) A rope

(as subscript, $4 + 1 = 1$ and $1 - 1 = 4$)indicate the remaining part of the previous season and the beginning of the next season. The three tokens in Fig. 4.1b tell the fact that the three accompanied events are all in progress. There is no clear-cut line between adjacent seasons. This is the way Nets deals with time: things are going on in harmony with no need of a timer. A calendar may tell you an accurate time (month, day, hour, and minute) for the next season to come, but it seems no one cares about it. Such a calculated prediction is based on the belief that time is linear like the axis of a real number.

Note that the tokens in Fig. 4.1a, b specify a current state instead of an initial one. No one knows how the alternating of seasons was started.

The difference between Fig. 4.1a, b is reflected by their respective occurrence nets shown in Fig. 4.2a, b.

Figure 4.2b has a rope structure, and each of its elements, say x, has a set $c(x)$ and a set $r(x)$ defined as below:

$$c(x) = \{y|(x,y) \notin F^+ \cup (F^-)^+\}$$

$$r(x) = \{y|(x,y) \in F^+ \cup (F^-)^+\}$$

$c(x)$ consists of all elements that are not on the same line with x, i.e., not ordered with x while $r(x)$ consists of all elements each of which is ordered with x. Now, $x \neq y \rightarrow c(x) \neq c(y) \wedge r(x) \neq r(y)$ for all elements x and y in (Fig. 4.2b). Every element in (Fig. 4.2b) distinguishes itself with structural individuality.

Now back to Fig. 4.2a. In contrast to (Fig. 4.2b), all elements in (Fig. 4.2a), share the above defined $c(x)$ and $r(x)$, i.e., $c(x) = r(x) = c(y) = r(y) = \{z| z \in R\}$, where R is the set of all net elements in (Fig. 4.2a). Thus, elements in Fig. 4.2a would shrink to one point, since they are not structurally distinguishable.

Accompanying condition for an event, as mentioned above, is obtained, not by chance, but by an operation on nets called S-completion. There are two kinds of operations on nets, namely S/T-completion and S/T-complementation. These operations will be introduced in Part III.

4.2 Fundamental Phenomena

The concepts of fundamental phenomena specify how individual transitions are related with each other. Definitions of these concepts for EN-systems will provide a sound foundation for understanding them in other systems, since EN-systems are at the lowest layer of the net system hierarchy.

Instead of "marking," a "case" has been used for the EN-system. A subset of B used to be called a constellation of B in the literature. If it is reachable from the initial case c_{in}, it is called a case; otherwise, it is a non-case. Besides, all definitions in this section are to be given in terms of predicates.

Case or non-case, they are all subsets of B. For simplicity, c is called a case in definitions below. Let e_1, e_2 be two events of $(B, E; F, c_{in})$.

Definition 4.1 Enabled Event and Successor Event e is enabled by case c, if $c[e>$,

$$c[e> \equiv {}^{\cdot}e \subseteq c \wedge e^{\cdot} \cap c = \varnothing$$

and if e occurs at c and c' is the successor, then $c[e > c'$,

$$c[e > c' \equiv c[e> \wedge c' = (c - {}^{\cdot}e) \cup e^{\cdot}$$

Fig. 4.3 $c[e > c'$

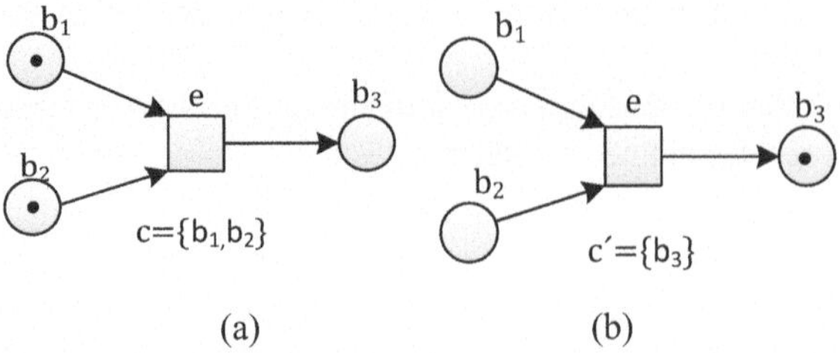

Fig. 4.4 Concurrent pair $c[e_1 \parallel e_2>$

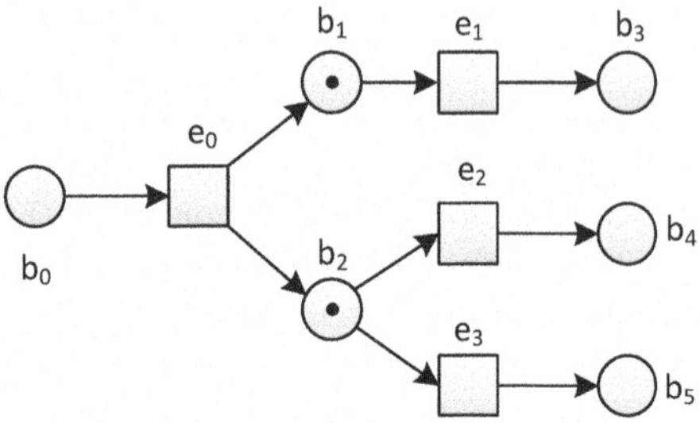

Here $c[e>$ is a binary predicate and $c[e > c'$ is a triple predicate. Such definitions are suitable for future automatic checking (Fig. 4.3).

Definition 4.2 Concurrency Events e_1 and e_2 are concurrent at c, if $c[e_1 \parallel e_2>$,

$$c[e_1 \parallel e_2> \equiv c[e_1> \wedge c[e_2> \wedge {}^{\cdot}e_1 \cap {}^{\cdot}e_2 = \varnothing \wedge e_1^{\cdot} \cap e_2^{\cdot} = \varnothing$$

The symbol "||" between e_1 and e_2 denotes "in parallel." In fact, e_1 and e_2 are structurally independent if they are in parallel. It is impossible to have ${}^{\cdot}e_1 \cap e_2^{\cdot} \neq \varnothing$, since otherwise $c[e_1> \wedge c[e_2>$ is impossible.

Let be $c = \{b_1, b_2\}$, c is reachable from initial case $c_{in} = \{b_0\}$ in Fig. 4.4. Now $c[e_1 \parallel e_2>$ and $c[e_1 \parallel e_3>$, but $\neg c[e_2 \parallel e_3>$, which means, concurrency is not transitive.

In all figures from Fig. 4.4 on, only those elements, that are related to figure titles, are named. This is to keep figures easier to read.

Definition 4.3 Ordered Event e_1 is before e_2, or e_1 and e_2 are ordered at c, if $c[e_1 \rightarrow e_2>$,

$$c[e_1 \rightarrow e_2> \equiv c[e_1 > c_1 \wedge c_1[e_2 > c_2 \wedge \neg c[e_2>$$

So, e_2 is enabled by the firing of e_1, either e_1 produces a token needed by e_2, or e_1 removes a token from a condition in $e_2^{\cdot}$ (Fig. 4.5).

This ordered relation is better called "immediate before" or "immediate after." The complete ordering relation among events can be derived since ordering relation is transitive.

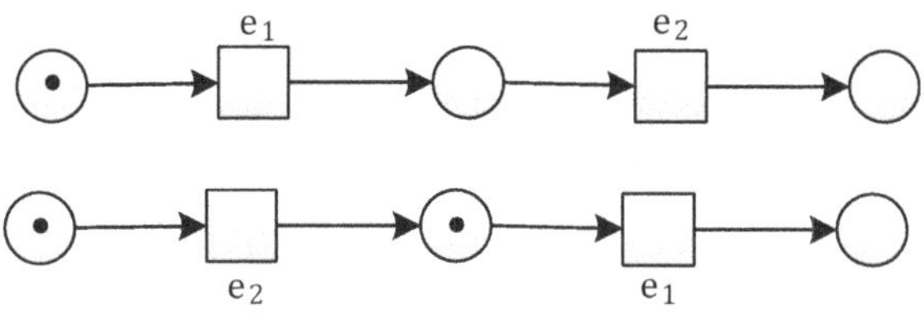

Fig. 4.5 Ordered pair $c[e_1 \rightarrow e_2>$

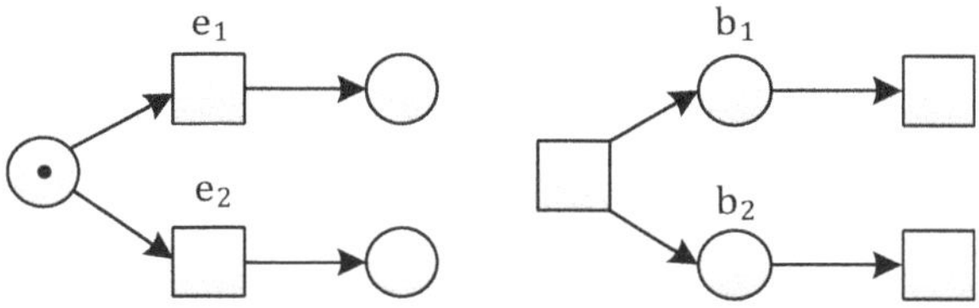

Fig. 4.6 A pair in conflict $c[e_1 | e_2>$ and the dual of the net

Definition 4.4 Conflict Events e_1 and e_2 are in conflict at c, if $c[e_1 | e_2>$,

$$c[e_1|e_2> \; \equiv c[e_1> \wedge \, c[e_2> \wedge \neg c[e_1 \parallel e_2>$$

So, only one of the conflicting events can fire at c, and that is what the symbol "|" means. The reason for $\neg c[e_1 \parallel e_2>$ is either ${}^{\cdot}e_1 \cap {}^{\cdot}e_2 \neq \emptyset$, or $e_1^{\cdot} \cap e_2^{\cdot} \neq \emptyset$.

Two nets are dual with each other if there is a correspondence f between their elements such that x is a T-element in this net, $f(x)$ is a S-element in the other net, and vice versa; besides, if (x, y) is an arc in this net, $(f(x), f(y))$ is an arc in the other net, and vice versa.

The nets in Fig. 4.6 are dual with each other, and as such conflict is dual to concurrency.

Definition 4.5 Contact Event e would lead to contact with condition b at case c, if $c[e \rightsquigarrow b>$,

$$c[e \rightsquigarrow b> \; \equiv \; {}^{\cdot}e \subseteq c \wedge b \in e^{\cdot} \cap c$$

The symbol "$\rightsquigarrow$" between e and b denotes that the arrow has been curved since the target condition b is true and it is, if e occurred, too "hard" to touch.

A contact situation is compared to a vehicle (e) with an obstacle (b) ahead ($b \in e^{\cdot} \cap c$) of it.

Definition 4.6 Potential Contact Event e is in potential contact with condition b at case c, if $c[e \dashrightarrow b>$,

$$c[e \dashrightarrow b> \; \equiv \; {}^{\cdot}e \cap c \neq \emptyset \wedge \neg({}^{\cdot}e \subseteq c) \wedge b \in e^{\cdot} \cap c$$

This is comparable to a vehicle stopped by a red light ($\neg({}^{\cdot}e \subseteq c)$) and an obstacle ahead ($b \in e^{\cdot} \cap c$). The symbol "$\dashrightarrow$" implies possible forward (irrational firing of e) (Fig. 4.7).

Fig. 4.7 Contact $c[e \rightsquigarrow b>$ and potential contact $c[e \dashrightarrow b>$

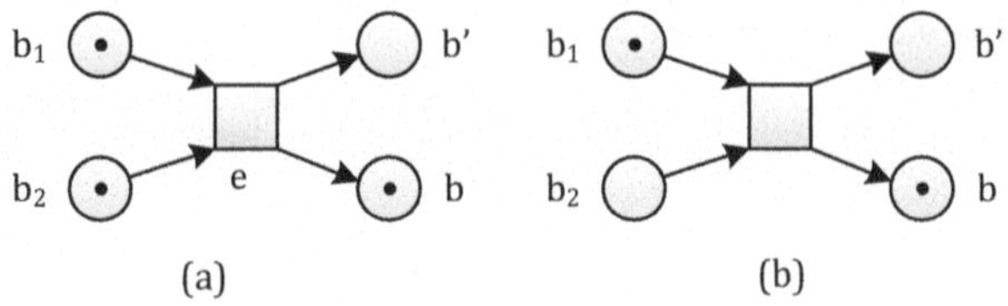

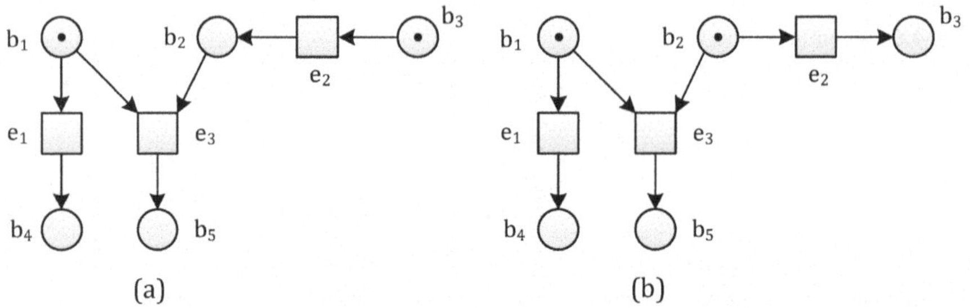

Fig. 4.8 A confusion triple $c[e_1 \overset{3}{-} e_2 >$

Let events e_1 and e_2 be concurrent at case c. Then there are 3 situations possible, i.e., e_1 and e_2 occur in parallel, or e_1 before e_2, or e_2 before e_1. Different firing ways of e_1 and e_2 may lead to different conflicts. Confusion is a mixture of parallel and conflict.

Definition 4.7 Confusion The triple (c, e_1, e_2) is in confusion if the above 3 situations lead to different conflicts: either the number of conflict pairs is increased/decreased, or conflict pairs are different. A confusion triple is denoted with $c[e_1 \overset{3}{-} e_2 >$ or $c[e_2 \overset{3}{-} e_1 >$. It is too complicated to formalize a confusion situation, and thus, $c[e_1 \overset{3}{-} e_2 >$ or $c[e_2 \overset{3}{-} e_1 >$ is not a formally defined predicate. Figure 4.8 below explains it better.

4.3 Application Examples

As said earlier, EN-systems would involve too many elements and too detailed descriptions in real applications. Examples given below are only toy applications. Though toys only, they serve to put together concepts defined separately into one system to show how they work in harmony.

Example 4.1 Dining Philosophers This example had long been taken to illustrate deadlock, and to explore ways to remove deadlock. But the real purpose is to study how to control (or manage) shared resources. Deadlock is but the result of no control. We have it here since it involves sequential events, concurrent events, and events in conflict.

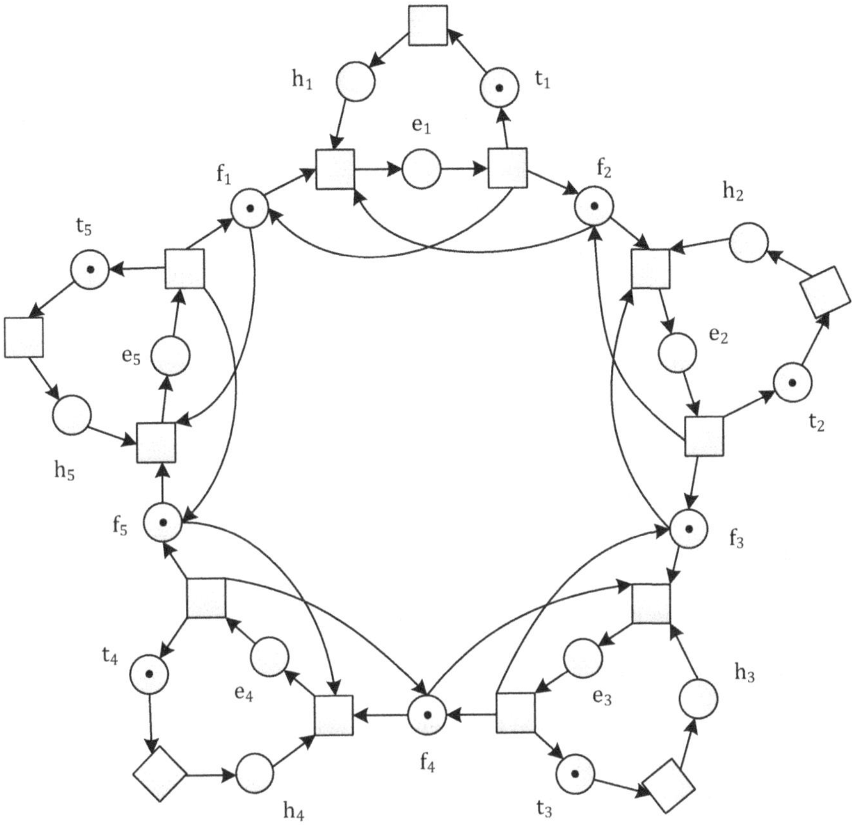

Fig. 4.9 Dining philosophers

Five philosophers are sitting at a round table thinking about human life. The sequential behavior of an individual philosopher is thinking → hungry → eating → thinking again. There on the table are 5 forks, each of which is in between two neighboring philosophers and ready for them to use. A hungry philosopher needs two forks on both his sides to start eating (Why two forks? Two chopsticks sound better). He would put back forks when he is satisfied. Figure 4.9 is a net describing the scene. In case forks are not controlled, every philosopher may pick up a fork at his own will. It is possible that every philosopher has a fork in his left hand, waiting for the one on his right. As such, all philosophers are deadlocked, and the whole system is dead.

Generally speaking, a deadlock is a mutually exclusive local property between two processes. A "hemiplegia" system (partly deadlocked) may still be alive. Formal definition of a deadlock is given below by Definition 4.8 after the discussion on fork control. Chained deadlock like philosophers is a special case.

A fair fork control aims mainly at efficiency of fork usage. Deadlock free is the minimum requirement for high efficiency. To be fair, to be deadlock free, etc., all these properties are related to an initial state, since they are semantic properties of a system.

As a start, the 5 tokens as shown in Fig. 4.9 indicate that all philosophers are thinking. Such an initial state does not lead to deadlock free or high efficiency of fork usage. A possibility is that two neighboring philosophers become hungry and try to pick up the shared fork at the same time. So a conflict appears. To avoid conflict, forks must be controlled. A straightforward way is to let forks be available in turn for neighboring philosophers as shown by Fig. 4.10 below. The problem is, which one of the two neighbors would be the first user? There are two directed circles in Fig. 4.10 consisting of arrows along that forks are to be passed. One circle includes f_i, and the other circle involves $f_i^{'}$, $i = 1, 2, 3, 4, 5$. A token in f_i denotes that the shared fork is for p_i to use, while a token in $f_i^{'}$ indicates that the same fork is available to p_{i-1}. There are 3 possible distributions of the 5 tokens on the two circles, i.e., 5:0, 4:1 and 3:2.

5:0 leads to deadlock: every philosopher has one fork available, while the other fork is available to his neighbor. They are all waiting, and no one would give up.

4:1 is a sequential solution; there is exactly one philosopher who has both forks available.

3:2 allows concurrency; two philosophers may be eating at the same time.

The net system in Fig. 4.10 gives the 3:2 solution. There are 3 tokens on the first circle and 2 tokens on the second one. Figure 4.10a is a complete description and (Fig. 4.10b) is a simplified version.

Definition 4.8 Deadlock, A Local Property Between Two Events Event e_1 and e_2 are deadlocked with each other, if $c[e_1 \leftrightarrow e_2>$,

$$c[e_1 \leftrightarrow e_2 > \equiv$$

$$\exists b_1, b_2 \in B : \left(b_1 \in {}^{\cdot}e_1 \cap e_2{}^{\cdot} \wedge b_2 \in e_1{}^{\cdot} \cap {}^{\cdot}e_2\right) \wedge b_1 = b_2$$

Figure 4.11 illustrates deadlock situations. It seems unreasonable to require $b_1 = b_2$ in the definition. But this does not require $b_1 = b_2$ to be always true. In case $b_1 = b_2$ becomes true, a deadlock is raised.

Deadlock is defined here as a fundamental phenomenon between two events. It does not include those deadlocks that involve more events, e.g., all 5 hungry philosophers may be deadlocked together.

Having introduced fundamental phenomena found in the example of dining philosophers, efficiency of fork usage should be studied to have a complete answer to satisfy philosophers. The question is, if a philosopher keeps thinking for a long time while forks are granted to him for use, then the fork would be idle before he becomes hungry. What could be done to keep the efficiency of fork usage? Figure 4.12 suggests an answer: to take back the idle fork for his neighbor to use. The net in Fig. 4.12 has an arrow with small circle as its head (⍰). This arrow is called an "inhibit arc." An inhibit arc requires the related condition to have no token (being false). So, in case a philosopher p_i remains not hungry for a certain time (agreed by

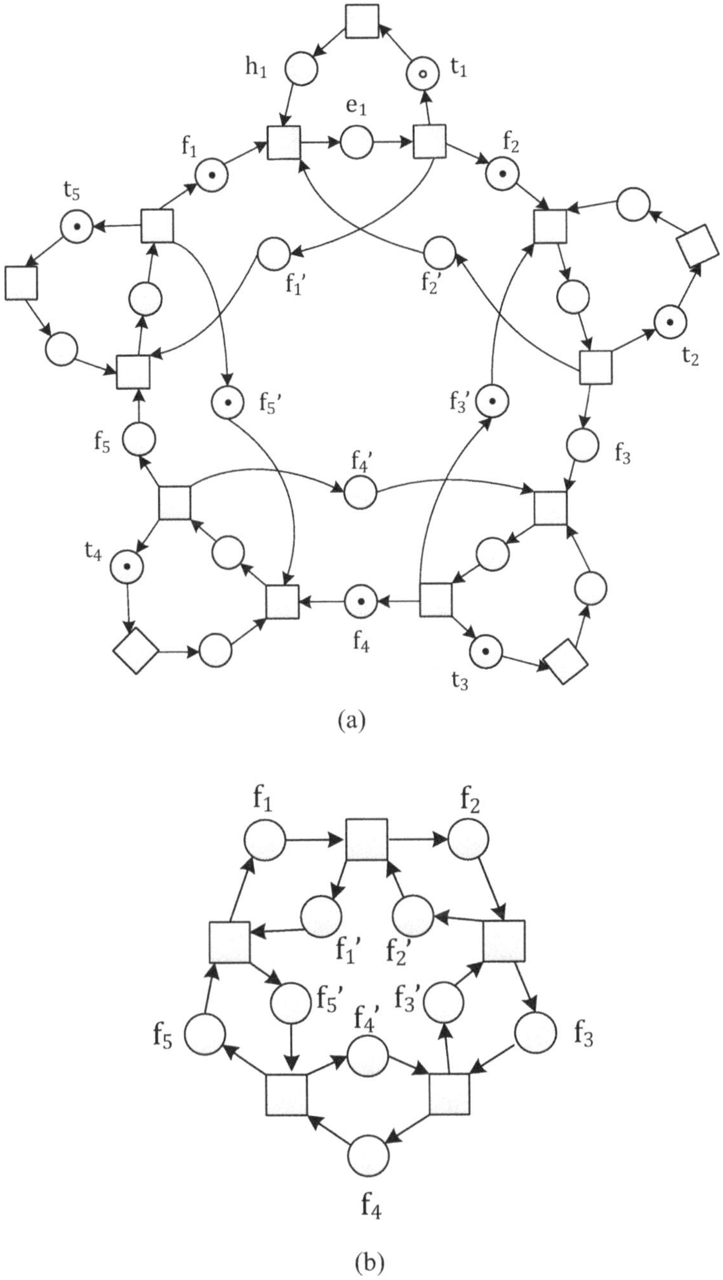

Fig. 4.10 The first users

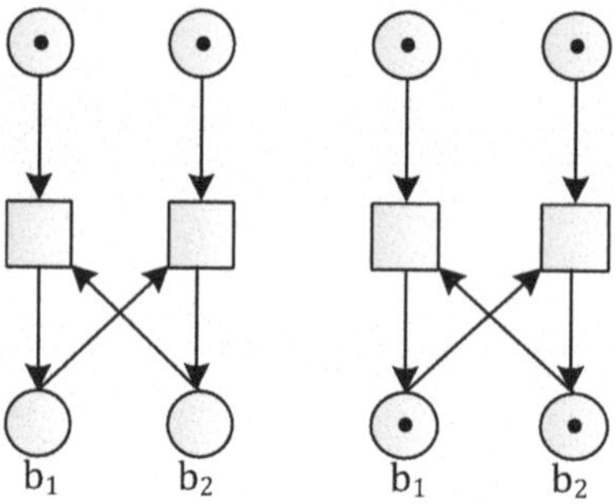

Fig. 4.11 Deadlock: $b_1 = b_2$

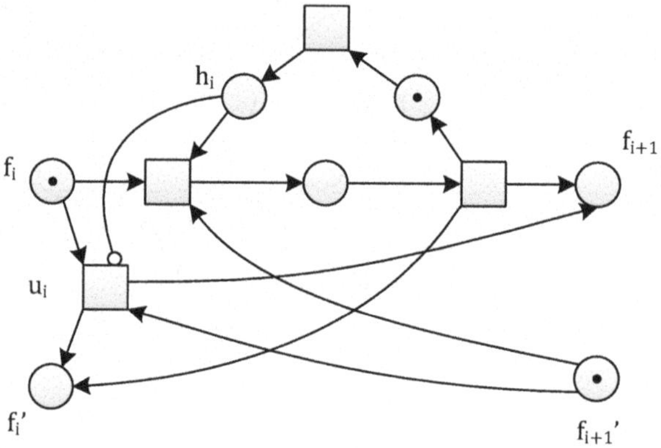

Fig. 4.12 Event u_i

all philosophers) and both forks are waiting for him to use, event u_i would re-assign the forks to his neighbors.

The concept of inhibit arcs enriches the net definition by allowing an input condition to have a side effect. To formally include an inhibit arc as consisting part of a directed net, the only thing to do is just to extend the flow relation F and to modify the definition of $c[e>$ and $c[e>c'$.

Definition 4.9 Inhibit Arc: Enabled and Successor An arc (b, e) in F is called an inhibit arc and e is enabled at c, if $c\lfloor e>$,

$$c\lfloor e> \equiv \left(b \in {}^{\cdot}e \wedge b \notin c\right) \wedge \left({}^{\cdot}e - \{b\}\right) \subseteq c \wedge e^{\cdot} \cap c = \varnothing$$

c' is the successor case, if $c\lfloor e > c'$,

$$c\lfloor e> c' \equiv c\lfloor e> \wedge\, c' = \left(c - {}^{\cdot}e\right) \cup e^{\cdot}.$$

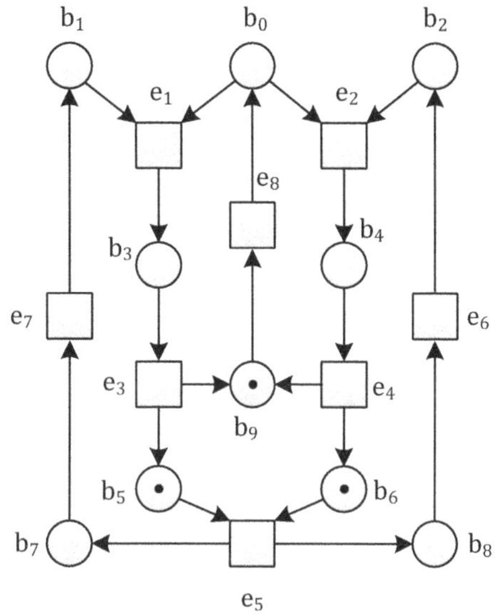

Fig. 4.13 Church wedding

Note that as the difference between $c\lfloor e>$ and $c[e>$, two points are important for $c\lfloor e>$: firstly, b is in the preset of e, but $b \notin c$, secondly, b remains to be false after the fire of e, i.e., $b \notin c'$. Formally, we have $b \in {}^{\cdot}e \wedge (c\lfloor e > c' \rightarrow b \notin c \wedge b \notin c')$.

Interested readers are encouraged to assemble transition u_i in Fig. 4.12 into the net system in Fig. 4.9 and to figure out how an inhibit arc functions.

Example 4.2 Wedding Ceremony Figure 4.13 below is a net system for church wedding. The token in conditions b_0, b_1 and b_2 are respectively the ready states of the wedding host, the bride, and groom. Events e_1, and e_2 are respectively the talking between host and bride/groom, e_3 and e_4 are respectively waiting for groom/bride, e_0 is the return of the host to ready state. Event e_5 is a combined event to keep the net simple. It includes the ring-exchange event, the leaving of the bride&groom, and the show up of next pair of bride&groom. Finally, the new comers step up (e_6 and e_7) to meet the host.

For those readers who has played "token game" based on the net system in Fig. 2.2 (a), this system is not new. With definitions of concepts for fundamental phenomena, the meanings of fundamental phenomena like conflict, non-transitivity of concurrency, etc., become concrete and clearer now. Event e_8 is concurrent with e_5, and also concurrent with e_6, e_7 (in case e_5 fires before e_8), but e_5 must fire before e_6, e_7.

Example 4.3 Stack for Data Management A memory cell is compared to a condition since it is either holding a data or no data (a meaningful value). It seems proper to use the EN-system.

There are two kinds of stacks, namely, FIFO and FILO, i.e., first-in first-out and first-in last-out. Furthermore, a stack may have a fixed or flexible capacity. It is easy to implement a FIFO/FILO with fixed capacity as shown in Fig. 4.14.

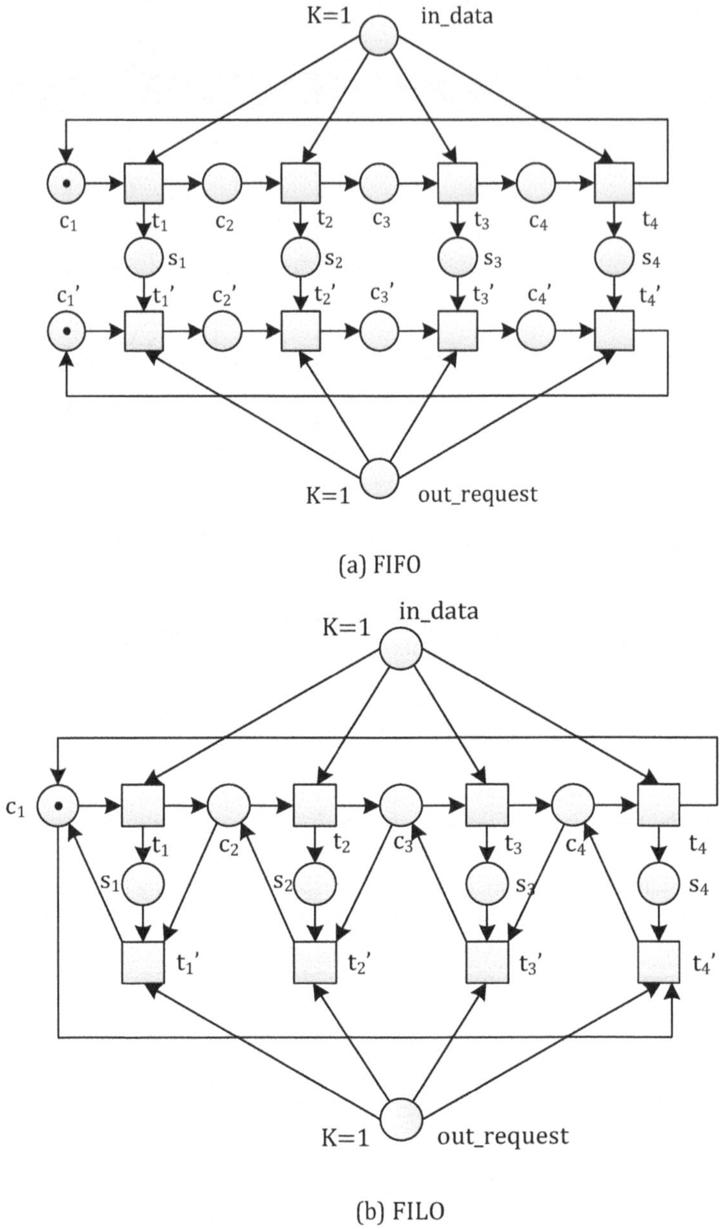

Fig. 4.14 Stack: FIFO (**a**) and FILO (**b**)

Here to be discussed is flexible capacity. This is, perhaps, a nice topic for a research paper, but not a good idea in practice. To implement a stack, certain memory locations must be assigned to it. The size of the assigned locations may

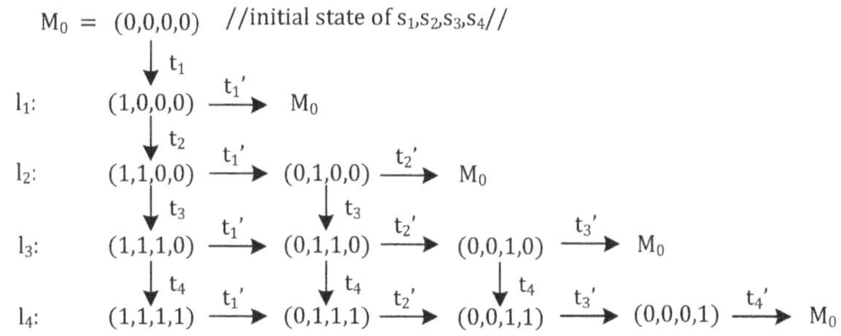

Fig. 4.15 Data in and out for FIFO

be great enough so the stack acts as if it is infinitely big, or in more attractive wording, it has a flexible capacity. It is in this sense that the above FIFO and FILO may have flexible capacity as well. So, "flexible" is meaningful to scholars only, not for software engineers.

The graphically presented FIFO stack in Fig. 4.14a corresponds to the triple (*S*, *T*; *F*) as given below:

$$S = \{in - data, out - request, s_1, s_2, s_3, s_4, c_1, c_2, c_3, c_4, c_1', c_2', c_3', c_4'\}$$

$$T = \{t_1, t_2, t_3, t_4, t_1', t_2', t_3', t_4'\}$$

$$F = \{(in - data, t_i)|i = 1, 2, 3, 4\} \cup \{(out - request, t_i')|i = 1, 2, 3, 4\}$$

$$\cup\{(t_i, s_i), (s_i, t_i')|i = 1, 2, 3, 4\}$$

$$\cup\{(c_i, t_i), (t_i, c_{i+1})|i = 1, 2, 3, 4\} \cup \{(c_4, t_4), (t_4, c_1)\}$$

$$\cup\{(c_i', t_i'), (t_i', c_{i+1}')|i = 1, 2, 3, 4\} \cup \{(c_4', t_4'), (t_4', c_1')\}$$

S-elements in-data and out-request are interfaces between stack users and stack. It is assumed that their capacity is 1. The stack does not care how to keep order in case there are more than one data waiting to get into the stack, or there are more users waiting to get a date from the stack. Note that it is not included in this FIFO stack structure where the out data is gone, since it varies from requester to requester.

To see how FIFO works, let's assume that data-in and data-out requests come one after another. Our attention concentrates on s_1, s_2, s_3, s_4, since these are where data are stored. $M(s_i) = 1$ and $M(s_i) = 0$ indicate that s_i is holding a data or no data respectively. Data-in will enable t_1, t_2, t_3, t_4 to occur one after another while the stack is not full. In case data-out is requested, then t_1', t_2', t_3', t_4' would fire one by one while the stack is not empty. Figure 4.15 below tells the dynamics of inside FIFO.

The order for in data is

$$(0, 0, 0, 0) \rightarrow (1, 0, 0, 0) \rightarrow (1, 1, 0, 0) \rightarrow (1, 1, 1, 0) \rightarrow (1, 1, 1, 1)$$

The order for out data is

$$(1,1,1,1) \rightarrow (0,1,1,1) \rightarrow (0,0,1,1) \rightarrow (0,0,0,1) \rightarrow (0,0,0,0)$$

It is clear that data are first in first out.

Figure 4.15 is another way to draw an occurrence net. It is also a reachable tree. A stack is a reactive system to provide storage service. Such a system does not have a complete initial state. With possible service requests in the future, the initial state would become complete. Figure 4.15 exposes the dynamics of it.

It must be admitted that Fig. 4.14 is just a reference for implementing FIFO and FILO. Dynamic management of memory locations is complicated. Nets may not be a proper means for this. But for teaching, Figs. 4.14 and 4.15 may be helpful to students.

Chapter 5
Place/Transition Net Systems

Abstract A Selement may hold resourses of the same kind that play the same role. Drinking water is different from water in rivers, and should be held by different places.

As defined earlier, a Place/Transition system, P/T-system for short, is a 6-tuple $\sum = (P, T; F, K, W, M_0)$, in which, $(P, T; F)$ is a directed net, K is a capacity function on P, W is a weight function on F, and M_0 is an initial marking, i.e., initial resource distribution.

For EN-systems, fundamental phenomena reflect mainly in structural properties, while for P/T-systems, fundamental phenomena tell semantic relations between transitions.

5.1 Fundamental Phenomena

Let M, t_1 and t_2 be respectively a marking and two transitions of $\sum$.

Definition 5.1 Concurrency Transitions t_1 and t_2 are concurrent at M, if $M[t_1 \parallel t_2>$,

$$\begin{aligned} M[t_1 \parallel t_2> \; &\equiv M[t_1> \wedge M[t_2> \\ &\wedge \forall p \in {}^{\bullet}t_1 \cap {}^{\bullet}t_2 : M(p) \geq w(p, t_1) + w(p, t_2) \\ &\wedge \forall p \in t_1^{\bullet} \cap t_2^{\bullet} : M(p) + w(t_1, p) + w(t_2, p) \leq K(p) \end{aligned}$$

Note that $M[t_1 \parallel t_2> \; = M[t_2 \parallel t_1>$ by definition, i.e., $\parallel$ is commutative. Besides, a place is different from a variable, no read/write conflict for places.

Definition 5.2 Sequence Transitions t_1 and t_2 are sequentially related at M, if $M[t_1 \rightarrow t_2> \; \equiv M[t_1 > M' \wedge M'[t_2> \; \wedge \; \neg M[t_2>$.

C. Yuan, *Principle of Petri Nets*, https://doi.org/10.1007/978-981-97-7336-7_5

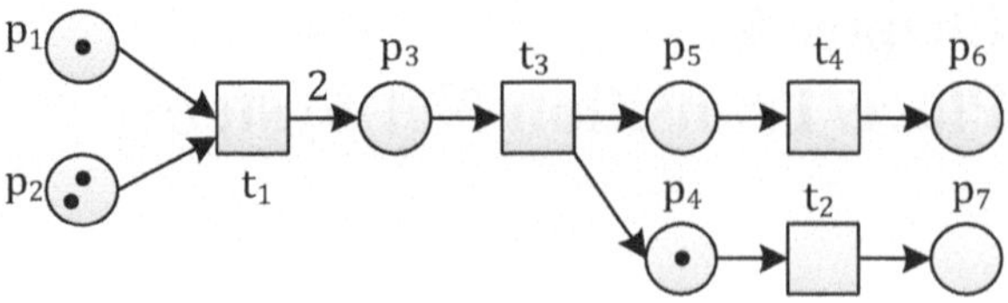

$$M_0 = (1,2,0,1,0,0,0)$$

$$M_1 = (0,1,2,1,0,0,0)$$

$$M_2 = (0,1,2,0,0,0,1)$$

Fig. 5.1 Concurrency $M_0[t_1 \parallel t_2>$ and sequence $M_2[t_3 \rightarrow t_4>$

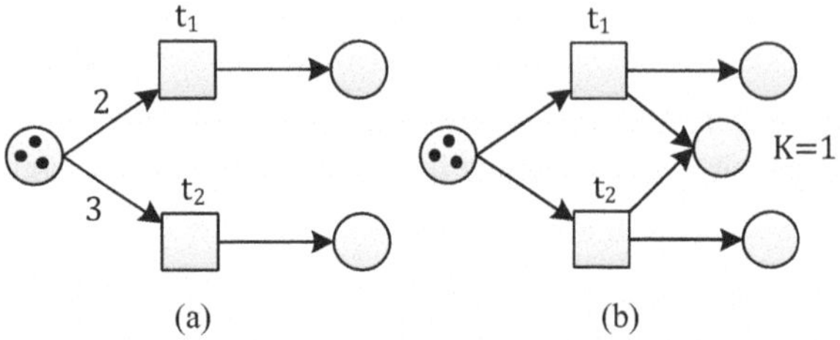

Fig. 5.2 Conflicts

That is, if the firing of t_1 enables t_2, the firing of t_2 must follow the firing of t_1.

The markings for the net in Fig. 5.1 are $M_0 = (1, 2, 0, 1, 0, 0, 0)$, $M_1 = (0, 1, 2, 1, 0, 0, 0)$, $M_2 = (0, 1, 2, 0, 0, 0, 1)$.

Note that $M_0[t_1 \rightarrow t_2>$ and $M_0[t_1 \rightarrow t_4>$ are not true, though t_2 and t_4 must fire after t_1. So, "$\rightarrow$" implies "immediately follow."

Definition 5.3 Conflict Transitions t_1 and t_2 are in conflict at marking M, if $M[t_1 \mid t_2>$,

$$M[t_1 \mid t_2 > \equiv M[t_1 > \wedge M[t_2 > \wedge \neg M[t_1 \parallel t_2 >$$

There are two cases that cause a conflict, either t_1 and t_2 are "fighting" for a shared token, or "fighting" for shared space. Figure 5.2 exhibits conflicts: fighting for token (a) and fighting for space (b).

Definition 5.4 Contact Transition t is in contact with place s at marking M, if $M[t \rightsquigarrow s>$,

$$M[t \rightsquigarrow s > \equiv \forall p \in {}^{\cdot}t : M(p) \geq w(p,t)$$
$$\wedge s \in t^{\cdot} \wedge M(s) + w(t,s) > K(s)$$

The firing of t is disabled by the lack of space at place s. In other words, should t fire, place s would have a token over flow.

Definition 5.5 Potential Contact Transition t is in potential contact with place s, at marking M, if $M[t \dashrightarrow s>$,

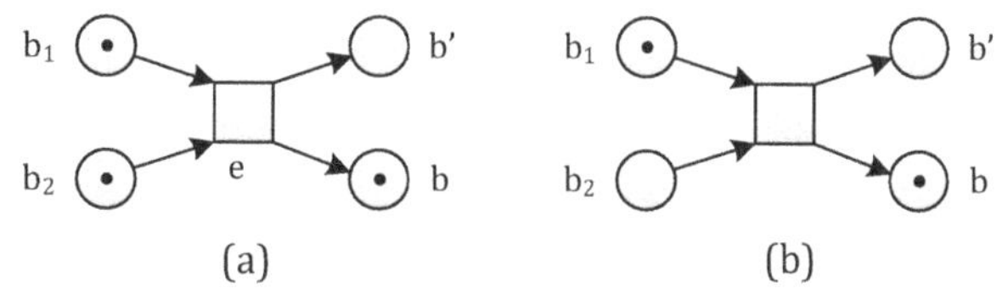

Fig. 5.3 Contact and potential contact

$$M[t \dashrightarrow s> \ \equiv s \in t^{\bullet} \wedge M(s) + w(t, s) > K(s)$$
$$\wedge \exists s' \in {}^{\bullet}t : M(s') < w(s', t)$$

The lack of tokens at the preset of t ($M(s') < w(s', t)$) has disabled transition t, so contact situation at place s ($M(s) + w(t, s) > K(s)$) is avoided. Though contact is only potential, it implies possible harm in practice, since rules are not always well followed.

Figure 5.3 includes both contact and potential contact in P/T-systems.

Confusion is one of the fundamental phenomena for EN-systems. It is possible, at least theoretically speaking, to define it for P/T-systems as well. But it would be too complicated to do so. As such, confusion in P/T-systems is not included in this book. Just remember that confusion is a mixture of concurrency and conflict. The conflict situation would be different due to the different ways of concurrent transition firings.

5.2 Properties and Analysis Methods

As a preparation, properties shared by net systems have been defined in Chap. 2. Respective application areas have their own requirements on system properties. For example, a fire extinguisher system in a city is required to respond as quickly as possible, a tall building needs a lift system to provide in-time service, the discipline of software engineering needs a system model for program analysis, etc. As an application example, a lift system will be discussed in Sect. 5.3 next. As for software engineering, a new system model called C-net has been proposed as mentioned earlier.

There are three different ways to understand a net system: focusing on system states, focusing on transition sequences, or focusing on both states and transition sequences.

With transition sequences, we have defined live and fair net systems. Both of them seem to be logically reasonable, but they rely on infinite transition sequences. We will redefine them, when synchrony is introduced.

With system states, the set of reachable markings, i.e., $[M_0>$, has been constructively defined and an algorithm to compute $[M_0>$ for finite net systems is given below. System properties will be discussed based on $[M_0>$.

The concept of system processes contains both transitions and markings. It is the main means to understand net systems. Before talking about processes, an algorithm for computing $[M_0>$ is given below.

Definition 5.6 Partial Ordering of Markings Marking M is greater than or equal to marking $M^{'}$, or $M^{'}$ is covered by marking M, denoted with $M \geq M^{'}$, if $\forall s \in S$: $M(s) \geq M^{'}(s)$. For place $p \in S$, $M > M^{'}$ is true at p, if $M \geq M^{'} \wedge M(p) > M^{'}(p)$.

Next is an algorithm to compute a reachable tree $T(\Sigma)$ so that every marking in $[M_0>$ is covered by a node of $T(\Sigma)$. As defined before, a marking does not allow infinity (ω or ∞) to be its element. In order to cover an infinite $[M_0>$ with a finite tree, the concept of marking is now extended to allow ω as its element.

Algorithm 5.1 To Compute $T(\Sigma)$ Every node u of $T(\Sigma)$ has a marking M_u attached to it.

1. To start with, $T(\Sigma)$ has only a root node r, $M_r = M_o$, Node r is now also a leaf of $T(\Sigma)$.
2. Select a leaf node x from $T(\Sigma)$, if it exists. If M_x enables no transition, then x is an end node. An end node is no longer counted as a leaf from the time it becomes an end leaf. Next, if there exists a node z on the route from r to x such that $M_x = M_z$, then x is also an end node. If $T(\Sigma)$ has no more leaf node, terminate. Otherwise, go to step 3).
3. If x is not an end node, for transition τ enabled by M_x and $M_x[\tau>M^{'}$, add a son node y to x on $T(\Sigma)$ with $M_y = M^{'}$. On the arc from M_x to $M^{'}$ is transition τ. If there is a marking M on the route from r to y, such that $M^{'} > M$ at p, then change $M^{'}(p)$ to ω. Do the same for every place like p. Do the same with every transition enabled by M_x. Back to step (2).

To prove the correctness of the above algorithm, termination is of primary importance. Then, it must be proved that every reachable marking is covered by a node on $T(\Sigma)$.

Theorem 5.1 Termination of Algorithm 5.1 Algorithm 5.1 terminates and every marking in $[M_0>$ is covered by a node of $T(\Sigma)$.

Proof

1. Treat M_0 as a positive integer (n digits integer), the number of positive integers smaller than M_0 is finite. Thus, sooner or later in the algorithm execution, some marking (as an integer) will reappear to end a subtree, or increasing number to have a ω invoked. Since n is just a positive integer, ω may appear at most n times. All subtrees and the whole algorithm will terminate.
2. Every marking M in $[M_0>$ corresponds to a transition sequence, and this sequence would be encountered in the process of algorithm execution to produce $T(\Sigma)$. The node on $T(\Sigma)$ reached by the transition sequence is either exactly M or a marking which contains ω that covers M.

Figure 5.4 contains two P/T-systems and their shared reachable tree.

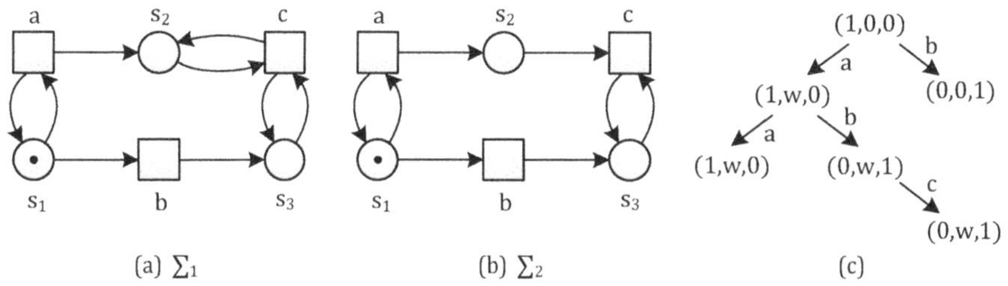

Fig. 5.4 P/T-system Σ_1, Σ_2 and their reachable tree

It is nice to have a finite tree to cover all reachable markings. But there are weak points of $T(\Sigma)$. The first problem is, as suggested by Fig. 5.4, two different systems share the same tree while they have different properties. For Σ_1, once transition c is enabled, it will be repeatedly enabled regardless of whether transition a fires again or not. For Σ_2, transition c has to wait for tokens from transition a. But we have $T(\Sigma_1) = T(\Sigma_2)$. The second problem is that the way how son nodes of the same father are related is not clear: they may be concurrent or in conflict. The third and more important problem is $T(\Sigma)$ does not make a difference among its leaf nodes. A leaf node may be a dead marking (enables no transition), or a repeatable marking. Next algorithm constructs a reachable graph $G(\Sigma)$ from $T(\Sigma)$, and $G(\Sigma)$ removes the last problem.

Algorithm 5.2 From Tree *T*(*Σ*) to Graph *G*(*Σ*) Check every leaf node of $T(\Sigma)$, if there is a node y on the route from root r of $T(\Sigma)$ to leaf node x such that $M_y \leq M_x$ (ω may appear in M_x), then overlay x on y.

This algorithm would terminate since $T(\Sigma)$ has only a finite number of leaf nodes.

The circle obtained by overlay x and y is called a "basic circle" and y is its start point. Transitions on arrows of a basic circle form a transition sequence called a basic sequence, y is also the starting point of this sequence. Here, a transition sequence is slightly different from a normal transition sequence since $M_y \neq M_0$.

To apply Algorithm 5.2 to Σ_2, in Fig. 5.2, some modification is required. Transition c of Σ_2 may fire many times before the firing of transition b. To express this "arbitrarily great, but not infinite" property $\omega - 1$ is used instead of ω. Thus, as $T(\Sigma_2)$, the node marking $(0, \omega, 1)$ after transition c should be $(0, \omega - 1, 1)$. Node $(0, \omega, 1)$ and node $(0, \omega - 1, 1)$ do not form a basic circle and transition c does not belong to a basic sequence.

With this fine change, Fig. 5.5 contains two reachable graphs obtained by Algorithm 5.2 from $T(\Sigma_1)$ in Fig. 5.4(c) and from modified $T(\Sigma_2)$.

Theorem 5.2 Properties Based on *G*(*Σ*)

1. If $G(\Sigma)$ has a leaf node, Σ is dead.
2. In case $G(\Sigma)$ has no leaf node, then transitions shared by all basic sequences are all live. Transitions not belonging to all basic sequences are dead.
3. Every live transition of Σ belongs to all basic sequences (circles).
4. If Σ is live, then every transition belongs to all basic circles of $G(\Sigma)$.

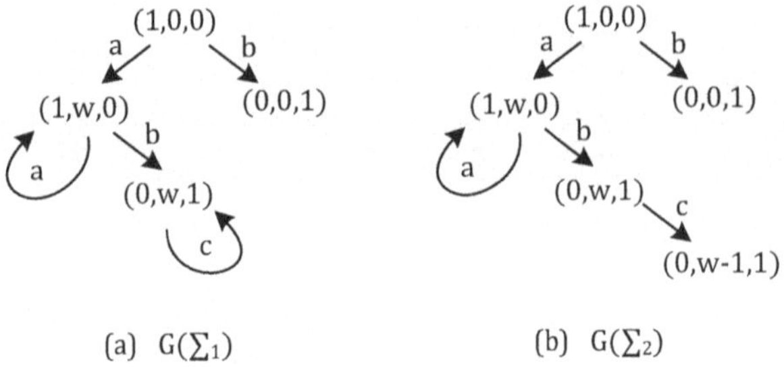

Fig. 5.5 $G(\Sigma_1)$ and $G(\Sigma_2)$

5. In case $G(\Sigma)$ contains a ω, then Σ is unbounded.
6. Every transition sequence (finite or infinite) must be a sequence of transitions attached to a route of $G(\Sigma)$, including repeatable basic circles. The reverse is also true since the use of $\omega - 1$ has removed false basic circles.
7. Σ is fair to transitions t_1 and t_2, if they belong to the same basic circles.

All properties listed above do not need a proof since a basic sequence is repeatable. Now, being live and being fair are no longer defined with infinite transition sequences.

More important properties for a real application are related with problems that demand a solution. The example of n-lift control will serve to illustrate it.

5.3 N-Lift Control

This is a conventional problem, involving concurrency, conflict, etc. To include this example here, do not tell readers how good Nets is, but rather, let readers get to know the dual character of Nets.

Given A M-floor building that has N lifts for service.

Buttons to request services are respectively:

$Fu(i) : i = 1, 2, \cdots, M$, floor up buttons;
$Fd(j) : j = 1, 2, 3, \cdots, M$, floor down buttons;
$\mathcal{L}(k) : k = 1, 2, \cdots, M$, lift buttons inside a lift.

The two button $Fu(M)$ and $Fd(1)$ do not exist in reality. They are included above, just for simplicity. Anyway, they will never be pushed since they do not exist.

Floor button $Fu(i)$ requests a lift to come to a stop at floor i in up direction; $Fd(j)$ requests a lift to come to stop at floor j in the down direction; $\mathcal{L}(k)$ requests the lift to go to floor k and to stop. Whenever a lift stops, it will always open the door and then close it. For simplicity, this process of open and close will not be repeated next.

It is of dual nature with Nets as system model for a lift system. It gains simplicity while it loses flexibility.

First, it gains simplicity.

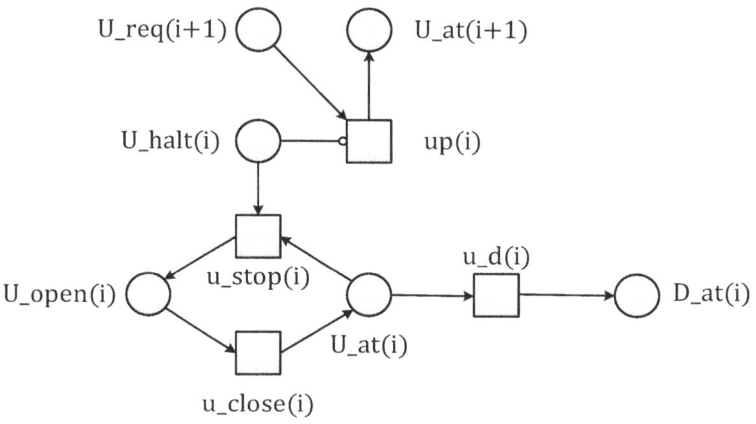

Fig. 5.6 Transitions at floor *i*

For global control, the complexity of N-lift problem is $(M, N, 2)$, M floors, N lifts, and 2 directions.

The author was told years ago that $N \leq 6$ is a must in practice. It is noticeable that 6 lifts are the general case for many of a tall building. The global states of 7 or more lifts may be too complicated to manage, or a group of 6 lifts can provide good service for a hotel or office building in general, including rush hours. The fact is that complaints are not rare. Experience in the past is: a lift in your direction might be passing by you without stopping since the lift was either full or dispatched before your push.

The wanted lift service should not disappoint passengers, i.e., whenever a lift passes by a floor, it responds to a floor button push by stopping unless "full" is displayed. So, passengers would not be complaining. But global dispatch is not flexible enough to do so, for service requests are not predictable. A simplest way to avoid "passing by without stopping" is to have no control. Let every lift go up from the bottom to top and then return to the bottom. Lifts stop at every floor to release/receive passengers. But low efficiency does not allow this way of "control by no control."

For Nets, the principle of local determination allows us to focus on one lift only. So, N is reduced to 1. Floor buttons are shared by all lifts in the way of "first arrive, first serve." As such, the complexity may be reduced from $(M, N, 2)$ to $(1, 1, 1)$, 1 lift, 1 floor, and 1 direction, since actions of a lift at every floor are the same (we have buttons $Fu(M)$ and $Fd(1)$) and up direction and down direction are anti-symmetric. Local determination is the merit of Nets.

Figure 5.6 includes transitions at floor i. This net is clear and easy to understand, except that element $U\_req(i+1)$ and $U\_halt(i)$ are explained below.

On the other hand, however, fixed extension of transitions in nets has made flexibility low. A lift in reality may go up/down from one floor to any other floor and stop in between as requested. But in Nets, atomicity of transitions allows only actions to go up/down one floor, since only these moves are atomic actions. As such,

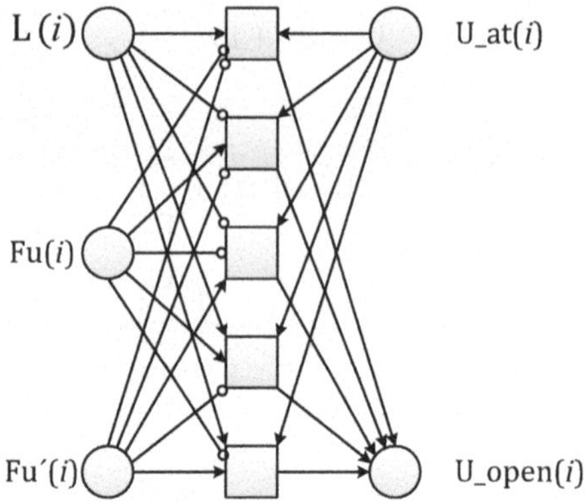

Fig. 5.7 To stop at floor *i* in up direction

many details have to be included to model lift control. This seems a draw back from practice. But, as far as system modeling is concerned, nets uses fewer achieve elements to represent lift moves. For example, only four moves are needed in up direction for a 5-floor lift, while there are possible $C_5^2 = 10$ floor combination lift moves.

Note that we have simplified the lift problem from $(M, N, 2)$ to $(1, 1, 1)$ and concentrate now on a single lift.

Figure 5.7 is a net for just one action, i.e., to stop at floor i in up direction. In Fig. 5.7, place $U\_at(i)$ is a lift state: having arrived (but not necessarily stops) at floor i. Place $U\_open(i)$ is also a lift state: having its door opened. State $U\_at(i)$ may enable two transitions: it enables $U\_stop(i)$ if required; otherwise (inhibit arc and $U\_halt(i)$ has no token), it goes on up to $U\_at(i+1)$.

Note that $Fu(i) \vee Fu'(i) \vee \mathcal{L}(i) = Halt(i)$, where $Fu'(i)$ is obtained when $Fu(i)$ has been read by some lift (becoming the responsible lift) and waiting to be served. $Fu'(i)$ requires just a pass-by service before the responsible lift arrives. The function of $Fu'(i)$ is to avoid the second lift to read $Fu(i)$ and to take the same responsibility.

The atomicity of transitions requires button pushes to be decomposed into atomic requests. $U\_req(i)$ is obtained from the decomposition of a floor up button or a lift button. In case the lift is at floor i. For $j, j > i$, the decomposition is as below:

$$U\_at(i) \wedge i < j \rightarrow$$
$$Fu(j) \cong U\_req(i) + U\_req(i+1) + \cdots + u\_stop(j)$$
$$\mathcal{L}(j) \cong U\_req(i) + U\_req(i+1) + \cdots + u\_stop(j)$$

"$\cong$" is used instead of "=", since $u\_stop(j)$ is a transition, rather than a place.

Note that $u\_stop(j)$ is a transition for the lift to stop. Up transitions are prefixed with "$u\_$" and places in up direction is prefixed with "$U\_$". All U_reqs are ended by a u_stop to ensure safety.

Above decomposition is illustrated by transition $u\_readFu(i,j)$. In Fig. 5.8, the lift is at floor i to read button $Fu(j)$. $U\_req(i+1, j)$ is abbreviation of $U\_req(i+1)$,

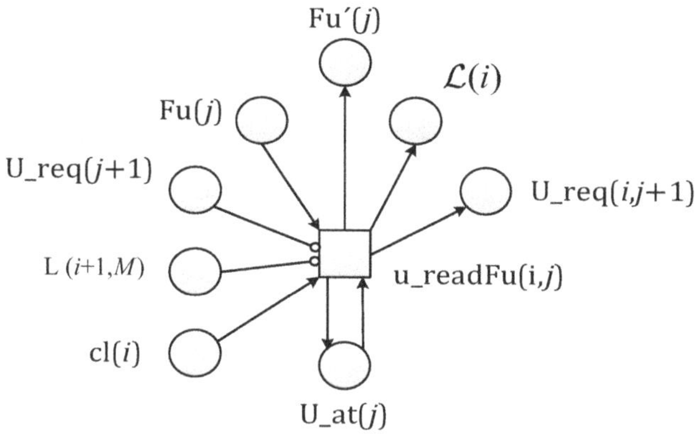

Fig. 5.8 Transition $u\_readFu(i,j)$

$U\_req(i+2),\cdots,U\_\mathrm{req}(j)$. A lift would read its own button first. Only if no lift button is pushed, a pushed floor button would be read. That is why transition $u\_readFu(i,j)$ has inhibit arcs from $\mathcal{L}(i+1,j)$, an abbreviation of $\mathcal{L}(i+1)$, $\mathcal{L}(i+2)$, $\cdots$, $\mathcal{L}(j)$.

Figure 5.9 includes almost all transitions at floor j in both directions. It is very complicated to understand. Human readers are very likely giving up reading. But for people working in the lift profession, nets may be of help in design stage.

To make clear the merit and the drawback of nets in modelling lifts, Fig. 5.6 is the net for one lift at one floor. The net seems simple and clear. But it requires explanation. When the lift reaches floor i, it may stop at request $U\_halt(i)$, otherwise it would go up to floor $i+1$ if required by $U\_req(i+1)$. In case of no stop request and no up request, the lift would change to down direction.

Atomicity of transitions has led to a complicated solution of N-lift problem. The algebraic presentation of this solution is also complicated since atomicity is the same, no matter what means to use for transition presentation.

We will return to this example when color net systems are discussed.

5.4 Toy Examples

Example 5.1 To Free a Prisoner This story came to me about 40 years ago when I was a visiting scholar abroad.

A prison cell has two openings, a and b. One opens to outside and leads to freedom, and the other one opens to the execution ground. Two guards, A and B, are standing outside a and b respectively, say A is guarding a, and B is guarding b. One of the guards is a truth teller while the other one is a liar. The prisoner is told that he may ask A or B one yes/no question, and based on the answer, he can choose a or b to go out and be freed or executed. Assuming that the prisoner asks guard A. The

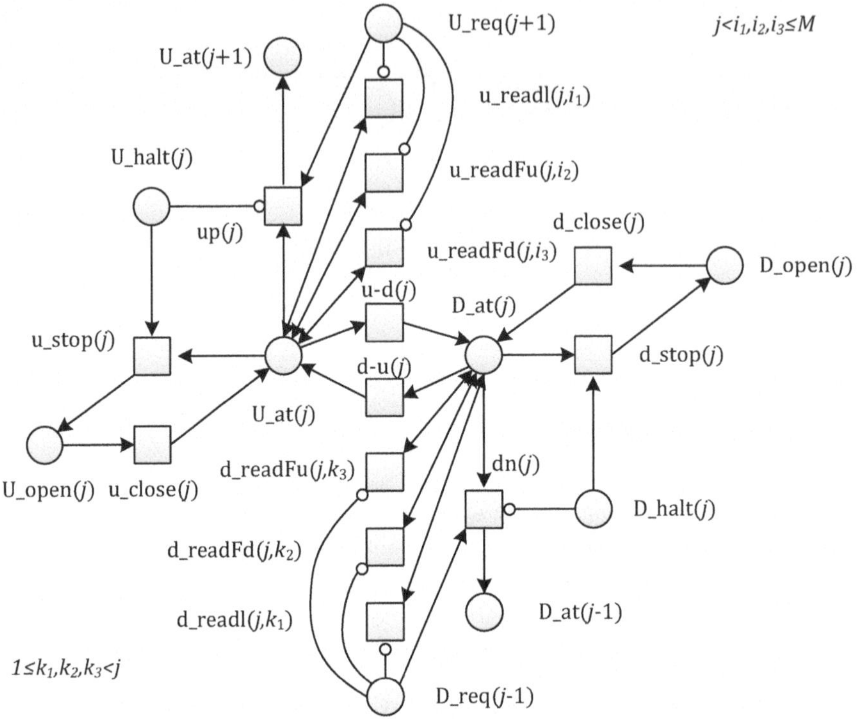

Fig. 5.9 Transitions at one floor in both directions

question should be in the form: "a complete statement plus yes or no," and it should be answered directly by the guard to be asked. This is because the answer from *B* to *A* (a liar and a truth teller) to the prisoner is always the opposite of truth. Now, if you were the prisoner, what question would you ask to ensure freedom? This problem has puzzled many. Readers may try it first, then go on reading.

Your question would be targeting at *a* or *b*, and be answered by *A* or *B*.

For the EN-system, a condition is just a single S-element; it is similar to a Boolean variable. But for our application, a condition is not the right means to describe states of *a*, *b* or *A*, *B*. Generally speaking, the state of an object like the openings and guards must be described by a bit of information. A condition is either true, or false. But a bit of information has three possibilities: being true, false, or unknown. It is also possible that an information is a constant. Figure 5.10 below illustrates it. Figure 5.10a is called an information station and Fig. 5.10b is a constant information. The box with a lying capital letter T represents a dead transition (not enabled by any reachable marking). A dead transition specifies a property of the related system, i.e., its precondition and postcondition at any case (i.e., marking consisting conditions) cannot enable it. The dead transition inside the big circle denotes a fact: $\neg(a = 1 \wedge a = 0)$, while the big circle itself represents information *a*.

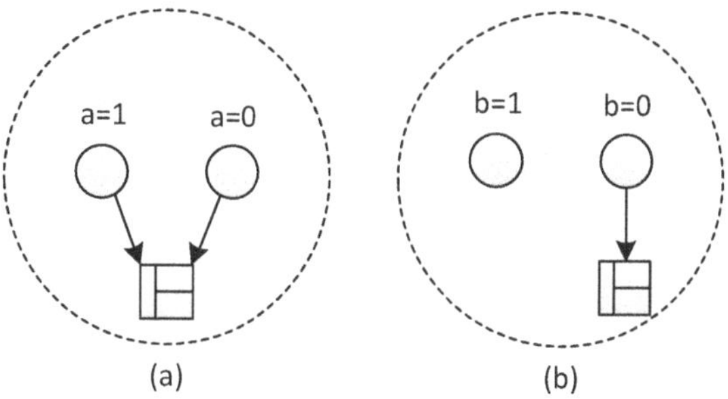

Fig. 5.10 Information station and dead transition

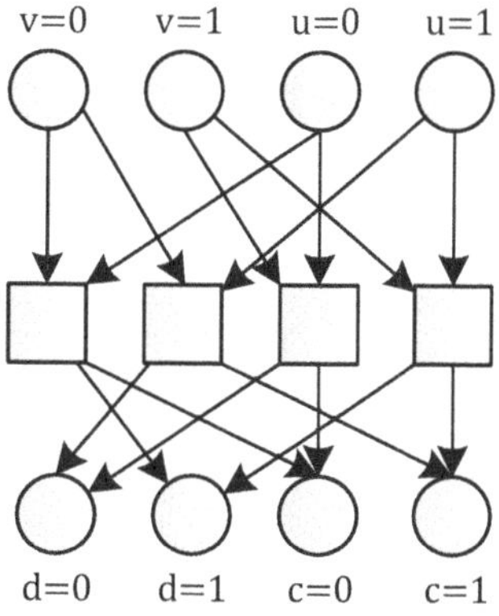

Fig. 5.11 Interaction of two one-bit information

Figure 5.10b specifies a constant information: $a = 1$. Note that $\neg(a = 1 \wedge a = 0)$ allows a to be unknown.

We will discuss information station and dead transition later when Enlogy is introduced.

Let us return to the above example of the prisoner. A single opening and a single guard must be modeled respectively with one bit information. Figure 5.11 below suggests a solution for the yes/no question. This is a simple net in which one bit information u and one bit information v represents the states of opening a and guard A respectively. Transitions t_1, t_2, t_3 and t_4 are interactions to the 4 possible combinations of u and v. Information c is the same as u, since they are the same information about opening a. Information d is the information, which is the answer. In case a yes/no question leads to the occurrence of some t_i, then the prisoner would be freed; otherwise, there is no solution to save him. This is because each of t_1, t_2, t_3 and t_4 corresponds to a different combination of the truth value of the opening and the truth value of the guard, as explained below.

Solutions are found by a careful study on the net in Fig. 5.11. More than one question can be asked: (T, L)? (T, D)? (F, L)? or (F, D)? where T = truth teller, F = liar, L = live and D = death. (T, L) = "The truth teller is guarding the opening to live, yes or no?". To go out from behind the guard if he answers "yes," otherwise to go out from the other opening. Readers are suggested to try it.

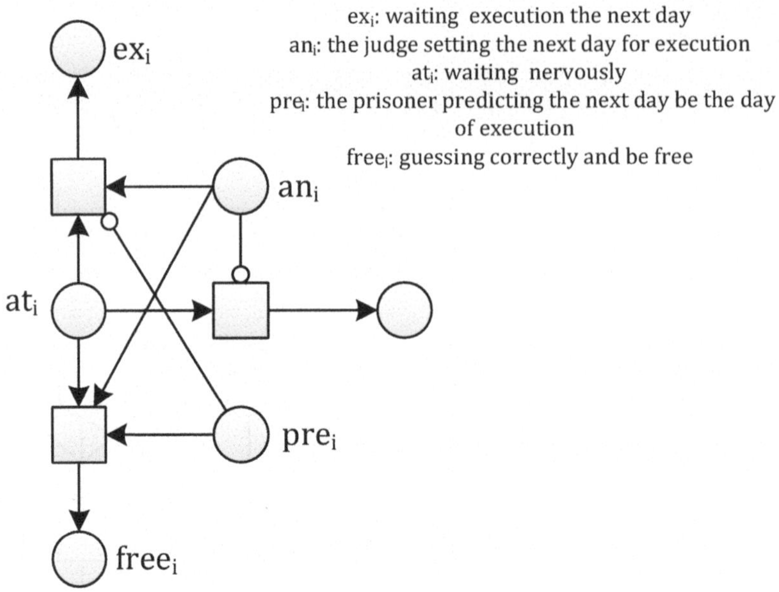

Fig. 5.12 One day in prison

Example 5.2 To Get Released This is also a story I heard when I was lined up in a cafeteria at Toronto University, Canada, in the late 1970s.

A prisoner is told that he would be released 1 day next week from Monday to Sunday. He has one chance to be freed if he predicts the execution day correctly 1 day prior. The judge is coming every day to listen to a possible prediction from the prisoner or to announce the execution decision the next day.

The prisoner thought that the execution day could not be Sunday, since otherwise he could make the right prediction on Saturday to make the execution impossible. So, Saturday is the last day for execution. But he continued with his logical reasoning and he could predict it on Friday to make Saturday's execution impossible. Finally, the prisoner slept sound with a smile, waiting to be freed.

Unfortunately, the prisoner was executed. The question is: what's wrong in his logic?

The author got to know this story 45 years ago. There was no answer to this question at that time. I had an idea about it many years later after I visited Petri's institute. It is Petri net that provides a hint to me.

Put the story in Petri nets, there are three transitions for the prisoner to participate in every day: one transition is from at(someday) to at(next-day); second transition is waiting to be executed next day and the last transition is waiting to be released next day. The kind judge lets the prisoner to make a prediction before he announces the decision. Figure 5.12 is the Petri net system for this story. Figure 5.12 shows transitions for 1 day and Fig. 5.13 includes transitions for all day.

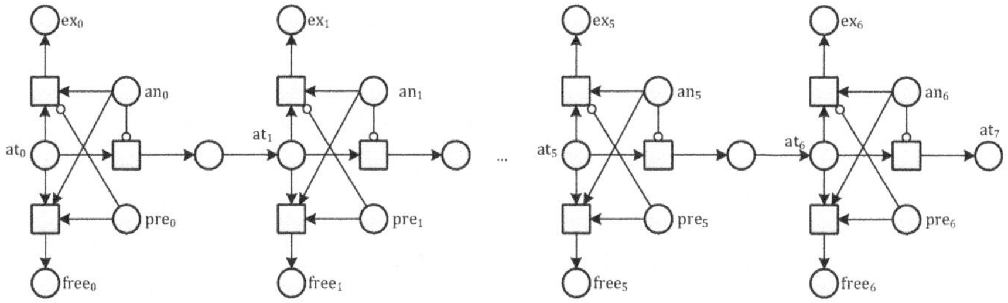

Fig. 5.13 More days in prison

The net in Fig. 5.13 shows more days in cell. It may be viewed as an unfolding from Fig. 5.12. There is but one token in all conditions a_i, $i = 1, 2, 3, \cdots$, since the token indicates that the execution time is the next day, and this "next day" is unique. There is but one token in all conditions pre_i, $i = 1, 2, 3, \cdots$, since the prisoner may make only one prediction. Condition at_0 has one token as well for the prisoner is alive at the beginning. The net contains 7 days of next week. It is clear by the net system that both being executed and being freed are possible. The logic of the prisoner is: he would be freed since he would not be freed. What a paradox.

Why these two small examples are difficult to answer at the beginning, and become simple when nets come into being? It is the graphical appearance of nets that provide a visual picture.

Chapter 6
High Level Net Systems: Pr/T-system

Abstract S-elements of Pr/T-systems are connected with predicates. A token held by an S-element makes the predicate true.

High level net systems include predicate/transition-system (Pr/T-system for short) and color net systems. They are folded from P/T-systems, as shown in Fig. 3.1.

The inflexibility of Nets leads to complicated systems while high level nets provide a way to reduce the degree of complexity by promoting a degree of abstraction. For example, the net system in Fig. 4.9 may be simplified to a Pr/T-system with 6 elements. The 6 elements in Fig. 6.1 are obtained by omitting the 5 transitions from "thinking" to "hungry." These 5 transitions are not deleted, but rather, they have all been made implicit, since philosophers cannot be thinking for too long, and sooner or later the transitions would occur to let tokens flow from "thinking" to "hungry." Similar to net folding, the action of hiding details is also a net morphism, a continuous mapping from nets to nets in net topology.

High level net systems are mainly for real applications, rather than for theoretical exploration. Thus, it is assumed that there is a fixed set D of individual objects to flow in the net. There, of course, may be objects that join or quit in the middle of the execution, i.e., D seems not a fixed set. To keep D fixed, special predicates may be included to shelter those that join or quit later.

Tokens to pass control from transition to transition are not counted as elements of D. Capacity of every place is assumed to be infinite (putting no restriction on token flow). Besides, the effect of a transition firing is conservative, i.e., it is just a redistribution of individuals among places in the extension. This is the basis to understand high level nets, say, understand the system $\sum_p$ in Fig. 6.1 below, of which some details are listed below to prepare for a formal definition.

The initial marking is given with symbolic sum: $M_0(A) = <p_1> + <p_2> + <p_3> + <p_4> + <p_5>$, $M_0(L) = <f_1> + <f_3> + <f_5>$, $M_0(R) = <f_2> + <f_4>$, $M_0(C) = < >$, and $D = \{p_i, f_i | i,j = 1,2,3,4,5\}$, i.e., 5 philosophers p_i and 5 forks f_i. Predicates A, C, L, R are respectively "x is a hungry

C. Yuan, *Principle of Petri Nets*, https://doi.org/10.1007/978-981-97-7336-7_6

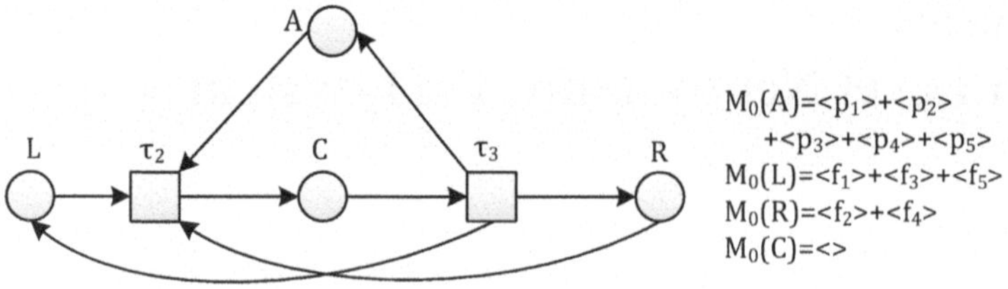

Fig. 6.1 System $\sum_p$: dining philosophers

philosopher," "x is eating with forks y (left hand) and z(right hand)," "y is ready for use" and "z is ready for use." Transitions τ_2, and τ_3 (τ_1 is implicit) are 3-ary static predicate *match*(x, y, z). Weights on arcs are as below:

$$A_F(A, \tau_2) = A_F(\tau_3, A) = <x>,$$

$$A_F(L, \tau_2) = <y>, A_F(R, \tau_2) = <z>,$$

$$A_F(\tau_2, C) = A_F(C, \tau_3) = <x, y, z>,$$

$$A_F(\tau_3, L) = <z>, A_F(\tau_3, R) = <y>,$$

Values that make *match*(x, y, z) true are $\{(p_i, f_{i-1}, f_i) | i = 1, 2, 3, 4, 5\}$, in which $1 - 1 = 5$. Substitution ($x \leftarrow d_1$, $y \leftarrow d_2$, $z \leftarrow d_3$) is feasible at marking M, if d_1 is a hungry philosopher ($<d_1> \in M(A)$), and forks d_2 and d_3 are ready to be used ($<d_2> \in M(L)$ and $<d_3> \in M(R)$) and *match*(d_1, d_2, d_3) is true. Feasible substitution ($x \leftarrow d_1$, $y \leftarrow d_2$, $z \leftarrow d_3$) enables τ_2, and then, after the firing of τ_2, τ_3 is enabled to fire, leading to a different fork distribution. Note that philosophers p_2 and p_4 may start eating concurrently at the given initial marking.

As said above, tokens are not counted as elements of D, but they still play a role in high level systems for system control, i.e., to force certain order beyond casual dependence. Besides, tokens may also be used to gain higher efficiency of resource usage by changing resource distribution from average score to distribution on demand.

To keep concepts as simple as possible, tokens would not be explicitly included in definitions next. Figure 6.2 illustrates token functions. The relation between transitions a and b have been changed, by extra places c_1 and c_2, from $M_0[a \parallel b>$ to $M_0[a \rightarrow b>$, and then to $M_0[a \rightarrow a \parallel b>$. Note that a transition of P/T-systems or high-level net systems may be concurrent with itself like $b \parallel b$. Tokens in places other than c_1 and c_2 represent resources that flow on the net. Besides, tokens may also change $M_0[a \rightsquigarrow b>$ (contact) to $M_0[a \dashrightarrow b>$ (potential contact), so safety is further ensured. To change $M_0[a | b>$ (conflict) to $M_0[a \rightarrow b>$ or $M_0[b \rightarrow a>$ may resolve the confusion situation.

6.1 Pr/T-system

The term "predicate" has been used above. Next is a more precise explanation of it.

A predicate is an incomplete proposition with the missing parts represented by variable names. Values of these variables belong to a domain called the definition

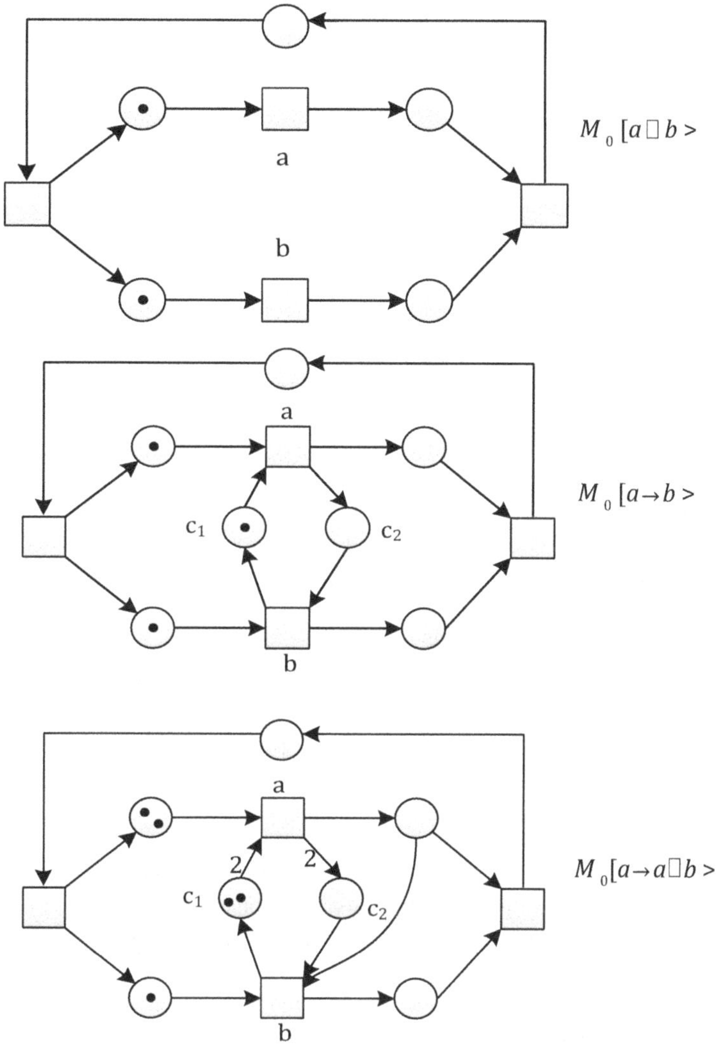

Fig. 6.2 How tokens in c_1 and c_2 work

domain of this predicate. Some values of this definition domain make the predicate true while other values make it false. This true-or-false divides the definition domain into two subsets. In case these two subsets are fixed, the predicate is a static one. Otherwise, it is dynamic. For example, in the domain $\{(p_i, f_i) | i = 1, 2, 3, 4, 5\}$, "$x$ is hungry" is a dynamic predicate, while "x is a philosopher" is a static predicate, since a hungry philosopher is no longer hungry after eating while a philosopher is a philosopher all the time.

Definition 6.1 Predicate/Transition-system $\sum = (P, T; F, D, V, A_p, A_T, A_F, M_0)$ is a predicate/transition system, Pr/T-system for short, if

$(P, T; F)$ is a directed net,

D is a nonempty set,

V is a set of variables on D,

A_p: $P \rightarrow \pi_1$, π_1 is the set of dynamic predicates on D.

A_T: $T \rightarrow \pi_2$, π_2 is the set of static predicates on D.

A_F: $F \rightarrow f_s, f_s$ is the set of symbolic sums on $D \cup V$,

M_0: $P \rightarrow f_s', f_s'$ is the set of symbolic sums on D, and for $p \in P$, $M_0(p)$ is in the definition domain of $A_p(p)$.

Remarks

1. If $A_p(p)$ is a n-ary dynamic predicate defined on D^n, the n-dimensional Cartesian product of D, then p is itself called a n-ary predicate as well. Besides, on all arcs from p or to p, the symbolic sums must be n-ary.
2. For $\tau \in T$, if static predicate $A_T(\tau)$ contains variables on D, then these variables must appear on input arcs to τ. The set of these variables is called the variable set of τ, denoted with $V(\tau)$. A combination of these variables required by $A_T(\tau)$ is called a pattern.
3. In case $V(\tau) = \varnothing$, the static predicate on τ is "true."
4. M_0 is a distribution of all objects of D.

To facilitate the understanding, let's go back to Fig. 6.1. Compared to above definition, A_T: $T \rightarrow \pi_2$ requires an explanation. $A_T(\tau_2)$ and $A_T(\tau_3)$ are both the static predicate $match(x, y, z)$, of which the value set is $\{(p_i, f_{i-1}, f_i) | i = 1, 2, 3, 4, 5\}$, $1 - 1 = 5$. As said before, each of these values is a pattern for τ_2 and τ_3 to fire.

Place C is a triple predicate. As its initial value, $<>$ is used: $M_0(C) = <>$. $<>$ is an empty symbolic sum. For C, $<>$ is 3-ary sum.

It is easy to check whether the set of predicates is "complete and mutually exclusive": a philosopher is either "hungry" (predicate A) or "eating" (predicate C), or "thinking" (implicit); a fork is either "ready for use" (predicate L or R) or "being used" (predicate C).

To assign an object of D to every variable in $V(\tau)$, obtained is a substitution of $V(\tau)$. It is denoted with $\{x \leftarrow d | x \in V(\tau) \wedge d \in D\}$.

The substitution $(z, x, y) \leftarrow (p_3, f_2, f_3)$ for τ_2 is a feasible (enabled) one at M_0, since $<p_3> \in M_0(A)$, $<f_2> \in M_0(L)$, $<f_3> \in M_0(R)$ and $match(x, y, z) =$ true. The substitution $(z, x, y) \leftarrow (p_5, f_4, f_5)$ for τ_2 is also feasible, and these two feasible substitutions are concurrent.

It is important to note that variable name y appears on both arcs (L, τ_2) and (τ_3, L), but it represents different forks. Philosopher p_3 picks up fork f_2 from L, but returns fork f_3 to L after eating. Though y is called a variable here, it is not a math variable to carry a value from one transition (statement) to another transition.

It is clear that with Pr/T-system as the means, a net structure is greatly reduced while markings on places (predicates) become complicated, so are the weights on arcs. Besides, transitions have to be marked with firing patterns. This is a trade-off.

For toy examples like dining philosophers, the merit of high-level net systems is not so obvious. Only in real applications, when the net structure looks like a net made by a spider, a simplified structure makes sense. It seems easier for an automatic tool to deal with a one-dimensional formula (predicates, symbolic sums etc.) than two or more dimensional graphic structures. It is not always possible to draw a net on a piece of paper without crossing arcs. Thus, a net is not always a two-dimensional graph (if arrow heads are removed).

In what follows, f_s' is the set of symbolic sums on D. A symbolic sum may be viewed as another way to write a set. In what follows, operators on sets are used on symbolic sums.

Definition 6.2 Marking of Pr/T-system A map $M : P \rightarrow f_s'$ is a marking on P, if

$$\forall d \in D \exists! p \in P : d \in M(p).$$

The symbol "∃ ! " requires not only "exists", but is also "unique." So, a marking is a distribution of objects in D on places of P, in the form of a symbolic sum. Σ is resource conservative since every marking is a distribution of resources in D. A resource conservative system requires every transition of it to be resource conservative.

Formal definitions for transition rules are complicated to write and to read. They will be given half-formally next.

Definition 6.3 Feasible Substitution For transition τ of Pr/T-system Σ, the substitution $\delta = \{x \leftarrow d | x \in V(\tau) \wedge d \in D\}$ for its variable set $V(\tau)$ is feasible at marking M, if

1. $D(\delta)$ is in the value domain of $A_T(\tau)$, where $D(\delta)$ consists of all objects used in substitution δ, i.e. $D(\delta)$ makes $A_T(\tau)$ true.
2. $\forall p \in {}^{\bullet}\tau : \delta(p, \tau) \subseteq M(p)$, where $\delta(p, \tau)$ is the symbolic sum $A_F(p, \tau)$ under substitution δ. So, $\delta(p, \tau)$ is a subsets of $M(p)$. Remember that a symbolic sum is treated as a set

Definition 6.4 Transition Rules for Pr/T-systems

1. For Pr/T-system $\sum = (P, T; F, D, V, A_p, A_T, A_F, M_0)$, transition τ is enabled by substitution δ at marking M, denoted by $M[(\tau, \delta)>$ or simply $M[\tau, \delta>$, if δ is feasible at M.
2. The successor marking M' for $M[(\tau, \delta)>$ is given by

$M'(p) = M(p) + \delta(\tau, p) - \delta(p, \tau)$ for all $p, p \in {}^{\bullet}\tau \cap \tau^{\bullet}$,
$M'(p) = M(p) + \delta(\tau, p)$ for all $p, p \in \tau^{\bullet}$,
$M'(p) = M(p) - \delta(p, \tau)$ for all $p, p \in {}^{\bullet}\tau$,
$M'(p) = M(p)$ for all $p, p \notin {}^{\bullet}\tau \cup \tau^{\bullet}$,

This successor relation is denoted as $M[(\tau, \delta)>M'$.

Definition 6.5 $[M_0>$, The Set of All Reachable Markings $[M_0>$ is the smallest set of markings that satisfies the two conditions:

$$M_0 \in [M_0>,$$
$$M \in [M_0> \wedge \exists(\tau,\delta) : M[(\tau,\delta)>M' \rightarrow M' \in [M_0>.$$

As said before for P/T-systems, $[M_0>$ must be the smallest.

6.2 Properties of Pr/T-systems

The pair (τ, δ) in Pr/T-systems plays the role of a transition t in P/T-systems, where τ is a transition name, δ is a feasible substitution. In what follows, φ represents (τ, δ), so $M[(\tau, \delta)>M'$ would be written as $M[\varphi>M'$.

Definition 6.6 Firing Sequence Sequence $\sigma = \varphi_1\varphi_2\cdots\varphi_n$ is a firing sequence of Pr/T-system $\sum = (P, T; F, D, V, A_p, A_T, A_F, M_0)$ if $n \geq 1$ and $M_0[\varphi_1>M_1[\varphi_2>M_2\cdots[\varphi_n>M_n$.

An infinite sequence $\sigma' = \varphi_1\varphi_2\cdots$ is a firing sequence if every prefix of σ' is a firing sequence.

Definition 6.7 Live System Transition τ is potentially enabled by marking M, if there exists a substitution δ, such that $M[(\tau, \delta)>$ or $\exists M' \in [M> : M'[\tau, \delta>$.

A transition τ is live if for every reachable marking M in $[M_0>$, there is a substitution δ, such that (τ, δ) is potentially enabled by M.

$\sum$ is live if every τ is live.

Fairness for Pr/T-systems will not be defined here. It is sufficient for readers to have it defined for P/T-systems. Fairness relies on infinity. It is meaningless to hunt for fair from infinity. Such fairness is meaningless for human beings, since no one could live forever. Such fairness is meaningless for application systems, since no parts of an application system would complain of being treated unfairly. So, fairness is a pure academic concept, not applicable in reality.

Fair or unfair, it mainly refers to human society. There is nothing in human society that could last forever. In other words, human society is always fair according to this definition. This is certainly untrue. As for wealth accumulation, no matter how great the distance between the rich and the poor, no one would have infinite wealth. So, wealth accumulation is always fair. This is not true either.

A concept called synchronic distance will be defined later, with which, the abovementioned distance between rich and poor will be quantified. So, instead of a clear cut between fair and unfair, a quantified measure for fairness will be suggested.

As means for system analysis, reachable tree $T[M_0>$ and reachable graph $G[M_0>$ can be constructed with algorithms similar to that for P/T-systems. Figure 6.3 is a simplified $T[M_0>$ for the dining philosophers, in which M_i is p_i eating and M_{ij} is p_i and p_j eating in parallel. Feasible substitutions on arcs from father node to son node are simplified to p_i (the eating philosopher) or $-p_j$, (p_j stops eating). Besides, all

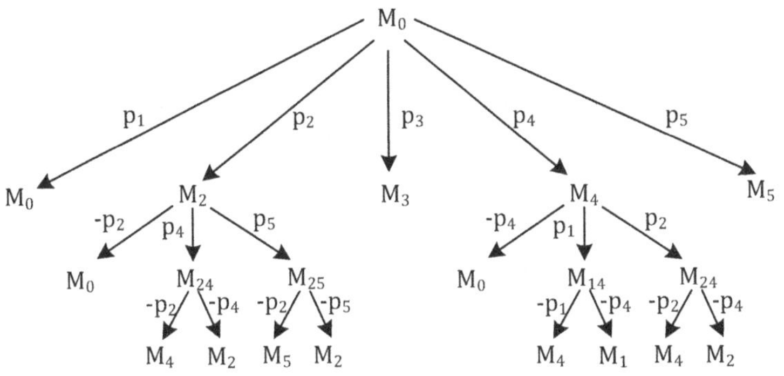

Fig. 6.3 $T[M_0>$ for dining philosophers

Fig. 6.4 Incident matrix for τ_2

$$a_1 =< p_1 > +< f_5 > +< f_1 >, a_2 =< p_2 > +< f_1 > +< f_2 >$$

$$a_3 =< p_3 > +< f_2 > +< f_3 >, a_4 =< p_4 > +< f_3 > +< f_4 >$$

$$a_5 =< p_5 > +< f_4 > +< f_5 >$$

$$\begin{array}{c} \\ A \\ L \\ R \\ C \end{array} \begin{array}{c} \begin{array}{ccccc} a_1 & a_2 & a_3 & a_4 & a_5 \end{array} \\ \begin{bmatrix} -p_1 & -p_2 & -p_3 & -p_4 & -p_5 \\ -f_5 & -f_1 & -f_2 & -f_3 & -f_4 \\ -f_1 & -f_2 & -f_3 & -f_4 & -f_5 \\ a_1 & a_2 & a_3 & a_4 & a_5 \end{bmatrix} \end{array}$$

offspring of the second generation share the same sub tree. Only two of these sub trees are explicit in Fig. 6.3.

A simple net (Fig. 6.1) and a complicated tree (Fig. 6.3), as the author has repeatedly stated, are situations that may be good for automatic treatment. Leave the simple for man and the complicated for AI.

The incidence matrix for the whole system is bound to be complicated. Fig. 6.4 below is a matrix for τ_2 in Fig. 6.1, in which

From each of the columns we see the conservative property of τ_2, and as such, τ_2 as a whole is conservative. The firing of τ_2 leads to a redistribution of individuals.

The incident matrix for transition τ_3 is similar.

6.3 Process

As means of analysis, we have defined firing sequences, $[M_0>$, $T(\Sigma)$and $G(\Sigma)$. The concept of system processes was originally defined for special P/T-systems in which the capacity of every place is ∞, and all arc weights are 1 (by the way, this is the original net model used by Prof. Petri himself) since otherwise the definition of

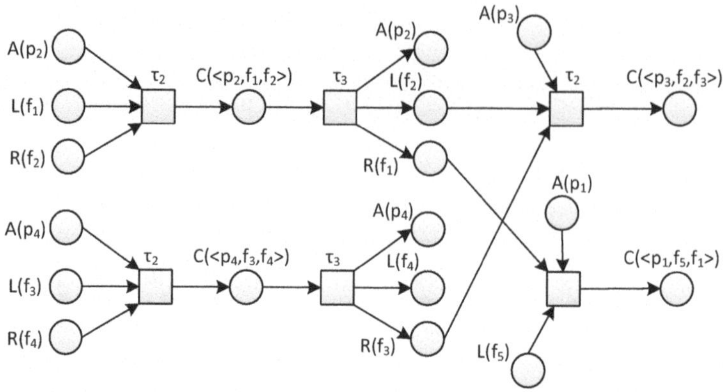

Fig. 6.5 A process of $\sum_p$

process would be too complicated to formalize. The most important thing is concept, not tiny details (i.e., various capacities and various arc weights). To involve complicated things to confuse oneself is not among the purpose of this writing.

The concept of processes is applicable to Pr/T-systems and color systems. A process is an unfolding from a system to occurrence net. So, informally speaking, a process of a net system is a pair consisting of an occurrence net and a mapping from this occurrence net to the net system. Figure 6.5 below is a process of the Pr/T-system $\sum_p$ for dining philosophers. The naming of the elements reflects the mapping from the occurrence net to $\sum_p$.

A system usually has more than one process and some processes may be infinite in size. The structure of such an infinite process would have certain regularities like a rational number, i.e., it is a repetition of one or more finite occurrence nets. Such a finite portion of an occurrence net is called an occurrence period. It is easy to find occurrence periods from $G(\sum)$. Every basic circle on $G(\sum)$corresponds to a period. Take every basic circle away from $G(\sum)$so that $G(\sum)$is divided into parts, then every connected part of the divided $G[M_0>$ corresponds to a period as well. This way, to obtain process periods from $G(\sum)$is already very close to an algorithm, so, it is left for readers to add details. The following theorem is obviously true since $G(\sum)$is finite.

Theorem 6.1 Process Periods Every finite net system has a finite number of finite periods.

Chapter 7
Color Net Systems

Abstract Tokens in color net systems are dyed with different colors to make a distincton.

A Pr/T-system names every individual and color net systems colors individually to make a distinction. A color system is simpler than a Pr/T-system since individuals of the same kind share the same color. As such, a color system is introduced with more details.

For color systems, every place has a set of token color and every transition has a set of occurrence color. Arc weights are mappings from occurrence color to token color. Let D be the set of available solid color. In addition to transition firing one after another, next definition includes various concurrent firings. Note that an occurrence color of the same transition may be concurrent with itself, i.e., a transition may fire concurrently more than once with the same color.

Definition 7.1 Color Net System $\sum = (P, T; F, C, I_+, I_-, M_0)$ is a color system, if

1. $(P, T; F)$ is a directed net, the foundation of $\sum$,
2. $C : P \cup T \rightarrow \wp(D)$, $\wp(D)$ is the power set of D, i. e., the set of all subsets of D. $C(p)$ is the set of token color of place p, and $C(t)$ is the set of occurrence color of t.
3. I_+ is the weight function for producing. For arc (p, t), $I_+(p, t)$ is a linear function from $C(t)_{ms}$ to $C(p)_{ms}$. I_- is a weight function for consuming. For arc (t, p), $I_-(p, t)$ is a linear function from $C(t)_{ms}$ to $C(p)_{ms}$.
4. $M_0 : P \rightarrow D_{ms}$ is the initial marking such that $M_0(p) \in C(p)_{mss}$. For every p in P.

Remarks

- A triple $(P, T; F)$ is often used to denote a directed net when P/T-systems and high-level net systems are discussed, though $(S, T; F)$ was used in the definition of directed nets.

C. Yuan, *Principle of Petri Nets*, https://doi.org/10.1007/978-981-97-7336-7_7

Fig. 7.1 A color system of church wedding

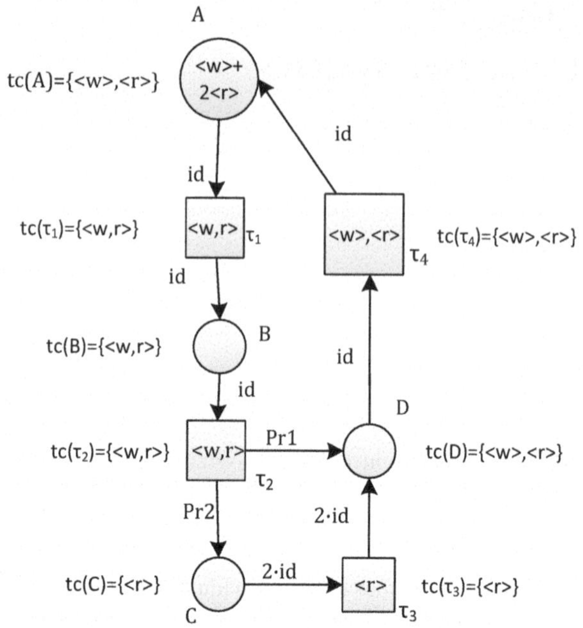

- The subscript "ms" is an abbreviation of "multiset". For example, D_{ms} is the multiset of D. Elements of a multiset are written as a symbolic sum. So, $2 < r > + < w > \in D_{ms}$ if r and w in D.
- $C(t)_{ms}$ and $C(p)_{ms}$ are respectively the multiset of occurrence color of t and the multiset of token color of p.
- A concurrent firing of occurrence color of t is an element in $C(t)_{ms}$, represented as a linear combination of occurrence color like $2a + 3b + c$, where a, b and c are occurrence color of t. A linear function from $C(t)_{ms}$ to $C(p)_{ms}$ computes effects of a concurrent firing: what is consumed and what is produced.
- Function f from $C(t)_{ms}$ to $C(p)_{ms}$ is linear if $f(2a + 3b + c) = 2f(a) + 3f(b) + f(c)$.
- I_+ and I_- are both linear functions from $C(t)_{ms}$ to $C(p)_{ms}$, computing respectively what a (concurrent) firing would produce or consume.
- It is the use of a multiset of color set that makes a color system better than a Pr/T-system.

An occurrence color is usually a composed color, represented as a vector like (r, w) or $(<r>, <w>)$. Thus, both functions I_+ and I_- are linear combinations of projection $pr1$, $pr2$, … , prn and the identity function id. For example, $pr2(x, y, z) = y$, $id(x, y) = (x, y)$ and $id(x) = x$. These math functions are not redefined here.

The problem of dinning philosophers is not a good example to exhibit the advantage of color net systems since all philosophers and forks must be dyed differently. To dye them and to name them makes no difference. The church wedding is a bit better, since the wedding couple shares the same color as shown in Figure 7.1 given below.

Fig. 7.2 Inhibit arcs (**a**) and (**b**)

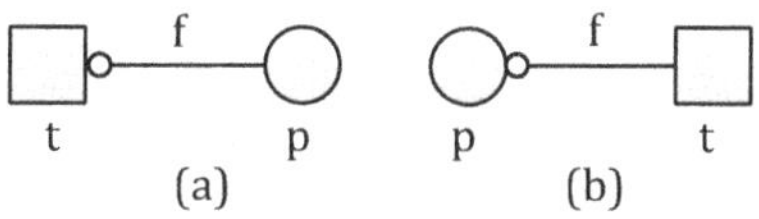

Fig. 7.3 Flexible arcs

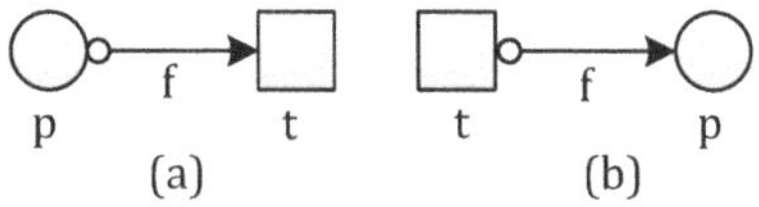

No good example of color system found that fits this book. A real application is expected.

To make better use of a color system, the following 4 kinds of directed arcs were proposed when the author tried to build a net for the lifts. These arcs may reduce structure complexity.

First kind: enriched inhibit arc

1. The arc (p, t) as shown in Fig. 7.2a is the first class of inhibit arc, if

$$M[t(a) > \rightarrow M(p) \cap f(a) = \varnothing$$

and

$$M[t(a) > M' \rightarrow M'(p) = M(p)$$

In which, $a \in C(t)_{ms}$, and f is the weight on (p, t), i.e., a linear function from $C(t)_{ms}$ to $C(p)_{ms}$.

2. The arc (p, t) as shown in Fig. 7.2b is the second class of inhibit arc, if

$$M[t(a) > \rightarrow M(p) \cap f(a) = f(a)$$

and

$$M[t(a) > M' \rightarrow M'(p) = M(p)$$

In which, $a \in C(t)_{ms}$, and f is the weight on (p, t), i.e., a linear function from $C(t)_{ms}$ to $C(p)_{ms}$.

Second kind: flexible arc

1. The arc (p, t) as shown in Fig. 7.3a is the first class of flexible arc, if

$$M[t(a) > \rightarrow M(p) \cap f(a) = \varnothing \vee M(p) \cap f(a) = f(a)$$

and

$$M[t(a) > M' \rightarrow M'(p) = M(p) - f(a)$$

So, $f(a)$ may have no common elements with $M(p)$, or be completely contained by $M(p)$, and the firing of t makes $M(p) \cap f(a) = \varnothing$.

2. The arc (t, p) as shown in Fig. 7.3b is the second class of flexible arc, if

$$M[t(a) > \rightarrow M(p) \cap f(a) = \varnothing \vee M(p) \cap f(a) = f(a)$$

and

$$M[t(a) > M' \rightarrow M'(p) = M(p) \cup f(a)$$

So, $f(a)$ may have no common elements with $M(p)$, or be completely contained by $M(p)$, and the firing of t makes $M(p) \cap f(a) = f(a)$.

Note that it is possible that $M(p) - f(a) \neq \varnothing$, i.e., $M(p)$ contains elements other than $f(a)$.

Third kind: combined arc

1. $(\{p_1, p_2, \ldots, p_n\}, t)$ is the first class of combined arc, if

$$M[t(a) > \rightarrow \forall i : 1 \leq i \leq n : M(p_i) \cap f_i(a) = \varnothing \vee M(p_i) \cap f_i(a) = f_i(a) \wedge \exists i \\ : 1 \leq i \leq n : M(p_i) \cap f_i(a) = f_i(a)$$

and

$$M[t(a) > M' \rightarrow \forall i : 1 \leq i \leq n : M'(p_i) = M(p_i) - f_i(a)$$

2. $(t, \{p_1, p_2, \ldots, p_n\})$ is the second class of combined arc, if

$$M[t(a) > \rightarrow \forall i : 1 \leq i \leq n : M(p_i) \cap f_i(a) = \varnothing \vee M(p_i) \cap f_i(a) = f_i(a) \wedge \exists i \\ : 1 \leq i \leq n : M(p_i) \cap f_i(a) = \varnothing$$

and

$$M[t(a) > M' \rightarrow \forall i : 1 \leq i \leq n : M'(p_i) \cap f_i(a) = f_i(a).$$

Figure 7.4 illustrates combined arcs, in which $n = 2$, and $f_1 \neq f_2$ in Fig. 7.5a, and $f = f_1 = f_2$ in Fig. 7.5b (Fig. 7.5).

Fourth kind: Causal arcs

1. (p_1, t) and (t, p_2) are a pair of first class of causal arcs if

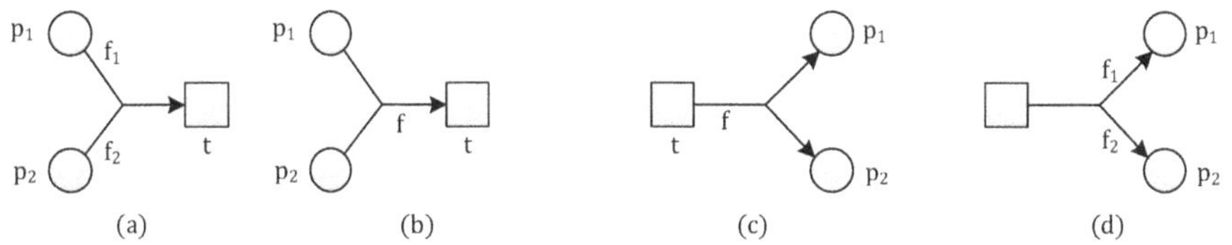

Fig. 7.4 Combined arcs

Fig. 7.5 Causal arcs

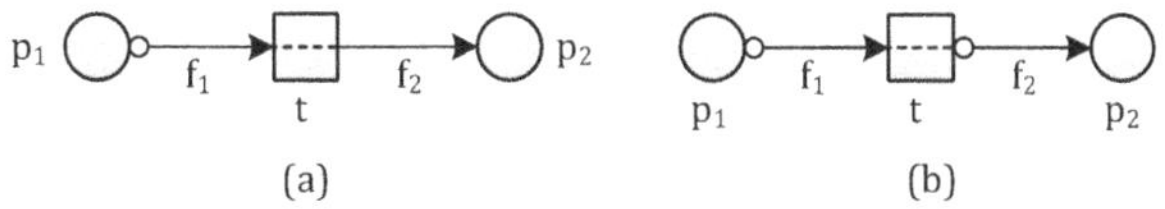

$$M[t(a)> \rightarrow M(p_1) \cap f_1(a) = \varnothing \vee M(p_1) \cap f_1(a) = f_1(a)$$

and

$$M[t(a) > M' \rightarrow M'(p_1) = M(p_1) - f_1(a) \wedge M'(p_2) \times \begin{cases} M(p_2) \text{ if } M(p_1) \cap f_1(a) = \varnothing \\ M(p_2) + f_2(a) \text{ if } M(p_1) \cap f_1(a) = f_1(a) \end{cases}$$

Or, with $\sim$ as the separator,

$$M'(p_2) = M(p_2) \text{ if } M(p_1) \cap f_1(a) = \varnothing \sim M(p_2) + f_2(a) \text{ if } M(p_1) \cap f_1(a) = f_1(a)$$

2. (p_1, t) and (t, p_2) are a pair of second class of causal arcs if

$$M[t(a)> \rightarrow (M(p_1) \cap f_1(a) = \varnothing \vee M(p_1) \cap f_1(a) = f_1(a)) \\ \wedge (M(p_2) \cap f_2(a) = \varnothing \vee M(p_2) \cap f_2(a) = f_2(a))$$

and

$$M[t(a) > M' \rightarrow M'(p_1) = M(p_1) - f_1(a) \wedge M'(p_2) = M(p_2) \text{ if } M(p_1) \cap f_1(a) = \varnothing \\ \sim M(p_2) \cup f_2(a) \text{ if } M(p_1) \cap f_1(a) = f_1(a)$$

The detailed net system for lifts is not included here since what interests us is not the lift system itself, but rather features of nets. Figure 7.6 is a net for lift button push, in which Fig. 7.6a is a P/T-system and Fig. 7.6b is a color system with causal arc. It seems that the complexity of Fig. 7.6a and the complexity of Fig. 7.6b are almost the same. But, Fig. 7.6a is a single push on one floor while Fig. 7.6b is a push for all M floors.

Place $cL(i)$ in Fig. 7.6a is mainly to keep the token number in $\mathcal{L}(i)$ not to exceed 1, no matter how many times the button is pushed. It is not as simple as it

Fig. 7.6 (a) P/T transitions (b) causal arcs

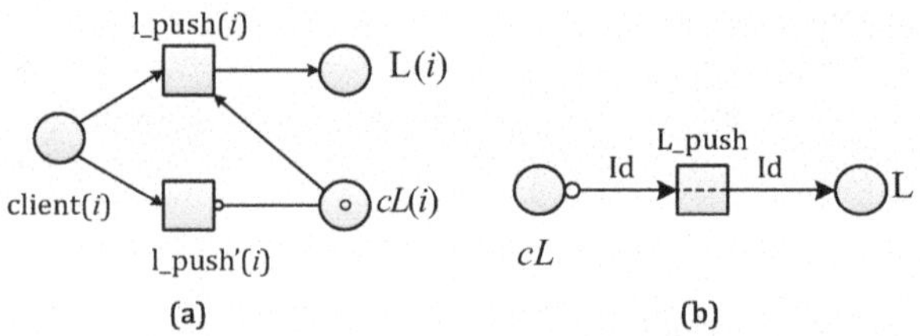

seems. An idle lift may read $\mathcal{L}(i)$ and comes to serve it. This lift is the candidate for $\mathcal{L}(i)$. It is possible that $\mathcal{L}(i)$ is served by a pass-by lift soon after there is a candidate. The token in $\mathcal{L}(i)$ should be removed by the pass-by lift on the one hand (since it has been served), while there must be a mark left to stop the candidate when it arrives at floor i. The token in *cL*(*i*) serves as the mark.

Place *cL* in (b) holds token color for floor buttons that are not pushed. A push (an occurrence color of transition l-push) would move the token color for due floor from *cL* to $\mathcal{L}$. This pair of causal arcs would solve the abovementioned problem of repeated button push.

So far, we have finished the presentation of a net system hierarchy. A problem is still in front us: how to make net systems more flexible for use. The limitations of P/T-systems include:

1. Transition extension is a fixed set of places.
2. Arc weights are invariable positive integers.
3. The only data type is positive integer, and the allowed operators are plus/minus on positive integers.

To amend these limitations, self-control systems and C-net systems have been proposed. The former allows variable arc weights, and the latter introduces data types into nets. These inventions fall into the category of engineering, no impact on net theory.

Chapter 8
Self-Control Systems

Abstract Weights on arcs of a net system represent the amount of tokens to be consumed or produced,and weights are usually remain constants. Self-control systems allow arc weights to vary from system state to states. It is the current amount of tokens held by a place that is the current weight on a arc if the name of that place is the weight on that arc.

Self-control systems have flexible arc weights and the flexibility comes from itself by allowing one or more arc weights being a name of its place, say p. The token number $M(p)$ at marking M would be taken as the weight on due arc at M.

Definition 8.1 Self-control System $\sum = (P, T; F, W, M_0)$ is a self-control net system if

$$
\begin{aligned}
& dnet(P, T; F) \\
& \wedge W : F \rightarrow \{1, 2, \ldots\} \cup P \\
& \wedge M_0 : P \rightarrow \{0, 1, 2, \ldots\}.
\end{aligned}
$$

Here, it is assumed that the capacities of places are all infinite.

In case $W(x, y) = p_1$ on arc (x, y), the real weight on (x, y) at marking M is $M(p_1)$. So, $W(x, y)$ varies from marking to marking. One way to show the weight graphically is to write the place name p_1 on arc (x, y), another way is to draw an arrow from p_1 to (x, y). Figure 8.1 illustrates it.

The alternating firing of t_1 and t_2 in Fig. 8.1a, b produces a Fibonacci series 0, 1, 1, 2, 3, 5, 8, ... The token numbers in place s_1 is 0, 1, 3, 8,..., and the token numbers in place s_2 is 1, 2, 5,.... By putting them together in the order $M(s_1)$, $M(s_2)$, a Fibonacci series is obtained.

The next definition makes the concept of flexible weights more flexible. The arc weights are extended from simply a constant or a place name to polynomials with place names as variables.

C. Yuan, *Principle of Petri Nets*, https://doi.org/10.1007/978-981-97-7336-7_8

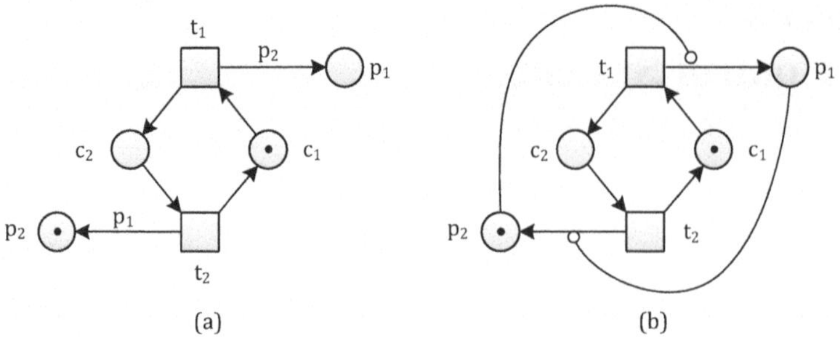

Fig. 8.1 Two ways to show flexible arc weight

Fig. 8.2 Self-control systems for progressions

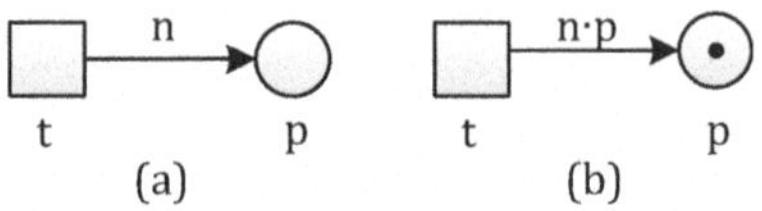

Fig. 8.3 Nonlinear net system

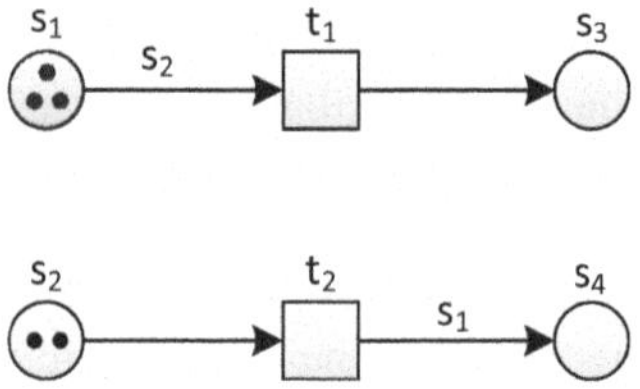

Definition 8.2 Extended Self-control Net System $\sum = (P, T; F, W, M_0)$ is an extended self-control net system if

$$dnet(P,\ \ T; F)$$
$$\wedge W : F \rightarrow \{1, 2, \ldots\} \cup E$$
$$\wedge M_0 : P \rightarrow \{0, 1, 2, \ldots\},$$

in which E is a N-ary polynomial of degree one with elements in P as variables and positive integers as coefficients. In case a polynomial reduces to a constant, it must be an integer greater than zero. N is the number of elements in P.

Figure 8.2 includes two examples of self-control net systems with extended flexible weights. Figure 8.2a computes an arithmetic progression, i.e., 0, n, $2n$, $3n$, …, and Fig. 8.2b computes a geometric progression, i.e., 1, $n + 1$, $(n + 1)^2$, $(n + 1)^3$, …. since $t(i + 1)/t(i) = n + 1$ for $i = 1, 2, 3, \ldots$, where $t(i)$ is the i_{th} item of this progression.

Figure 8.3 contains a self-control net system, in which transitions are related with each other with flexible weights. In this system, $M_0 = (3, 2, 0, 0)$, and both t_1 and t_2 are enabled for firing. We know that there are three ways for concurrent transitions to fire.

$$M_0 = (3,2,0,0)\vec{t}_1 M_1 = (1,2,1,0)\vec{t}_2 M_2 = (1,1,1,1)$$

$$M_0 = (3,2,0,0)\vec{t}_2 M_1 = (3,1,0,3)\vec{t}_1 M_2 = (2,1,1,3)$$

$$M_0 = (3,2,0,0)\vec{t}_1 \parallel \vec{t}_2 M_1 = (1,1,1,3)$$

The three ways of transition firings end up at different markings. Thus, self-control net systems are not linear.

Transition t_2 in Fig. 8.3 may fire concurrently with itself to produce the successor marking $M_0 = (3,0,6,0)$. At this marking, the weight $M(s_2)$ on arc (s_1, t_1) becomes zero. $M[t_1>$ is true or not? If $M[t_1>$ is true, then t_1 may fire arbitrarily many times since the capacity of s_3 is assumed to be infinite.

As an abstract transition, and as long as its extension is not empty, its dynamics is decided by transition rules, no matter how many times it may fire. High level systems aim at real applications, and as such, endless firing should be considered whether it is reasonable or not. Endless firing is very likely not realistic. So, as a suggestion, when all weights on input arcs become zero, the transition is disabled.

Definition 8.3 Transition Rule

1. For arc weight e, $e \in E$, the value of e at marking M, denoted by e_M, is obtained by taking $M(p)$ as the value of p in e, for all place p, that is,

$$e_M = e|_{M(p) \to p}, p \text{ takes the integer } M(p) \text{ as its value.}$$

2. The extended weight $W'(x, \; y)$ on arc $(x, \; y)$ is defined as

$$W'(x,y) = W(x,y) \text{ if } (x,y) \in F \sim 0 \text{ if } (x,y) \notin F,$$

3. The value of $W'(x,y)_M$ at marking M is computed by

$$W'(x,y)_M = e_M \text{ if } W(x,y) \in E \sim W'(x,y) \text{ if } W(x,y) \notin E$$

   in which $e_M = e|_{M(p) \to p}$ for $W(x,y) = e$.
4. $M[t> = \exists p \in P : W'(p,t)_M \neq 0 \wedge \forall p \in P : W'(p,t)_M \leq M(p)$, $M[t>M' \equiv M[t> \wedge \forall p \in t : M'(p) = M(p) - W'(p,t)_M \wedge \forall p \in t : M'(p) = M(p) + W'(t,p)_M - W'(p,t)_M$

Definition 8.4 Concurrent Step

1. Let $u = \sum_{i=1}^{n} u_i t_i$ be a multiset on T, $T = \{t_1, t_2, \ldots, t_n\}$ and u_i, $i = 1, 2, \ldots, n$, are positive integers, $\sum_{i=1}^{n} u_i \neq 0$, u is a concurrent step at marking M, denoted with $M[u>$, if

$$\forall p \in P : u_1 W'(p,t_1)_M + u_2 W'(p,t_2)_M + \cdots + u_n W'(p,t_n)_M \leq M(p),$$

2. The successor marking M' of u at M, denoted with $M[u>M'$, is given by

Fig. 8.4 Incidence matrix

$$\begin{array}{c} \\ s_1 \\ s_2 \\ s_3 \\ s_4 \end{array} \begin{array}{c} \begin{array}{cc} t_1 & t_2 \end{array} \\ \begin{bmatrix} -s_2 & 0 \\ 0 & -1 \\ 1 & 0 \\ 0 & s_1 \end{bmatrix} \end{array}$$

Fig. 8.5 Successor marking of let concurrent step $u = (1, 2)$

$$M' = \begin{bmatrix} 3 \\ 2 \\ 0 \\ 0 \end{bmatrix} + \begin{bmatrix} -s_2 & 0 \\ 0 & -1 \\ 1 & 0 \\ 0 & s_1 \end{bmatrix}^{u_1 \quad\; u_2} \begin{bmatrix} 1 \\ \\ \\ 2 \end{bmatrix}$$

$$= \begin{bmatrix} 3 \\ 2 \\ 0 \\ 0 \end{bmatrix} + \begin{bmatrix} -2 & 0 \\ 0 & -1 \\ 1 & 0 \\ 0 & 3 \end{bmatrix} \begin{bmatrix} 1 \\ \\ \\ 2 \end{bmatrix}$$

$$= \begin{bmatrix} 3 \\ 2 \\ 0 \\ 0 \end{bmatrix} + \begin{bmatrix} -2 \\ -2 \\ 1 \\ 6 \end{bmatrix} = \begin{bmatrix} 1 \\ 0 \\ 1 \\ 6 \end{bmatrix}$$

$$\begin{aligned} &\forall p \in P \\ &\quad : M'(p) = M(p) - \left(u_1 W'(p, t_1)_M + u_2 W'(p, t_2)_M + \cdots + u_n W'(p, t_n)_M\right) \\ &\qquad + \left(u_1 W'(t_1, p)_M + u_2 W'(t_2, p)_M + \cdots + u_n W'(t_n, p)_M\right) \end{aligned}$$

For linear systems, transitions in a concurrent step may fire in an arbitrary order to end up at the same successor marking. A self-control system is not linear, and different ways of firing lead to different successors. The incidence matrix reflects this nonlinear property.

Definition 8.5 Incidence Matrix

1. For self-control system $\sum = (P, T; F, W, M_0)$, $P = \{p_1, p_2, \ldots, p_n\}$ and $T = \{t_1, t_2, \ldots, t_n\}$, the $n \times m$ matrix $A = [A(i,j)]$ is the incidence matrix of $\sum$, if $A(i, j) = W(t_i, p_i) - W(p_i, t_i)$.
2. For marking M, let be $A(i,j)_M = W(t_i, p_i)_M - W(p_i, t_i)_M$, and $A_M = [A(i,j)_M]$, then A_M is the incidence matrix of $\sum$ at M.
3. Let u be a concurrent step at M and $M[u>M'$; the formula $M' = M + A_M u^T$ is called the successor formula, in which $u^T = (u_1, u_2, \ldots, u_m)^T$. u^T is a column vector.

The incidence matrix of the system A in Fig. 8.3 is given in Fig. 8.4 below:

Note that the addition of M and $A_M u^T$ is not a normal matrix operation, since A_M contains variables (place names) whose concrete values come from M. The successor formula for the system in Fig. 8.3 is given in Fig. 8.5 below, in which $u = (1, 2)$ is a concurrent step.

According to transition rules of self-control systems, variables s_1 and s_2 in Fig. 8.3 take $M_0(s_1)$, i.e., 3, and $M_0(s_2)$, i.e., 2, as their respective values. It must carry out a substitution to replace $M_0(s_1)$ with 3, and $M_0(s_2)$ with 2, before the matrix addition. This "substitution then addition" operation is proposed just for computing successor marking in self-control systems. This operation is named subplus, and the operator is $\leftrightarrow$. This operation is formally given by next definition.

Definition 8.6 Subplus Operation For n-dimensional column vector $a = (a_1, a_2, \ldots, a_n)^T$, all a_i are positive integers, and $e = (e_1, e_2, \ldots, e_n)^T$, all e_i are polynomials of degree one that contain variables $x_1, x_2, \ldots, x_n$, then $b = a \leftrightarrow e$ is defined by

$$b = (b_1, b_2, \ldots, b_n)^T$$

in which

$$b_i = a_i + e_i(a) \text{ for } i = 1, 2, \ldots, n,$$

where $e_i(a) = e_i|_{x \to a}$, i.e., all x_j in e_i is replaced with a_j.

To put subplus operation in vector form, we have

$$a \leftrightarrow e = a + e|_a$$

in which $e|_a = (e_1|_{x \to a}, e_2|_{x \to a}, \ldots, e_n|_{x \to a})^T$

As an example and for simplicity, let be $n = 3$, and $a = (1, 2, 3)^T$, $e = (x_2, x_1 + x_3, x_1)^T$, then we have

$$e|_a = \left(e_1|_{x \to a}, e_2|_{x \to a}, e_3|_{x \to a}\right)^T = (2, 1 + 3, 1)^T = (2, 4, 1)^T$$

$$a \leftrightarrow e = a + e|_a = (1, 2, 3)^T + (2, 4, 1)^T = (3, 6, 4)^T$$

Subplus is now a non-commutative operation between two column vectors. It has a priority, which is higher than matrix plus but lower than matrix multiplication.

The next definition extends subplus to a column vector and a matrix inductively.

Definition 8.7 Extended Subplus For column constant vector $a = (a_1, a_2, \ldots, a_n)^T$ of positive integers and $n \times k$ matrix E, if all elements of E are polynomial of degree one that contain variables $x_1, x_2, \ldots, x_n$, then

$$a \leftrightarrow E = (a \leftrightarrow e) \leftrightarrow E'$$

where e is the first column vector of E and E' is the $n \times (k - 1)$ matrix obtained from E by deleting its first column.

Lemma 8.1

1. For a concurrent step u at marking M, its successor formula is

$$M' = M \leftrightarrow Au$$

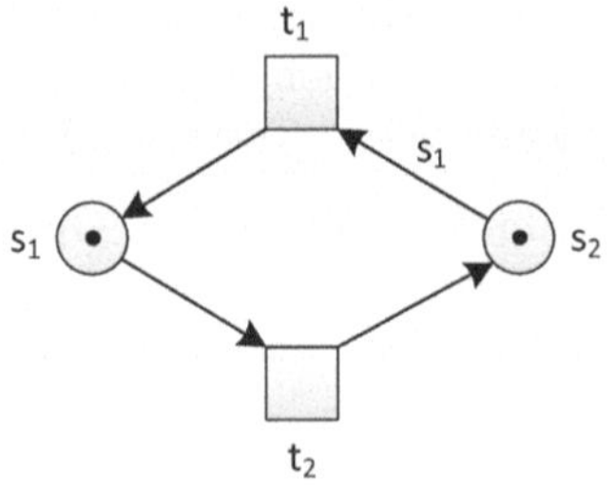

Fig. 8.6 A simple self-control system

in which $u = (u_1, u_2, \ldots, u_n)^T$. Au is the product of matrix A times column vector u.

2. For concurrent step series α_1, α_2, …, α_n and α is the matrix of which the ith column is the column vector for α_i, then the successor marking for α is given by the successor formula

$$M' = M \nrightarrow A\alpha,$$

where M' is the successor: $M_0[\alpha_1{>}M_1[\alpha_2{>}\cdots M_{n-1}[\alpha_n{>}M'$.

The concepts of $T(\sum)$, $G(\sum)$, S-invariant, T-invariant, etc. are all applicable to self-control net systems. The nonlinear property has made their detailed definitions much more complicated. With Example 8.1, the concept of T-invariant is illustrated.

Example 8.1 Invariant The self-control net system in Fig. 8.6 has two T-invariants while no S-invariant.

$\begin{pmatrix} 1 \\ 1 \end{pmatrix}$ and $\begin{pmatrix} 1 & 0 \\ 0 & 1 \end{pmatrix}$ are T-invariants while $\begin{pmatrix} 0 & 1 \\ 1 & 0 \end{pmatrix}$ is not.

$\begin{pmatrix} 1 \\ 1 \end{pmatrix}$ is the concurrent firing of t_1 and t_2, $\begin{pmatrix} 1 & 0 \\ 0 & 1 \end{pmatrix}$ is t_1 before t_2. Concurrent firing of t_1 and t_2 or t_1 before t_2, the successor marking regress to initial marking.

$\begin{pmatrix} 0 & 1 \\ 1 & 0 \end{pmatrix}$ is t_2 before t_1, leading to a marking in which place s_1 has no token. It is impossible now to return to the initial marking. Thus, $\begin{pmatrix} 0 & 1 \\ 1 & 0 \end{pmatrix}$ is not a T-invariant. Besides, since $w(s_2, t_1) = s_1$, and s_1 has no token, The weight on the only input arc of transition t_1 is 0. The question arises again now: is transition t_1 enabled or not? According to transition rule for P/T-systems, t_1 is enabled and it may fire arbitrarily often, since $K(s_1) = \infty$ is assumed. Self-control systems aim at real applications, arbitrary transition firing should not be allowed. That is why the transition rule for self-control systems demands that at least one input arc with nonzero weight for a transition be enabled. So, t_1 is not enabled after t_2.

It is worth repeating that if a T-invariant is enabled at marking M, then its firing would have the same M as its successor. Such a marking M may exist, but it is not necessarily reachable from M_0. This is because a T-invariant is a structure property, irrelevant to initial marking.

Computer programming is among the main application areas of Petri nets. Nets, as it is defined so far, may provide a block diagram at the design stage. But, the lack of variables has prevented Nets to be applicable to real programming. Next, a new kind of nets is proposed for asynchronous concurrent programming.

Chapter 9
C-net

Abstract C-net is for compution and communication. Variables are consisting features. It is variables that receive and hold information from a transition for later use. This has greatly extended the areas of net application.

C-net = Nets + variables (data types), aiming at programming. Letter "C" is the initial of computing and communication, that is what programming is all about.

Nets is a concurrent and asynchronous system model. Programming on top of Nets results at programs with no extra control on statements, except causal dependence. C-net opens the door for Petri nets to computer programming.

Global control flow is in fact a heavy burden on programmers. They are forced to think in a sequential way. Programming in C-net would let programmers concentrate on solutions to an application, rather than considering how to arrange statements into a sequence.

The example below is to solve a simple problem with Nets. This example shows the power of Nets in presenting concurrency on the one hand, and on the other hand, it tells of the limitations of Nets as it is now.

Example 9.1 Chicken and Rabbit Chicken with rabbit in a cage is an ancient Chinese problem. Given the total numbers of heads (red beans) and legs (green beans) of chickens and rabbits in the same cage, to compute the respective numbers of chickens and rabbits. It is assumed that the cage is invisible.

Figure 9.1 is a P/T system with inhibit arcs that computes the answers by counting beans. The initial marking M_0 is $M_0(h) = m$, $M_0(l) = n$, $M_0(s_1) = 0$ and $M_0(s_2) = 0$, i.e., the numbers of red beans and green beans are m and n respectively. Numbers of tokens held by places s_1 and s_2 at marking M are respectively the number of chickens and rabbits counted so far when marking M is reached.

This is a simple arithmetic problem of positive integers. There are formulas to compute answers to this problem. The net system in Fig. 9.1 simulates real human counting. The merit of Nets, compared with programs, is concurrency. Transitions t_1

C. Yuan, *Principle of Petri Nets*, https://doi.org/10.1007/978-981-97-7336-7_9

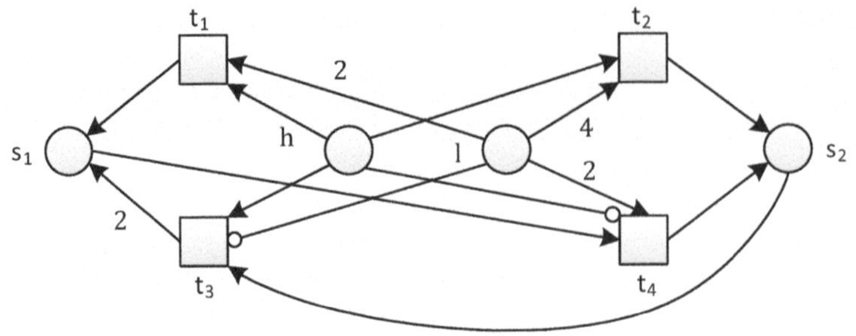

Fig. 9.1 Chicken with rabbit cage

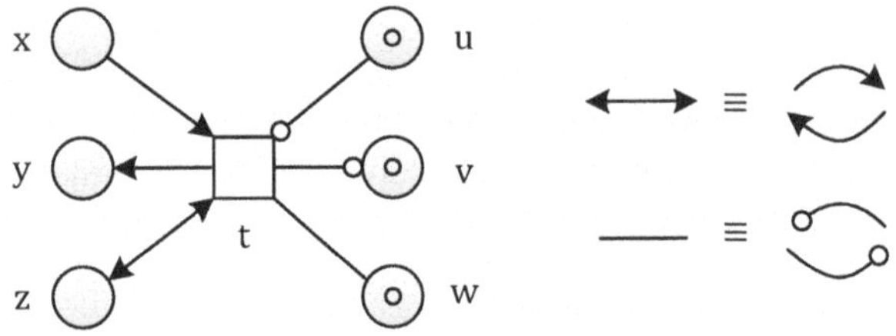

Fig. 9.2 Extension of C-net transition

and t_2 are concurrent when $h \geq 2$ and $l \geq 6$ simulate two persons' independent counting. In contrast to conventional programming, there is no read-write conflict between t_1 and t_2 according to transition rules. An arithmetic computing of positive integers may be represented as a process of P/T-systems. It is easy to prove that in order to have correct answers to this problem, i.e., places s_1 and s_2 end up at no token, m and n must satisfy the formula $2m \leq n \leq 4m \wedge even(n)$. Figure 9.1 will end up at $M(s_1) = M(s_2) = 0$ if the above formula is true.

Disadvantage of nets is the lack of data types. This fact has limited Nets to do only very simple integer arithmetic. The only data type in a net is "positive integer" (token number) with limited plus and minus operations. The capacity of a place sets an up bound on plus operation, and the non-negative nature of token numbers at any marking sets the low bound.

Targeting at concurrent programming, C-net introduces variables of various types as a new kind of S-elements, and read/write operations as new kinds of transitions. Figure 9.2 illustrates graphically represented extension of such a new transition t. The extension of t consists of three places x, y, and z and three variables u, v, and w: x is input, y is output, and z is both input and output; t reads u, write v, and read&write w. To distinguish a variable from a place graphically, a variable is represented by a double-circle, as shown in Fig. 9.2. The extension of a transition in real applications is certainly not as complete as shown in the figure. It varies from application to application. Besides, places are not a necessary part of a C-net transition.

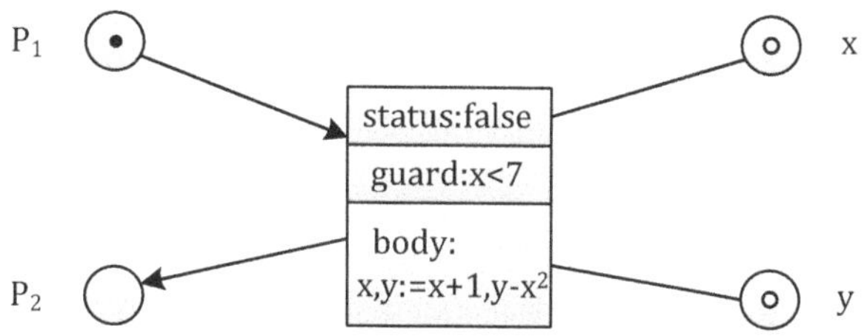

Fig. 9.3 C-net transition

9.1 C-net Transition

As shown in Fig. 9.3, a C-net transition involves too many factors. It would be complicated to define its transition rules formally. All concepts of C-nets will be first given informally to prepare for formal definition and to facilitate understanding.

C-net is a two-faced object. It is first a net, and then it is also a program. As a net, its transition acts according to transition rules. As a program, every single transition is itself a simple program called transition program. Transition program or program transition, it depends on which facet of it you mean. Tokens flow from transition to transition to reflect causal dependence of transition programs. As such, a two-faced transition requires a two-fold way to be enabled, i.e., token enabled and variable enabled. It is token enabled, T-enabled for short, if it is enabled as a normal net transition. It is variable enabled, V-enabled for short, if its program part has meaningful initial values for all its variables. For variables not initialized, C-net would let ψ be their initial value. So, ψ would disable a program transition.

Figure 9.3 shows an overall look of a C-net transition.

The box representing a C-net transition in Fig. 9.3 is divided into three parts; the top part provides its status (having been executed with initialized variables or not), and the middle part indicates a condition called "guard" to decide whether the statement(s) is conditional and, if yes, what the condition is. The third part is the statement(s) or the program body, telling what to do. The transition in Fig. 9.3 tells: "Status: false, guard: $x < 7$, body: $x, y := x + 1, y - x^2$." The body assigns variables x and y in parallel, i.e., to have expression $x + 1$ and $y - x^2$ evaluated before assigning them to x and y.

Here expressions $x + 1$ and $y - x^2$ share variable x, the two assignments are related with each other. Parallel execution requires the evaluation of expressions $x + 1$ and $y - x^2$ to be completed before assigning. The difference between "parallel" and "concurrent" is that the latter requires the respective expressions to share no variables at all.

There are three key words: status, guard, and body. "Status = false" indicates that initial values of variables in the program has not been used for execution. Once initial values are used, false is changed to true. It becomes false again if at least one of the values of the input variables is renewed. For example, to execute $x := x + 1$,x requires a meaningful initial value. Once it is executed, it would assign a new value to x, status remains false. So, it is executed again for the second time. To stop such endless renew → false → renew → false, guard set a condition. In Fig. 9.3, guard is $x < 7$. The execution of $x := x + 1$ (the body) would sooner or later make $x < 7$ false, $x := x + 1$ stops execution, and x is not renewed, and the program terminates. The set of all transitions with x as input is called T-extension of x. A new value of x will lead all transitions in its extension to be V-enabled. In case more than one transition is V-enabled by x, only one of them should be T-enabled to avoid uncertainty.

A guard is a Boolean expression, it serves as the condition for body execution. Body is a program by itself.

Token decides whether a transition is T-enabled, and key words "status" and "guard" decide whether a transition is V-enabled.

The body is written in OE (operation expression) for C-net. It is of course allowed to write it in any other programming language, but OE has its unique merits. OE is a completely new programming language. Its syntax and semantic axioms are defined side by side. And as such, semantics of OE programs can be computed from program text based on semantic axioms. Next is a brief introduction of OE, to prepare for transitions program in C-net.

9.2 OE: Operation Expression

To understand why OE is needed and why it is good, conventional programming languages and conventional formal semantics are briefly recalled first.

9.2.1 Conventional Formal Semantics

Conventional programming languages have inherited the concept of variables from conventional mathematics. A variable allows a write operation and a limited read operation. By "limited," we mean two things: first, a read operation is applicable only in the course of evaluating a math expression; second, what is obtained from such a read operation is the current value held by the variable being read. A pure value does not tell how it relates to the initial state. Such a read operation is helpless in the study of formal semantics. That is why the concept of variables is of no importance in conventional formal semantics. Instead, an assignment is the basic brick for constructing disciplines of formal semantics.

Conventional formal semantics take the assignment sequences of programming execution as program semantics. Thus, semantics = {possible execution sequences}, i.e., the set of all legal execution sequences. There are different ways to view and to study an assignment. It is either defined as a mapping (function) from program state to program state, or as an operation. Thus, an execution sequence is a series of functions composed one after another like $f_n(f_{n-1}(\cdots))$, or a series of operations like $p_1, p_2, \ldots, p_n$. Properties of such sequences include predicates like "$x < y$ is stable," "sooner or later $x > y^2 + 2$," etc. The former is a stable property and the latter is a progress property.

Hoare logic is the most successful algebraic semantics, the Turing award winner of 1980. The key concept in Hoare logic is assertion. For program (or program segment) S, $\{p\}S\{q\}$ is an assertion on S, where p and q are predicates on states of S. This assertion is true if the truth of p at the initial state of S leads to the truth of q at the final state of S. For example, $\{x > 5\}x := x + 1\{x > 6\}$. This assertion is true at a glance. In order to prove $\{p\}S\{q\}$, the concept of the weakest precondition $wp(S, q)$ was proposed. By definition, if $wp(S, q)$ is true at the initial state of S, then q must be true after p. The most fundamental axiom in Hoare logic is $(p \rightarrow wp(S, q)) \rightarrow \{p\}S\{q\}$, i.e., if p implies $wp(S, q)$, then $\{p\}S\{q\}$. For assignment $x := e$, $wp(x{:=}e, q) = q|_e^x$, i.e., $wp(x := e, q)$ is obtained by replacing every appearance of x in q with expression e. In the above example, $wp(x{:=}x + 1, x{>}6) \equiv (x{>}6)|_{x+1}^x \equiv (x + 1){>}6 \equiv x{>}5$. So, $\{x > 5\}x := x + 1$ $\{x > 6\}$ is true.

As a program, S must consist of a series of statements, say $S \equiv s_1, s_2, \ldots, s_n$. For simplicity, let $n = 3$, the way to prove $\{p\}S\{q\}$ is to prove $\{p\}s_1, s_2, s_3\{q\}$, i.e., to compute $wp(s_3, q)$, $wp(s_2, wp(s_3, q))$, and $wp(s_1, wp(s_2, wp(s_3, q)))$, and finally to prove $p \rightarrow wp(s_1, wp(s_2, wp(s_3, q)))$. For programs of hundreds of statements, such sequential computing is hard work. This is just to prove one property, namely q of S.

All in all, what is discussed by these formal semantics are program properties. They have, up till today, failed to give a precise definition of program semantics. The set of execution sequences is the semantics for computers, telling a computer what to do, but not the semantics for human users.

9.2.2 *What Is Program Semantics for Human Users*

Example 9.2 Shared Semantics of Two Programs Below are two programs s_1 and s_2:

$$s_1 \quad a{:=}x; x{:=}y; y{:=}a$$

$$s_2 \quad x{:=}x + y; y{:=}x - y; x{:=}x - y$$

It is easy to see that both s_1 and s_2 exchange values initially held by x and y. It is also easy to see that s_1 and s_2 have completely different assignments and different assignment sequences.

All conventional formal semantics would conclude that s_1 and s_2 have different semantics although what they do is the same.

Is such a conclusion curious?

Informally speaking, the semantics of a program is "What" it does, not "How." But, all conventional formal semantics have targeted at "How," instead of "What"

OE aims at a formal description of "What."

Such a what/how mistaken is rooted in the misunderstanding of program variables. As mentioned above, programming languages have copied the concept of variables from mathematics, and formal semantics have inherited it from programming languages. But, the concept of math variables does not capture the complete nature of program variables. A program variable is the name of a computer memory location, a math variable is just the name of a value with no connection to any hardware object. A memory location may be read any time while a math variable allows read operation only in the course of evaluating a math expression. OE recognized this difference and has, based on this recognition for the first time, formally defined read and write operations on memory locations via their names, i.e., program variables.

All read and write operations in OE are precisely defined with respect operators and operands. As such, semantic axioms have been given side by side with operation definitions. The operator for write is an up bar " $^{-}$ ". A complete write operation (conditional writes, concurrent writes, and loops) is called a program term, including operator and operand. Program terms form an operation expression (i.e., OE) if they are connected with a semicolon. A single term is also an operation expression. Semicolon is not only a connector (or punctuation mark), but also a semantic object with formally defined semantics. So, $x := x + 1$ becomes $\overline{x}(x+1).s_1$ and s_2 above become:

$$s_1 \quad \overline{a}(x); \overline{x}(y); \overline{y}(a)$$

$$s_2 \quad \overline{x}(x+y); \overline{y}(x-y); \overline{x}(x-y)$$

The operator for read-after is an under bar "__", read-before operator is a curved under bar "~". A read-before operation and a read after operation are both necessary for semantic description. It tells how the initial state of S and the final state of S are related, i.e., tells what program S does.

To see how the semantics of S_1 and S_2 are computed from S_1 and S_2, the semantic axioms for a simple write operation $\overline{u}(e)$ and $\overline{v}(e)$ are given below, where V_p is the set of variables in that OE program p writes.

Semantic axioms for a simple write:

(A0) $V_\varepsilon = \varnothing$, ε is the "skip" in OE, it writes no variable.
(A1) $\underline{u}(\overline{u}(e)) = e$, $\underline{u}(\overline{v}(e)) = u$, for $u \neq v$,
(A2) $\underset{\sim}{u}(\overline{v}(e)) = u$, for all variable u, including v.

Remarks

1. Variable u is not changed by $\overline{v}(e)$, so $\underline{u}(\overline{u}(e)) = e$.
2. The initial value of any variable before a write operation is itself, so $\underset{\sim}{u}(\overline{v}(e)) = u$.

By the above axioms, the semantic of $\overline{x}(x+1)$ is computed as given below with newly proposed concepts, including semantic functions, semantic predicate, semantic formula, semantic calculus etc.

$$\overline{x}(x+1)/\text{assignment}/$$

$$\underset{\sim}{x}(\overline{x}(x+1)), \quad \underline{x}(\overline{x}(x+1)) = x+1/\text{semantics axioms}/$$

So, x is the initial value (irrelevant to concrete value) and $x + 1$ is the final value. This relation may be written as

$$\underline{x} = x+1 \text{ and } \underset{\sim}{x} = x$$

in which $\underline{x}$ and $\underset{\sim}{x}$ and are semantic functions defined on programs (not only OE programs). Assignments in all sorts of program languages share semantic axioms given above.

To clear up concepts first, let's consider a simple program consisting of 2 assignments with two variables x and y:

$$P: \quad s_3; s_4, \text{where } s_3 \text{ is } \overline{x}(x+y) \text{ and } s_4 \text{ is } \overline{y}(x-y).$$

It is not difficult to find that $\underline{x}(P) = x+y$ and $\underline{y}(P) = x$ in which x and y are initial values of P. What to do next is to illustrate how to compute $\underline{x}(P)$ and $\underline{y}(P)$ with semantic axioms to show a way of automatic semantic computation. Semantic axioms used below will not be mentioned explicitly.

First, an informal description of computing semantics of s_3; s_4

The initial values before s_3 is x and y:

$$\underset{\sim}{x}(s_3) = x \wedge \underset{\sim}{y}(s_3) = y.$$

The final value after s_3 is

$$\underline{x}(s_3) = \underset{\sim}{x}(s_3) + y \wedge \underline{y}(s_3) = \underset{\sim}{y}(s_3).$$

That is $\underline{x}(s_3) = x+y \wedge \underline{y}(s_3) = y$.

The initial values of x and y before s_4 are the final values of x and y after s_3:

$$\underset{\sim}{x}(s_4) = \underline{x}(s_3) \wedge \underset{\sim}{y}(s_4) = \underline{y}(s_3).$$

That is $\underset{\sim}{x}(s_4) = x+y \wedge \underset{\sim}{y}(s_4) = y$.

Thus, the final values after s_4 are

$$\underline{x}(s_4) = \underset{\sim}{x}(s_4) = x + y$$

$$\wedge \underline{y}(s_4) = \underset{\sim}{x}(s_4) - \underset{\sim}{y}(s_4) = x + y - y = x.$$

So, $\underline{x}(P) = x + y$ and $\underline{y}(P) = x$.

To extract concepts and terms from above example, we have:

Semantic proposition: $\underline{x}(P) = x + y$ and $\underline{y}(P) = x$.

By removing subject P from proposition, we obtain predicates:

$$\underline{x} = x + y, \quad \underline{y} = x.$$

They are semantic predicates, since semantic functions are their consisting elements.

$\underset{\sim}{x} = x$ is also a semantic predicate, and it is useful in automatic semantic computing from program texts consisting of more than one assignment. The way to automatically compute semantics of s_3; s_4 is as given below.

First, replace s_3; s_4 with semantics (s_3); semantics (s_4) to obtain a semantic predicate formula:

$$s_3; s_4 \rightarrow \underline{x} = x + y; \ \underline{y} = x - y$$

Add unassigned variables to it (italic):

$$s_3; s_4 \rightarrow \underline{x} = x + y \wedge \underline{y} = y; \ \underline{y} = x - y \wedge \underline{x} = x,$$

Remove ";" and to replace s_3; s_4 with $s'_3; s'_4$, where s'_3 is obtained by replacing $\underline{x}$ with $\underset{\sim}{x}$ and $\underline{y}$ with $\underset{\sim}{y}$, s'_4 is obtained by replacing x with $\underset{\sim}{x}$ and y with $\underset{\sim}{y}$:

$$\rightarrow \underset{\sim}{x} = x + y \wedge \underset{\sim}{x} = y; \underline{y} = \underset{\sim}{x} - \underset{\sim}{y} \wedge \underline{x} = \underset{\sim}{x}$$

Remove s'_3 when $\underline{x}$ and $\underset{\sim}{y}$ are passed to $\underline{x}$ and $\underline{y}$:

$$\rightarrow \underline{y} = x + y - y \wedge \underline{x} = x + y$$

$$\rightarrow \underline{y} = x \wedge \underline{x} = x + y$$

The above process of computing semantics from a semantic predicate formula to semantic predicate is formalized as below:

$$
\begin{aligned}
& x = x + y \wedge \underline{y} = y; \underline{y} = x - y \wedge \underline{x} = x \wedge \underset{\sim}{x} = x \wedge \underset{\sim}{y} = y \\
\equiv\ & \underline{x} = x + y \wedge \underline{y} = y; \underline{y} = \underset{\sim}{x} - \underset{\sim}{y} \wedge \underline{x} = \underset{\sim}{x} \\
\equiv\ & \underline{y} = \underset{\sim}{x} - \underset{\sim}{y} \wedge \underline{x} = \underset{\sim}{x} \wedge \underset{\sim}{x} = x + y \wedge \underset{\sim}{y} = y \\
\equiv\ & \underline{x} = x + y \wedge \underline{y} = x.
\end{aligned}
$$

This process of automatic semantics computation is called semantic predicate calculus.

Now, back to the two small programs s_1 and s_2 mentioned earlier above. The semantics of s_1, s_2 are given, respectively by semantic formulas below, in which each assignment has been replaced by their respective semantics:

$$s_1 \quad \underline{a} = x;\ \underline{x} = y; \underline{y} = a$$

$$s_2 \quad \underline{x} = x + y;\ \underline{y} = x - y;\ \underline{x} = x - y$$

s_1 and s_2 are now semantic formulas that may be reduced to a semantic term by semantic calculus in the way as shown above. For s_1 and s_2, their semantics are given below:

$$s_1 \quad \underline{x} = y \wedge \underline{y} = x \wedge \underline{a} = x$$

$$s_2 \quad \underline{x} = y \wedge \underline{y} = x$$

So, omitting the auxiliary variable a, $\underline{x} = y \wedge \underline{y} = x$ is precisely the semantics of s_1 and s_2.

OE, as a new programming language, is not as important as concepts derived from it. These concepts include:

Semantic functions like $\underline{x}$, $\underline{y}$; with semantic axioms, the semantics of assignments, $\underline{x}$, $\underline{y}$ can be computed for given assignments.

Semantic predicates: a predicate that contains semantic functions.

Semantic term: semantic predicates connected with logic operators.

Semantic formula: a formula consisting of semantic terms and semantic operators like the sequential operator ";".

Semantic calculus: to reduce a semantic formula to a semantic term.

A semantic term contains final results evaluated for all semantic functions.

Semantic predicates and semantic calculus may also be used for program specification and specification refinement. Such specification and refined specification can be analyzed with semantic calculus.

Interested readers are referred to the author's book 《OESPA: Semantic Oriented Theory of Programming》(Science Press, Beijing, 2019).

9.3 Formal Specification with an Example

Requirement: to sort integer array $A[0..n-1]$ into ascending order.

Specification in terms of semantic predicate:

$$\text{Goal}: \quad \underline{A}[0] \leq \underline{A}[1] \leq \cdots \leq \underline{A}[n-2] \leq \underline{A}[n-1] \wedge \underline{A}_M = A_M$$

in which $\underline{A}[i]$ is the final value of the i(th) element of $\underline{A}$ after sorting, $\underline{A}$ is the final value of the array A as a whole after sorting, $\underline{A}_M$ is the multi-set of $\underline{A}$, and $\underline{A}_M = A_M$ required to keep the multi-set of A invariant.

Strategy towards goal: hunting for index k such that

$$0 \leq \underline{k} < n \wedge \underline{A}[0..\underline{k}-1] \leq \underline{A}[\underline{k}] \leq \underline{A}[\underline{k}+1..n-1] \wedge \underline{A}_M = A_M$$

This is a specification for Dijkstra's quick sorting: hunting for index k as required above with $\underline{A}_M = A_M$, that is to keep the multi set of A invariant all the time.

As the first step, hunting may start from both $A[0]$ and $A[n-1]$: keep the head-segment smaller than or equal to $A[0]$ and the tail segment grater than or equal to $A[0]$.

The next step is to sort, also with Dijkstra's quick sorting, $\underline{A}[0..\underline{k}-1]$ and $\underline{A}[\underline{k}+1..n-1]$ into ascending order, respectively and in parallel.

The algorithm of quick sorting is not included here, since our aim is to introduce OESPA for C-net. All nice properties of OE and concepts derived from OE will benefit C-net, since the program for a C-net transition is written in OE.

9.4 Formal Definition of C-net

Definition 9.1 C-net 6-Tuple $CN = (P, V, T; F, R, W_r)$ is a C-net, if

$$\begin{aligned} & P \cup V \cup T \neq \varnothing \wedge (P \cap T = \varnothing \wedge P \cap V = \varnothing \wedge V \cap T = \varnothing) \\ & \wedge (F \subseteq (P \times T \cup T \times P) \wedge R \subseteq V \times T \wedge W_r \subseteq V \times T) \\ & \wedge (dom(F) \cup cod(F) \cup cod(R) \cup cod(W_r) = P \cup T) \\ & \wedge (dom(R) \cup dom(W_r) = V) \end{aligned}$$

Remarks C-net may have just one segment of program, i.e., just one program transition. That is why *dnet*$(P, T; F)$ is not required.

In addition to $(P, T; F)$,

1. V is the set of variables.
2. R is a read relation between V and T.
3. W_r (W is reserved for weights on arcs) is a write relation between V and T.
4. A C-net transition is a program transition.

From now on, we will make a distinction between C-net and a C-net system. The former refers to the static structure without initial marking, while the latter emphasizes dynamics, i.e., how it acts for a given initial marking, including initial variable values.

Before defining the concept of a C-net system, some terms are defined below. The concepts of presets and post-sets of transition and places are applicable to C-net, and as such, they are not redefined here.

Definition 9.2 Basic Terms For C-net $CN = (P, V, T; F, R, W_r)$ and $x \in V, t \in T, p \in P$,

1. $r(x) = \{t | (x, t) \in R\}$ is the read-set of x, $w(x) = \{t | (x, t) \in W_r\}$ is the write-set of x. Read-set of x is also called extension of x.
2. $r(t) = \{x | (x, t) \in R\}$ is the read-set of t, $w(t) = \{x | (x, t) \in W_r\}$ is the write-set of t.
3. $tp(x)$ is the data type of x, it is also the value domain of this data type. It depends on the context.
4. $Type = \cup_{x \in V} tp(x)$ is the value domain of all variables.

Definition 9.3 From C-net to C-net System For C-net $CN = (P, V, T; F, R, W_r)$,

1. $K : P \rightarrow \{1, 2, \cdots\} \cup \{\infty\}$ is the capacity function of CN.
2. $M_p : P \rightarrow \{0, 1, 2, \cdots\}$ is a flow marking of CN if $\forall p \in P : M_p(p) \leq K(p)$.
   $M_v : V \rightarrow Type$ is a value marking if $\forall x \in V : M_v(x) \in tp(x)$,
   $M = (M_p, M_v)$ is a marking of CN, i.e. marking = (place marking, variable marking).
3. $W : F \rightarrow \{1, 2, \ldots\}$ is the weight function of CN.
4. $status : T \rightarrow \{true, false\}$ is the state function of CN,

   $guard : T \rightarrow E_b$ is the whistle function of CN, where E_b is a set of Boolean expressions. For $t \in T$, $guard(t)$ contains only variables in $r(t)$, the read-set of t.
   $body : T \rightarrow E_o$ is a transition program function of CN, if $body(t)$ is a parallel assignment in OE for all variables in $w(t)$. E_o is the set of OE expressions such that $body(t)$ reads all variables in $r(t)$.

5. $M_T = (status, guard, body)$ is the transition marking of CN.

Note that a guard may have auxiliary variables, and body may assign values to them.

Definition 9.4 C-net System $\sum = (P, V, T; F, R, W_r, K, W, M_t, M_0)$ is a C-net system if $CN = (P, V, T; F, R, W_r)$ is a C-net, and K, W, M_t, and M_0 are, respectively, a capacity function, a weight function, a transition marking, and a marking of CN. As the initial setting, $\forall t \in T : M_T(t) = false$.

Note that a marking of CN is a pair (M_p, M_v), initial state of P and initial state of V.

Definition 9.5 Transition Rule

1. Transition t is value-enabled or V-enabled by (M_T, M_V), denoted with $(M_T, M_V)[t\rangle$, if $\neg status(t) \wedge \forall x \in V : guard(t, x) = M_v(x)$. Note that $guard(t, x)$ is the value

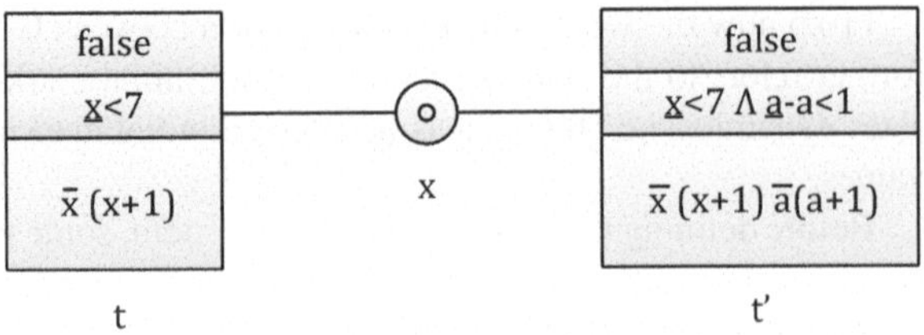

Fig. 9.4 Program transition

of x in *guard*(*t*). So, *guard*(t, x) $= M_v(x)$ requires that the initial value of x given by M_v is still the current value in *guard*(*t*).

2. Transition t is token-enabled or P-enabled by M_p, denoted with $M_P[t>$, if t is enabled at M_P by transition rules of P/T-system.
3. Transition t is enabled at (M_T, M), denoted with $(M_T, M)[t>$, if $(M_T, M_V)[t> \wedge M_P[t>$, or, $(M_T, M)[t> \equiv (M_T, M_V)[t> \wedge M_P[t>$. Note that $M = (M_P, M_V)$. So, t is enabled at (M_T, M) if t is V-enabled at (M_T, M_V) and P-enabled at M_P.
4. If $(M_T, M)[t>$, t may occur to produce its successor $\left(M'_T, M'\right)$ as given below.
   For all t' in T,

$$M'_T(\text{status}(t')) = \begin{cases} \text{status}(t') & \textit{if } \; t' \neq t \wedge t' \notin \cup_{x \in w(t)} r(x) \\ \text{true} \;\; \text{if} \;\; t' = t \wedge t' \notin \cup_{x \in w(t)} r(x) \\ \text{false} \;\; \text{if} \;\; t' \in \cup_{x \in w(t)} r(x) \end{cases}$$

in which $w(x)$ and $r(x)$ are, respectively, the write set and read-set of x. For all x in $w(t)$, the new value $M'_v(x)$ of x is given by $\underline{x}$

$$M'_v(x) = \begin{cases} \underline{x}(B) & \text{if } \; w(t) \cap r(t) = \varnothing \\ \underline{x}(B') & \text{if } \; w(t) \cap r(t) \neq \varnothing \quad \text{where} \quad B' = B^n \end{cases}$$

Note B = *body*(*t*), and n is the smallest positive integer such that n times execution of B would make *guard*(*t*) = *false*.

The successor marking on places, i.e., M'_P, is computed according to transition rules of P/T-systems.

There are two program transitions t and t' in Fig. 9.4 below. As a convention, the key words "status," "guard," and "body" are omitted and to be recognized by their positions in the transition box. They are pure V-transition since they share variable x but are not connected to any place elements. A V-transition is always considered P-enabled. If the value of x is not ψ, then t and t' are V-enabled.

The guards of t and t' are both $x < 7$, since $\overline{a} - a < 1$ is always true before the first execution. Note that a is auxiliary. For all initial values of x that is greater than 6 (*tp*(x) = integer), the guard is false, both t and t' are not V-enabled. As a C-net system, t and t' are dead. In case $x < 7$, say $x = 4$, both t and t' are V-enabled, and they are in read/write conflict since they share x. Transition t' may occur if the conflict is solved in favor of it. The execution of *body*(t'), i.e., $\overline{x}(x + 1)\overline{a}(a + 1)$ will lead to $\overline{a} - a = 1$, and *guard*(t') = *false*. Auxiliary variable a controls the execution of t'. In case $\overline{a} - a = 1$ is replaced with $\overline{a} - a = 2$, t' may be executed more than once.

In contrast to t', *body*(t) may be executed repeatedly until $x \geq 7$. For initial value 4 of x, 3 times of executing would lead to $x \geq 7$. This number "3" is an example of n in B^n for transition rules in above Definition 9.5.

After above informal description of C-net systems, next are some formal definitions. In all these definitions, $\sum = (P, V, T; F, R, W_r, K, W, M_t, M_0)$ is a C-net system.

Definition 9.6 Basic Relations

1. For transition t_1 and t_2 of $\sum$, if

$$w(t_1) \cap (w(t_2) \cup r(t_2)) = \varnothing \wedge w(t_2) \cap (w(t_1) \cup r(t_1)) = \varnothing,$$

then t_1 and t_2 are read/write independent, denoted by $WRInd(t_1, t_2)$.

2. Transition t_1 and t_2 are in V-conflict at (M_T, M), denoted with $WRC(t_1, t_2, (M_T, M))$, if $(M_T, M)[t_1\!> \wedge (M_T, M)[t_2\!> \wedge \neg\, WRInd(t_1, t_2)$:

$$WRC(t_1, t_2, (M_T, M)) \equiv (M_T, M)[t_1 > \wedge (M_T, M)[t_2 > \wedge \neg WRInd(t_1, t_2).$$

3. Transition t_1 and t_2 are concurrent at (M_T, M), denoted with $(M_T, M)[t_1 \parallel t_2\!>$, if they are both enabled and there is no conflict, i.e.,

$$(M_T, M)[t_1 \parallel t_2 > \;\equiv\; (M_T, M)[t_1 > \wedge (M_T, M)[t_2 > \wedge\, WRInd(t_1, t_2) \wedge \neg \mathrm{P} \\ - \mathrm{conflict}(t_1, t_2, M_p).$$

Example 9.3 Bubble Algorithm as a C-net System Bubble algorithm sorts array $A[0..n-1]$ into ascending order. It compares $A[0]$ with array elements from $A[1]$ to $A[n-1]$, hunting for the maximum, and moves the maximum (first bubble) to $A[n-1]$ by swapping. It repeats this "compare and swap" process on $A[0..n-2]$ to find the second bubble, the third bubble, and so on till $A[0..n-1]$ becomes an ascending array. This is a sequential process. Sorting, similar to the lineup of new-face pupils for a physical education class, is concurrent and asynchronous by nature. It is control flow that forced programmers to invent a way to bubble up. To capture the concurrent and asynchronous nature of hunting for bubbles, C-net is a nice model as shown by Fig. 9.5. Interested readers are suggested to fill up the blanks in the figure.

This C-net system simulates pupils' lineup to a great degree. It has no control, and what transitions do is just to compare and swap concurrently and asynchronously. The only thing worth mentioning is the read-and-write conflict between the transition to compare $A[i]$, $A[i-1]$ and the transition to compare $A[i]$, $A[i+1]$. A shared place does not necessarily lead to conflict, but a shared variable does. To resolve these conflicts between variables, transitions are divided into two concurrent sets: those that compare $A[i]$ and $A[i+1]$ for even indexes $i = 0, 2, \ldots$, and those that compare $A[i]$ and $A[i+1]$ for odd indexes $i = 1, 3, \ldots$. Written in OE, we have:

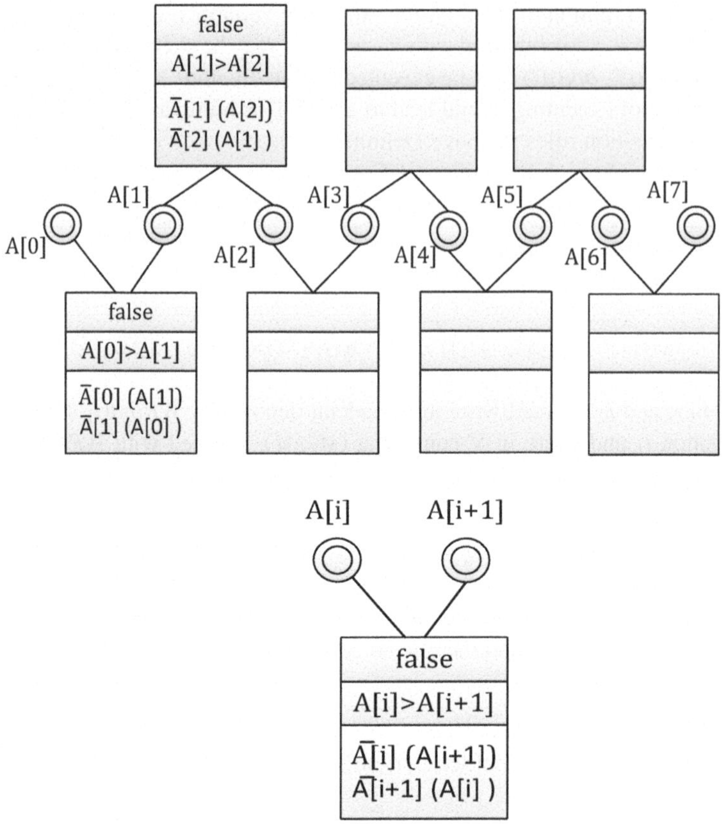

Fig. 9.5 Concurrent sorting in C-net

$$\equiv < \parallel i : \text{even}(i) \wedge 0 \leq i < n : \left(\overline{A}[i](A[i+1])\overline{A}[i+1](A[i])\right)^{A[i] > A[i+1]} >$$
$$\equiv < \parallel i : \text{odd}(i) \wedge 0 < i < n : \left(\overline{A}[i](A[i+1])\overline{A}[i+1](A[i])\right)^{A[i] > A[i+1]} >.$$

In above OE programs, "$\|$" is the concurrent connector between write-operations, and $\overline{A}[i](A[i+1])\overline{A}[i+1](A[i])$ is also a concurrent writing: it swaps $A[i]$ and $A[i+1]$, i.e., to write $A[i]$ and $A[i+1]$ with expressions $A[i+1]$ and $A[i]$, respectively under the condition given by superscript $A[i] > A[i+1]$.

The semantics of concurrent writing $\overline{x}(e_1)\overline{y}(e_2)$ is $\overline{x}=e_1 \wedge \overline{y}=e_2$, that is to evaluate e_1 and e_2 first, then to write the obtained results into x and y, respectively. Above semantic of $\overline{x}(e_1)\overline{y}(e_2)$ is in fact a semantic axiom for OE. This axiom applies to concurrent writing given by "$\|$".

It is easy to modify the C-net in Fig. 9.5 so that asynchronous concurrency can be controlled as given by S_0 and S_1 above. Let one program transition take S_0 as its program body and all elements of array A as its input variables, and another program transition take S_1 as its program body with all elements of A as its input as well.

Fig. 9.6 Two C-net transition program

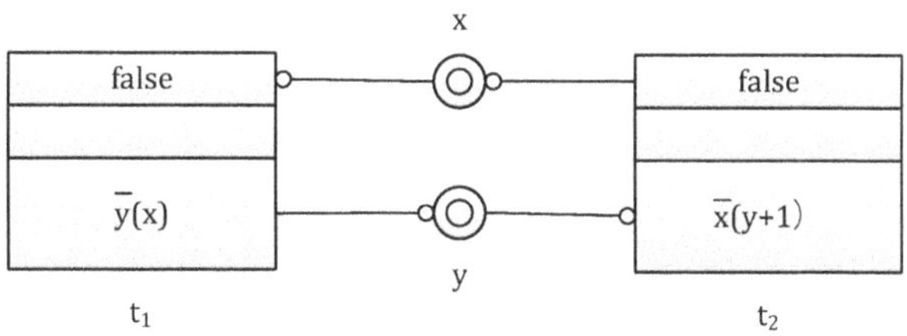

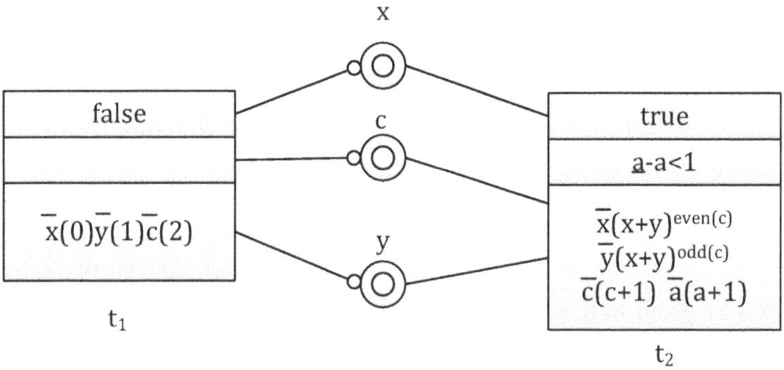

Fig. 9.7 How an auxiliary variable functions

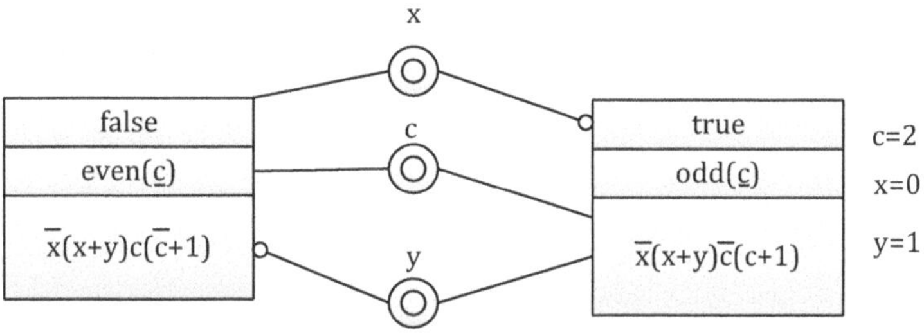

Fig. 9.8 Alternating computing of Fibonacci series

Another way to implement asynchronous concurrency among transitions in Fig. 9.5 is to use a synchronizer to be defined in Chap. 11.

Example 9.4 An Endless Loop Figure 9.6 has two C-net program transitions t_1 and t_2, writing into variables x and y, respectively. As long as ψ is not the initial value of x and y, both t_1 and t_2 are V-enabled since their status is "false" and guard is "true" (by default). Once this initial conflict is resolved, t_1 and t_2 will execute their transition program in turn without an ending.

To see more on what a C-net may do, Figs. 9.7 and 9.8 show two ways to produce the Fibonacci series.

The transition t_1 in Fig. 9.7 is enabled but t_2 is not (status is true). The execution of transition program t_1 assigns initial values to x, y, and c and then becomes dead, since it reads no variable. The firing of t_1 leads to status change of t_2 from true to false, t_2 is enabled. The guard of t_2 in Fig. 9.7 is given with the auxiliary variable a; $\underline{a} - a < 1$ is initially true, but will become false after a one-time execution of $\overline{a}(a + 1)$. However, the new values of x and y keep the status of t_2 false. Note that as an auxiliary variable, the final value $\underline{a}$ is not remembered after termination of t_2, and as such, $\underline{a} - a < 1$ is always true for the first firing of t_2. So, auxiliary variable a ensures that t_2 occurs time after time in the way of to occur → terminate → to occur → terminate ⋯1.

The initial values of x and y given by t_1 is the first two numbers in the Fibonacci series: $\underline{x} = 0$, $\underline{y} = 1$, and $\underline{c} = 2$, which is the index of the next Fibonacci number to be computed by t_2. A one-time execution of t_2 produces one Fibonacci number. We have $\text{even}(\underline{c}) \rightarrow \underline{y} = \text{Fib}(\underline{c})$ and $\text{odd}(\underline{c}) \rightarrow \underline{x} = \text{Fib}(\underline{c})$. Transition program t_2 will not stop repeating unless extra control is added to *guard*(t_2).

In the C-net system in Fig. 9.8, initial values : $\underline{x} = 0$, $\underline{y} = 1$, and $\underline{c} = 2$ are given implicitly outside the transition. One of the two transition programs computes even-indexed Fibonacci numbers, while the other computes odd-indexed Fibonacci numbers, and they occur in turn.

The formal definition of C-net systems are seemingly hard to grasp. But it is very useful, since it builds a bridge between conventional Petri nets and computer science. Without the C-net system, the study of business process management (BPM) would not be able to make progress in terms of Nets, since all business processes need variables to pass data from assignment (transition) to assignment. BPM modeling will be discussed in Chap. 11. To prepare for BPM modeling, the concept of synchrony is presented next.

Chapter 10
Synchronizer

Abstract This chapter is a preparation for application in business process management (BPM). The key concept "synchronizer" is proposed and precisely defined.

This chapter is a preparation for net application in business process. modeling (BPM).

Synchronizer is a special kind of S-element. It plays a role in BPM modeling to make transitions (BPM tasks) in its scope act according to their causal dependence and guild regulations while maintaining flexibility towards BPM cases. Recall that scope of a S-element, similar to extension of a transition, is the union of its preset and its post set. Synchrony, as a branch of general net theory, will be introduced in Part III. Synchronizer, as a means to implement synchronization, is briefly described here, since it is the key concept for BPM to be introduced next in Chap. 11.

A synchronizer connects two sets of transitions to force transitions in its preset and transitions in its post-set to act consistently. To see how a synchronizer p functions, let $p = \{t_{1i} | i = 1, 2, ..., n\}$ and $p = \{t_{2j} | j = 1, 2, ..., m\}$. The weights on all arcs (t_{1i}, p), $i = 1, 2, \ldots, n$, are constant a_2 and the weights on all arcs (p, t_{2j}), $j = 1, 2, \ldots, m$, are constant a_1. In addition, $k(p) = a_1 \times a_2$ and $0 < a_1 \leq n$, $0 < a_2 \leq m$.

Denote p with $p = (T_1, T_2\ ,\ (a_1, a_2))$ and let M be the marking in consideration. The transition rules around p is: when exactly a_1 transitions in T_1 are concurrently enabled by M and $M(p) = 0$, these a_1 transitions fire. When $M^{'}(p) = a_1 \times a_2$ at successor marking $M^{'}$, i.e., $M^{'}(p) = K(p)$, a_2 transitions in T_2 are enabled to fire. More importantly, no transition in T_2 may fire more than once for one case, since a single business case does not need to redo the same task.

Graphically, p is represented as given in Fig. 10.1a.

To put above concepts into definition, we have:

C. Yuan, *Principle of Petri Nets*, https://doi.org/10.1007/978-981-97-7336-7_10

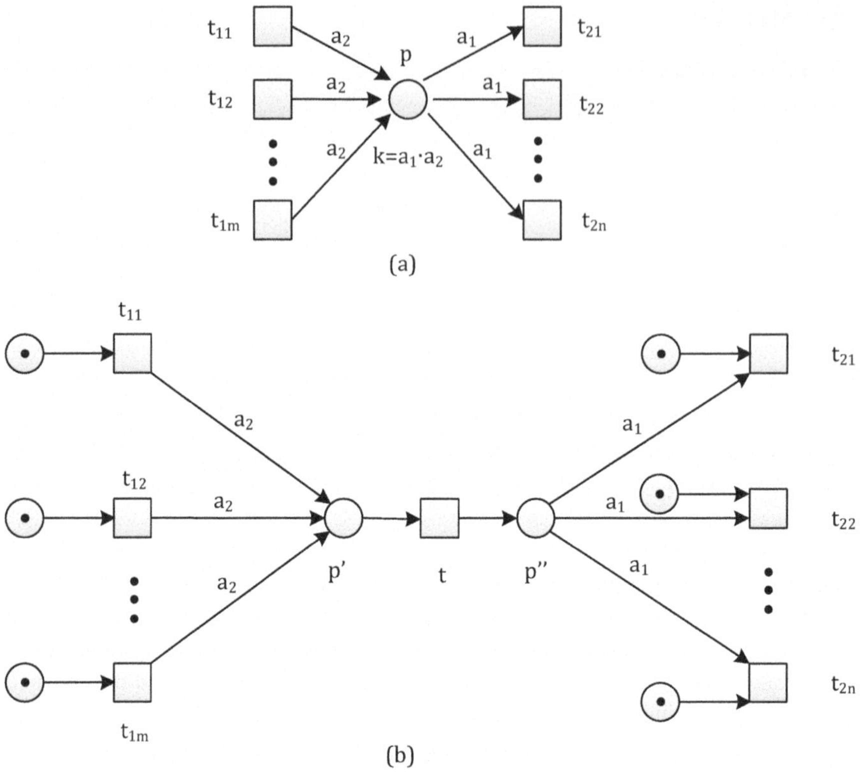

Fig. 10.1 Synchronizer p

Definition 10.1 Synchronizer S-element $p = (T_1, T_2, (a_1, a_2))$ is a synchronizer if $T_1 = p = \{t_{1i} | i = 1, 2, \ldots, n\}$, $T_2 = p = \{t_{2j} | j = 1, 2, \ldots, m\}$, $W(t_{1i}, p) = a_2$, $W(p, t_{2j}) = a_1$ and $0 < a_1 \leq n$, $0 < a_2 \leq m$, and $k(p) = a_1 \times a_2$.

Definition 10.2 Transition Rule Around a Synchronizer When a_1 transitions in T_1 are enabled concurrently and $M(p) = 0$, these a_1 transitions fire; only if $M(p) = K(p)$, a_2 transitions in T_2 are concurrently enabled to fire. No transition is allowed to fire twice.

Transition rules given above seem different from the conventional transition rules. Figure 10.1b is the detailed structure of synchronizer p, in which each of all transitions in T_1 has an extra S-element in its preset, and this extra S-element has a token when a new case is initiated. It is easy to see that the conventional transition rules applied on the net in Fig. 10.1b have the same results as given above in Fig. 10.1a.

A single synchronizer keeps transitions in its scope consistently synchronized as stated above.

There are different situations for the synchronizer in Fig. 10.1a.

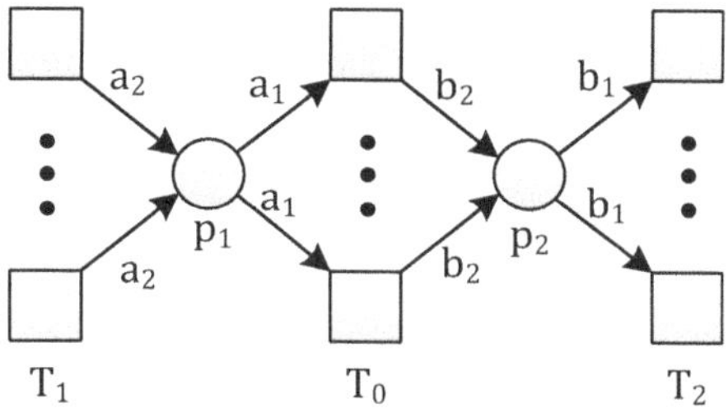

Fig. 10.2 Two consecutive synchronizers

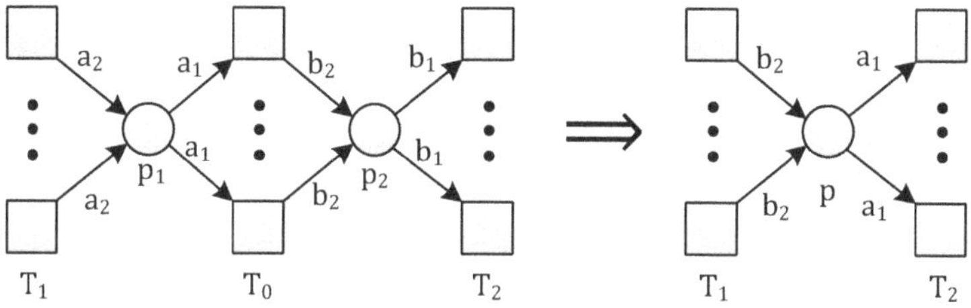

Fig. 10.3 From p_1 and p_2 to p

$m = n = a_1 = a_2 = 1$: a line synchronizer,
$m = a_1 \wedge a_1 > 1$: fork-in concurrently,
$m > a_1 \wedge a_1 > 1$: fork-in with case dependent flexibility,
$n = a_2 \wedge a_2 > 1$: fork-out concurrently,
$n > a_2 \wedge a_2 > 1$: fork-out with case dependent flexibility.

Fork-in and fork-out may be combined freely to form a complete synchronizer.

A business process in reality has certainly more steps to accomplish a business case. Thus, it is necessary to prove a process with more synchronizers consistently synchronized. Figure 10.2 includes two consecutive true synchronizers p_1 and p_2.

In Definition 10.3 below, $T_1 = \{t_{1i} | i = 1, 2, \ldots, n\}$, and $T_2 = \{t_{2j} | j = 1, 2, \ldots, m\}$.

Definition 10.3 Consistent Consecutive Synchronizers Let $^{\bullet}p_1 = T_1$, $p_1^{\bullet} = {}^{\bullet}p_2 = T_0$, $p_2^{\bullet} = T_2$. If weights on all input arcs from T_1 to p_1 are a, and weights on all output arcs from p_2 to T_2 are d, then p_1 and p_2 are said to be consistent at T_0 with each other if $a = d$.

In above definition, synchronizer p_1 makes a transitions in T_0 fire, synchronizer p_2 waits for d transitions in T_0 to fire. Thus, if and only if $a = d$, p_1 and p_2 agree with each other at T_0.

The consistency of p_1 and p_2 at T_0 makes it feasible to have T_0 implicit as inner structure of synchronizer p as shown by Fig. 10.3. In other words, p_1 and p_2 are combined (or simplified) to a new synchronizer p. This is the key to prove correctness of business process by simplification.

There are 7 simplification rules now for proving consistently synchronized property of a business process. This property is also called unimpeded, since an initial token may go through to an end.

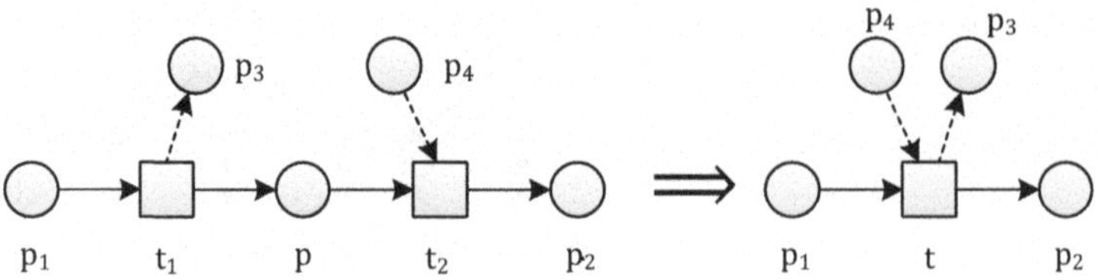

Fig. 10.4 Rule 2 for simplification

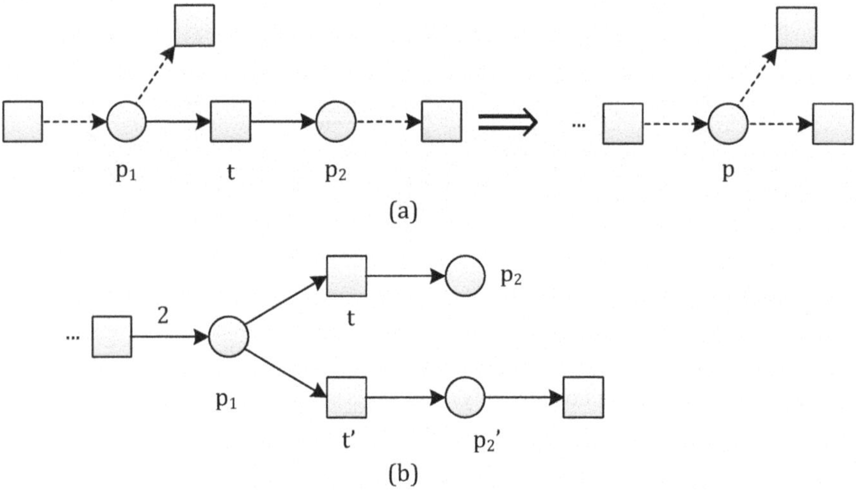

Fig. 10.5 Rule 3 for simplification

Rule 10.1

For $p_1 = (T_1, T_0\,,\ (a_1, a_2))$ and $p_2 = (T_0, T_2\,,\ (b_1, b_2))$, if $a_2 = b_1$, then p_1 and p_2 can be simplified to $p = (T_1, T_2\,,\ (a_1, b_2))$.

This is the rule presented by Fig. 10.3 above.

Theorem 10.1 Consistency Between Synchronizers If $p_1$and p_2 are synchronizers of business process $\sum = (P, T; F, K, W, M_0)$, and $\sum' = (P', T'; F', K', W', M_0)$ is obtained by combining p_1 and p_2 to p', i.e., $P' = \{P - \{p_1, p_2\}\} \cup \{p'\}$, $T' = T - T_0$, F' is obtained by deleting all input arrows to p_1 and out arrows from p_2, and adding arrows from all transitions in T_1 to p and adding arrows from p to all transitions in T_2.

This theorem is just a version of Fig. 10.3 in terms of words.

Rule 10.2

For $p = (\{t_1\}, \{t_2\}, (1, 1))$, if $t_1 \cap t_2 = \{p\}$, then p may be made implicit as shown in Fig. 10.4. The dotted arrow may or may not exist.

Rule 10.3

For transition t and synchronizers $p_1$and p_2, if $p_1 \cap p_2 = \{t\}$, and $W(p_1, t) = W(t, p_2) = 1$, then t may be made implicit as shown in Fig. 10.5. Dotted arrows represent possible existences.

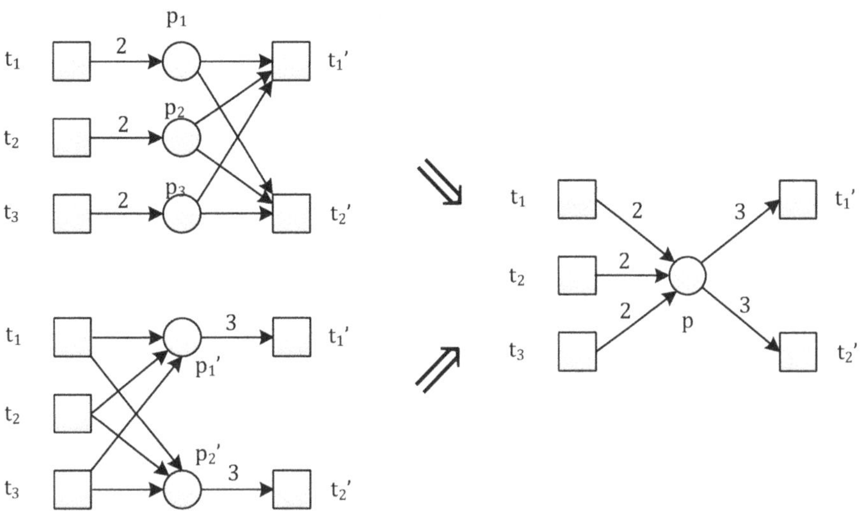

Fig. 10.6 Rule 4

Transitions t and t' in Fig. 10.5b are both fulfil conditions of Rule 10.3. In case t and p_2 are combined into p_1, what is obtained is no longer a business process. The reason is that (b) is not unimpeded, since the two end places would both have a token at the end of a business process execution.

Rule 10.4
Let be $T_1 = \{t_i | i = 1, 2, \ldots, a\}$ and $p = \{t_j | j = 1, 2, \ldots, b\}$, If $p_i = (\{t_i\}, T_2, (1, b))$ for $i = 1, 2, \ldots, a$, are all synchronizers, then these synchronizers may be combined to a single synchronizer $p = (T_1,\ T_2\ ,\ (a, b))$. If $p_j = \left(T_1, \left\{t'_j\right\}, (a, 1)\right)$ are all synchronizers for $j = 1, 2, \ldots, b$, then these synchronizers may be combined to a single synchronizer $p = (T_1, T_2\ ,\ (a_1, b_2))$.

Figure 10.6 is the graphical representation of Rule 10.4 in which $a = 3$ and $b = 2$.

This rule is to remedy possible misdoings. Synchronizers p_i for $i = 1, 2, \ldots, a$, and p'_j for $j = 1, 2, \ldots, b$ may be designed as $p = (T_1, T_2\ ,\ (a_1, b_2))$ at the very beginning.

Rule 10.5
Synchronizers $p_i = (\{t\}, \{t_i\}, (1, 1))$, $i = 1, 2, \ldots, a$ may be combined to synchronizer $p = (\{t\}, \{t_1, t_2, \ldots, t_a\}, (1, a))$.

Synchronizers $p_i = (\{t_i\}, \{t\}, (1, 1))$, $i = 1, 2, \ldots, a$ may be combined to synchronizer $p = (\{t_1, t_2, \ldots, t_a\}, \{t\}, (a, 1))$.

Figure 10.7 is the graphical presentation of Rule 10.5.

Rule 10.6
Let $T = \{t_1, t_2, \ldots, t_a\}$, $T_i = \{t_{i1}, t_{i2}, \ldots, t_{ib}\}$, $i = 1, 2, \ldots, a$ be subsets of transitions, then synchronizers $p_i = (\{t_i\}, T_i, (1, b))$, $i = 1, 2, \ldots, a$ can be combined to a place

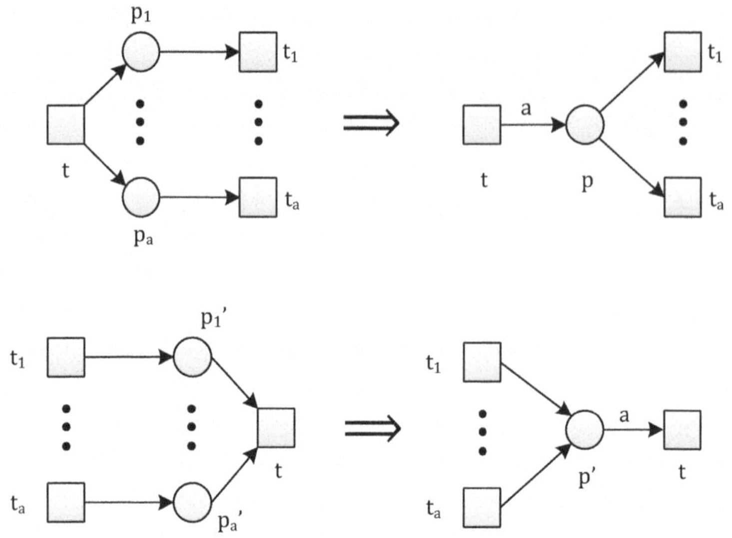

Fig. 10.7 Rule 10.5

p, $K(p) = a \times b$, $p = T$, $p = \cup_{i=1}^{a} T_i$, $W(t_i, p) = b$, $W(p, t_{ij}) = 1$, $i = 1, 2, \ldots, a$, $j = 1, 2, \ldots, b$. Place $p = \left(T, \cup_{i=1}^{a} T_i, (1, b)\right)$ with the way the synchronizer is represented, though p is not qualified as a synchronizer. The capacity of p is not the product of weights on its in-arcs and its out-arcs as required by a synchronizer.

Similarly, synchronizers $p_i' = (T_i, \{t_i\}, (b, 1))$, $i = 1, 2, \ldots, a$, can be combined to place p', $K(p') = a \times b$, $p' = \cup_{i=1}^{a} T_i$, $p' = T$, $W(t_{ij}, p) = 1$, $W(p', t_{ij}) = b$, $i = 1, 2, \ldots, a$, $j = 1, 2, \ldots, b$. Place p' is not qualified as a synchronizer for the same reason.

Figure 10.8 is the graphical presentation of Rule 10.6.

Places p and p' are called virtue synchronizers. But they have the main features of a synchronizer, i.e., transitions in its pose-set are enabled at marking M only if $M(p) = K(p)$, or $M(p') = K(p')$. Besides, the number of concurrently firing transitions are decided by $K(p)$, $K(p')$ and the weights on arcs around p and p'.

Definition 10.4 Virtue Synchronizer A place $p = (T_1, T_2, (a, b))$ is a virtue synchronizer if

$$\forall t \in T_1 : W(t, p) = b \wedge \forall t \in T_2 : W(p, t) = a \wedge K(p) \neq a \times b,$$

But, $K(p)/b = n$ and $K(p)/a = m$, in which n,m are respectively the element numbers in T_1 and T_2.

Virtue synchronizers are just intermediate objects by Rule 10.6. They can be further simplified to synchronizers by modified Rule 10.1.

Rule 10.1'

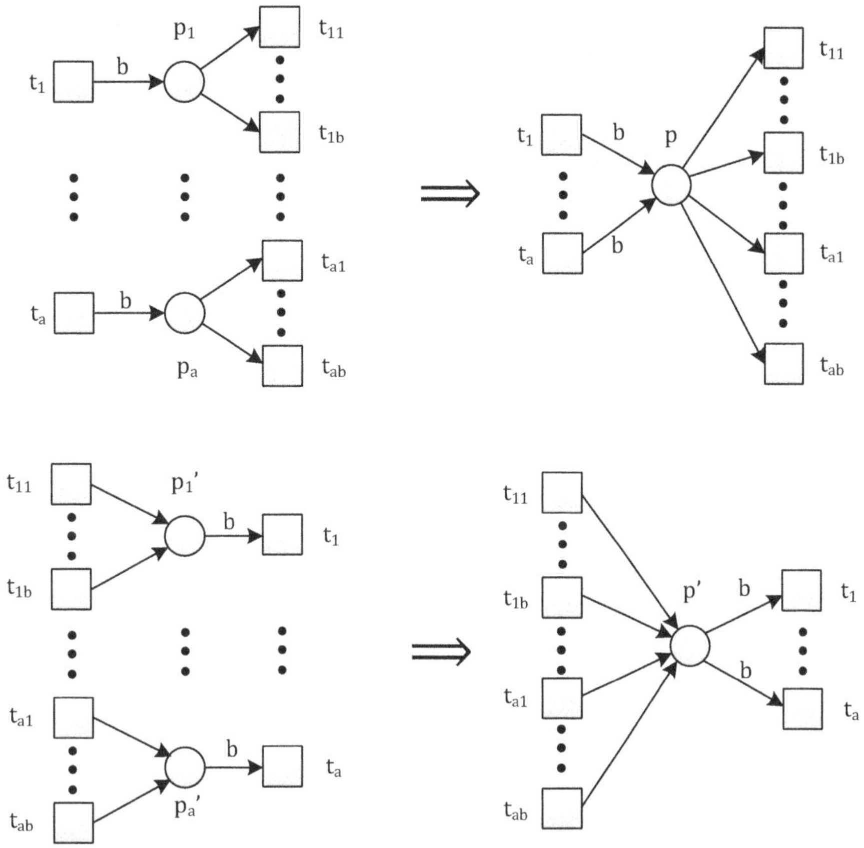

Fig. 10.8 Rule 10.6

Let $p_1 = (T_1, T\ ,\ (a_1, b_1))$ and $p_2 = (T, T_2, (a_2, b_2))$ be synchronizer or virtue synchronizer. If $K(p_1)/a_1 = K(p_2)/b_2$, then p_1 and p_2 can be combined to $p_1 = (T_1, T_2\ ,\ (a, b))$, in which $a = K(p_1)/b_1$, $b = K(p_2)/a_2$,

$$\forall t \in T_1 : W(t,p) = b \wedge \forall t \in T_2 : W(p,t) = a \wedge K(p) = a \times b.$$

Figure 10.9 is an example of simplification from a complete process to a place with empty scope.

The inner structures of S-element with empty scope are consistent with each other. Thus, we have

Definition 10.5 Harmony The S-element with empty scope is called harmony.

Figure 10.10 contains a well-synchronized business process; interested readers may try to simplify it to harmony.

Figure 10.11 below illustrates various situations where synchronizations are not consistent. In Fig. 10.11a, the token will reach the two end places, the token in

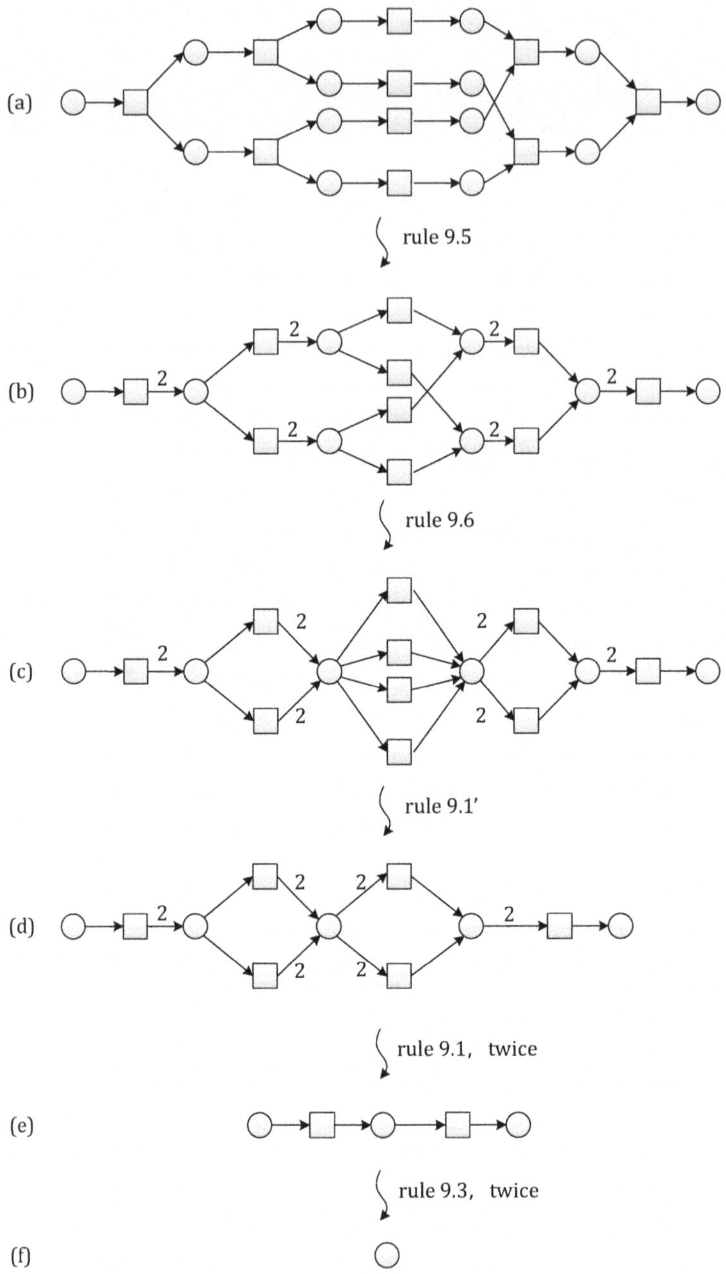

Fig. 10.9 Simplification to "harmony"

Fig. 10.11b will not be able to reach the end, and for Fig. 10.11c, the end place e_1 is idle, it would never have a token.

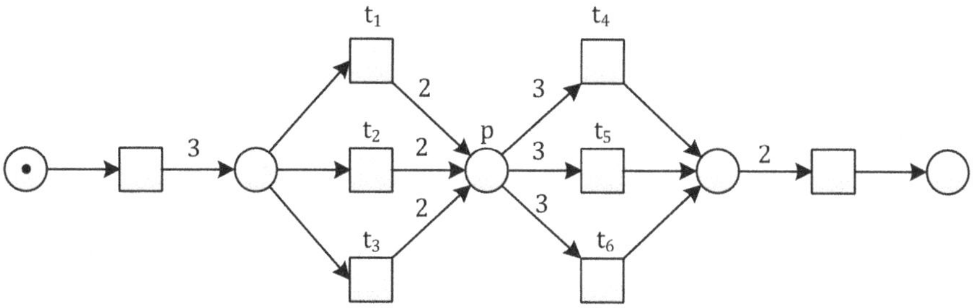

Fig. 10.10 Consistent synchronization

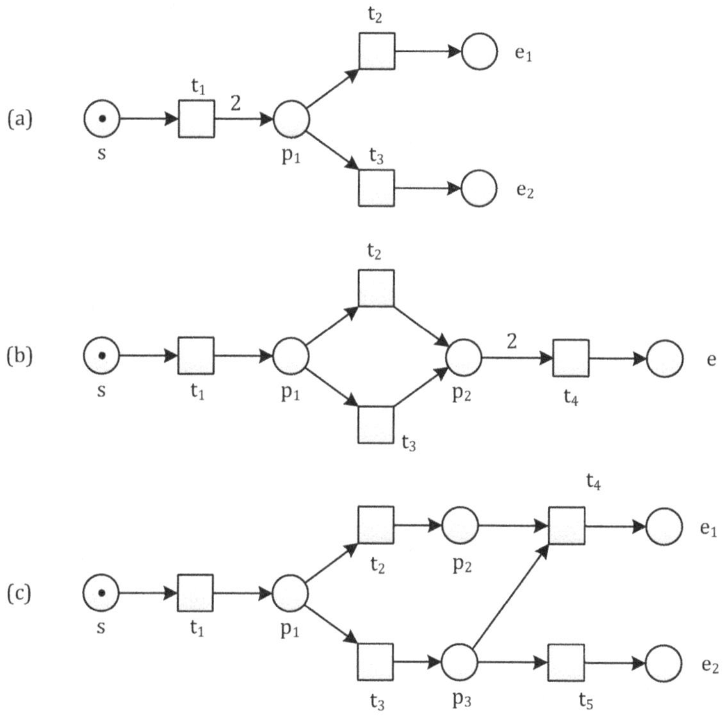

Fig. 10.11 Three ill-synchronized situations

Note that these ill-synchronized structures may become substructure of consistently synchronized process.

Figure 10.12 shows mixed synchronization, transitions t_1 and t_2 would be concurrent, while t_3 and t_4 would be in conflict. This mixed synchronization must be a part of a greater process.

A synchronizer may have flexible demand on what is to be synchronized. Such a flexible synchronizer must appear pairwise as shown in Fig. 10.13 in which variable x plays the role of a positive integer. The value of x varies from case to case.

The concept of synchronizers is the key in business process modeling.

Fig. 10.12 Mixed synchronization

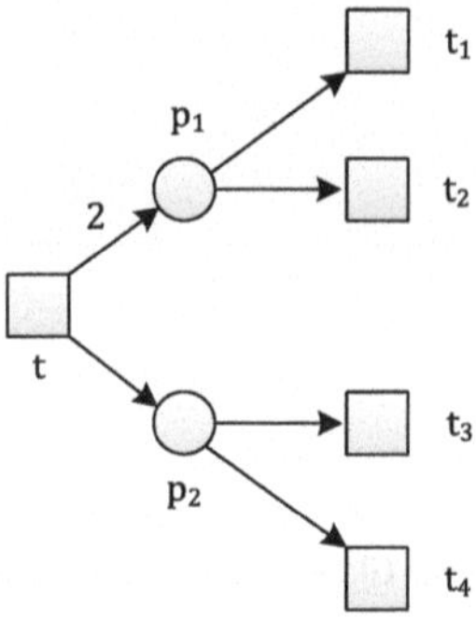

Fig. 10.13 Flexible synchronization

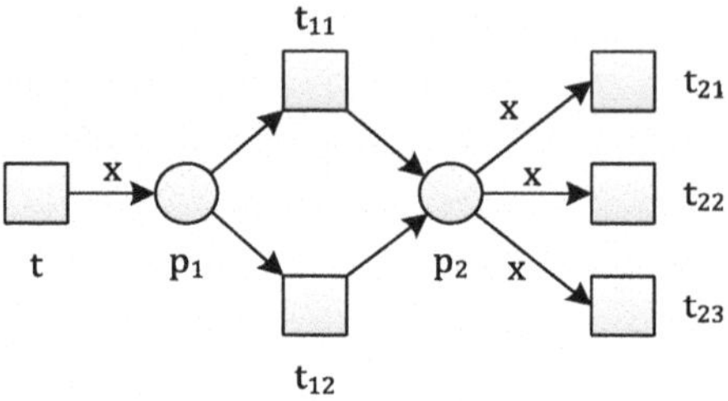

Chapter 11
Business Process Management (BPM)

Abstract A three-leyer business process model is proposed here for the presentations of causal dependence among process tasks, individual business case semantics and finally logical dependence of management tasks.

BPM was called workflow management. About in the year 2002, the Workflow Management Coalition defined the concept of workflow (the workflow reference model) as:

> The computerized facilitation or automation of a business process, in whole or part.

The concept of workflow management system was defined as:

> A system that completely defines, manages and executes "workflow" through the execution of software whose order of execution is driven by a computer representation of the workflow logic.

The author tried to make "*computerized facilitation or automation of a business process*" true. What is introduced here in this chapter is what the author had done in this direction.

To understand "computerized facilitation," it is necessary to know what a computer brings with it to business process management.

Long before the birth of digital computers, there existed business processes. Where enterprises exist, there is business process, then and now. The difference comes from what is used to record the progress, a paper form or digital form? A traveling form must be signed by persons in charge of different duties. As such, a paper form must travel a well-designed sequential route so as to have all signatures in the same form, while digital forms may travel in parallel and have all copies of signed digital forms combined into one. It is digital form that makes parallel traveling possible to achieve higher efficiency and accuracy.

There are two key words in business process management, i.e., business and management. As such, there are two kinds of tasks to be distinguished: business

C. Yuan, *Principle of Petri Nets*, https://doi.org/10.1007/978-981-97-7336-7_11

tasks and management duties. Instead of task, what management does is called duty. It is the right of an enterprise to divide its business into tasks, and it is the responsibility of management to decide how to carry out its duty. A business task requires professional knowledge and its execution must be explicitly recorded in the business form. A business task may be in charge of certain dispatch in addition to business affairs. A management duty requires no professional knowledge, what it requires to know is management rules. What such a management duty is responsible for includes:

- To check whether the prior business task has done a good job
- If so, to select someone (person or computer program) to do each of the business tasks that follow
- If not, to return the form for redo or modification

The criteria for a business task to be well done varies from task to task, but there are things in common, say which blanks for a business task to fill out and the types of contents required by these blanks, say words, numbers or charts.

It is not necessary to put what such a management task has done into a business form. As long as a business is well done, it must have been well managed. There might be a blank for comments on errors for later improvement. Such a blank is for all management duties, in case something unexpected occurs.

11.1 What a Business Process Consists of

Every enterprise has its professional business to carry out to make money. Every enterprise has also to keep its inner affairs in order. Inner or outer management is the only means to have it well done. In what follows, inner business and outer business will both be called business, since their managements are the same in the eye of formal treatment.

It is the foundation for management to ensure what is to be managed is well organized and formally presented.

Next words may include some repetition of what has been said before this section. It is for the need of formalization.

To carry out a business in a company, a group of tasks must be designated by that company. To initiate a business case, a business form, as mentioned above, must be filled out with case specific data. New data will be added to the initialized form in the course of the form traveling. Some of the data will be used for selecting successor tasks from all possible successors, while the rest data are just kept on the form. Thus, a business is abstracted as a pair (T, D), where T is the set of tasks and D is the set of variables to hold data for successor selection. In addition to (T, D), a "one way road map" for the form to travel through tasks in T is necessary. This road map comes from casual dependence among tasks and possible guide regulations (denoted with C). So, (T, D, C) is the basis for BPM. A one-way road map is in fact a partial ordering relation $<: x < y$ means that x is earlier than y. To replace C with $<$, $(T, D,$

$<).(T, D, <)$ is obtained, which provides a foundation for constructing a formal model to serve automatic management in a business.

$(T, D, <)$ for a concrete business, given by a professional company, must be checked to see whether it satisfies certain requirements to give rise to an executable procedure.

Definition 11.1 Process Logic (or Business Logic) $(T, <)$ is the process logic of a business, if $< \subseteq T \times T$ is a connected asymmetric partial order and $< \cup >^* = T \times T$.

Note that $>$ is the reverse relation of $<$ and $< \cup >^*$ is the transitive closure of $<$. Note also that asymmetric partial order contains no loop.

The transitive closure of binary relation R is defined as below.

Let R be a relation defined on $T \times T$, then $R^0 = \{(r, r) | r \in R\}$, $R^1 = R$, $R^2 = R \times R = \{(x, y) | \exists z \in T : (x, y) \in R \wedge (z, y) \in R\}$, $R^n = R \times R^{n-1}$, $\ldots$, $R^* = R^0 \cup R^1 \cup R^2 \cdots \cup R^n \cdots \cup \cdots = \sum_{i \in \text{integer}} R^i$, in which the "integer" is non-negative.

It is important that a process logic contains no loop. It is more important to distinguish a process logic and a concrete case.

Loops may be needed in the course of carrying out a task due to shortage of resources. A document may be returned to its drafter by reviewer, or returned to reviewer by judge (final reviewer). A loop requires repetition of the same thing. A returned work requires modification. Modification belongs to case execution; it does not belong to process logic for all cases.

$<$ must be connected, since it belongs to the same business; $<$ must be a partial order, since full order is just a special case; $< \cup >^* = T \times T$, since $<$ is connected.

Petri net is the best choice for BPM modeling, since token flow is very much similar to form flow. In fact pioneers in BPM modeling area had realized the importance of Petri nets at an early stage. A recall of what they have achieved is discussed first in Sect. 11.1.1 below.

11.1.1 Conventional BPM and New Trend

(a) WF-net

Figure 11.1 below is an early model for insurance claim. It consists of 5 tasks: *ac* (accept), *cc* (check claim), *cp* (check policy), *pay* (claim is agreed), and *dn* (claim is denied). Figure 11.1a contains 4 basic node structures to be used in Fig. 11.1b. The meaning of triangles inside boxes is as given in Fig. 11.1a.

Apparently, this is not a true Petri net. Triangles do not belong to Nets. But it is called WF-net in the literature and is assumed to be an EN-system consisting of conditions and events.

Correctness is not defined for WF-net (maybe the inventors have no idea about it at all). Instead, soundness is the key property of WF-net. The proposed

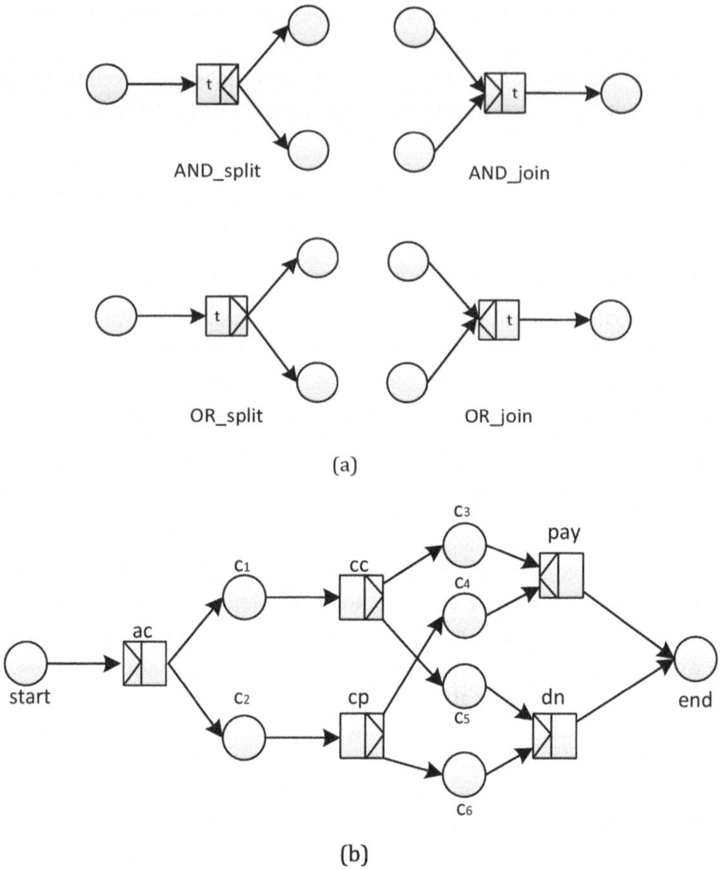

Fig. 11.1 Insurance claim—EN-system(?)

analysis method requires an extra event to be added to (b). This extra event is not included in (b) since it is not part of the process.

A WF-net is sound if the token in the initial place *start* would, via the extra event, flow back to *start* and leave no token behind. Besides, every event should have a chance to occur in dealing with this or that case. For a cooperative action with another company, a shadow of a man is attached to the event box (not shown in (b)). In case an envelope is attached to action box (not shown in (b)), that means extra data from outside is required.

No wonder that such a model for business processes has not been used in reality, though many followers of workflow pioneers have written hundreds of papers about it. The reason for not being used in reality, the author guesses, is not only because of the complexity (special factors for individual cases and factors for all cases squished together), but also because it failed to be complete; the concept of correctness is missing. Correctness requires a different model for BPM.

(b) BPMN (business process modeling notation)

It would take too much time and space to give a detailed introduction to BPMN. Below is a list of its gateways.

Gateways include: exclusive gateway (), event gateway (), parallel gateway (), inclusive gateway (), complex gateway (), parallel event gateway () and exclusive event gateway ().

Compared with the only binder "synchronizer", gateway is a complicated concept. The reason may be traced back to it being informal. The three layer model, to be introduced in Sect. 11.1.3 below, distinguishes, as said above, a "one-way road map" (process logic) for all legal cases and one route for a single case traveling (case semantics). Process logic is the bottom layer, while case semantics is the second layer. It distinguishes a management task and a management that is not a task (pure management). So pure management is separated from process logic and case semantics. This is an example of "divide and conquer." BPMN squishes all case-specific situations into one picture, so that all elements are put in front of people working in this area. It seems they have got used to it.

Theory development often lags behind practical needs. When practical methods have been widely used for certain time, theory may still be a "baby." A good theory is deeply rooted in professional knowledge as well as accumulated practical experiences. Though there exists a gap between theory and practice, it is worthy to absorb "nutrition" from theory.

(c) The study of BPM is now closely following new developments in software, like cloud computing and AI. The author keeps his fingers crossed for these researches.

(d) Process mining is now becoming a hot topic in BPM study. But, without a qualified log, process mining would not contribute much.

(e) The importance of BPM correctness is now ignored by many. It will become a must for complicated applications in the future.

11.1.2 Correctness of BPM

Tasks in the insurance claim example are determined by the insurance company. Insurance professionals with vast experience would have all their business processes well designed and well executed in their daily practice. But it is possible that they have no idea about a formal model; potential errors would be discovered only when such errors arise, leading to disagreement with customers. So, a formal model is needed to express procedures for insurance personals to follow. Insurance claim is but a simplified example.

The Petri net used in this chapter is a special kind, since it uses special S-elements called synchronizers, defined in Chap. 10, as binders between adjacent tasks.

The first thing to do in our approach is to construct a net model for $(T, <)$, then try to simplify this net, with simplification rules given in Chap. 10, to see whether or not it may be reduced to the special S-element with empty scope. As said above, this special element is called "harmony." A so-constructed net is called process logic (or business logic).

Definition 11.2 Process Logic in Terms of Petri Nets

1. A Petri net is a process logic, if it has exactly one initial place; synchronizers are the unique binders between transitions. Besides, all its end elements are places.
2. A process logic is correct if and only if it can be simplified to harmony with simplification rules given in Chap. 10.

11.1.3 Three-Layer Model for Insurance Claim

In our $(T, D, <)$ way of thinking, T consists of all business tasks, and D is a set of variables to hold data that decides how to select immediate successor transitions (tasks). $<$ is a partial order to specify causal dependence and possible guild regulations among tasks.

Back to the insurance claim example, we have:

$$T = \{ac, cc, cp, pay, dn\},$$

$$D = \{x, y : Boolean\},$$

$$< \ = \{[ac \to cc>, [ac \to cp>, [cc \parallel cp>, [cc \to pay>, [cc \to dn>, [cp \to pay>, [cp \to dn>\}$$

The arrow $\to$ above denotes immediate follow: *cc* and *cp* are immediately executed in parallel (concurrent) after *ac*. $(T, <)$ above gives out the process logic for an insurance claim. Figure 11.2 contains this logic expressed in terms of Petri net. So, $x \to y$ means $x < y$ and $\{z | x < z < y\} = \varnothing$.

The dual net of process logic is management logic. Two nets are dual with each other if there exists a one-to-one correspondence between T-elements of this net and S-elements of that net, and vice versa. Let's call the dual element of a synchronizer "judge," since its duty is quality testing. Figure 11.2 contains the management logic as well.

Boolean variables x and y are for task *cc* and task *cp* to write (output) their respective decisions to pay or to deny a claim, and for task *pay* and task *dn* to read (input) these decisions.

Process logic is the bottom layer for a business since it is the "one-way road map" for all possible cases to travel.

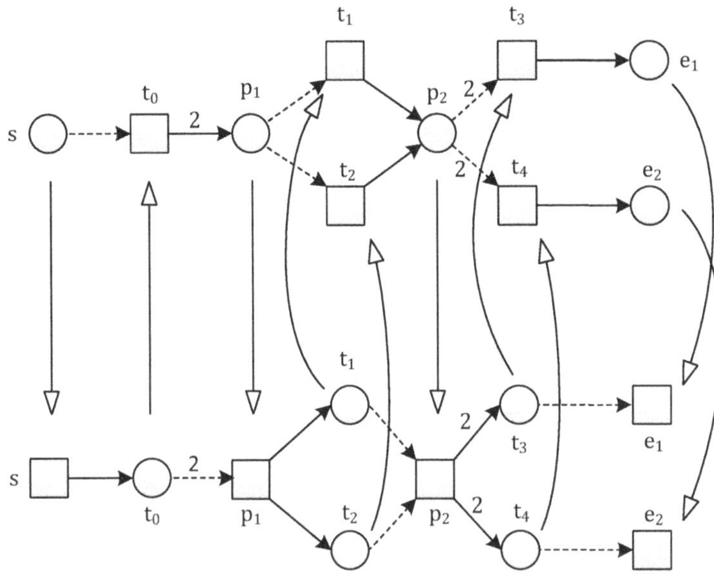

Fig. 11.2 Process logic and management logic

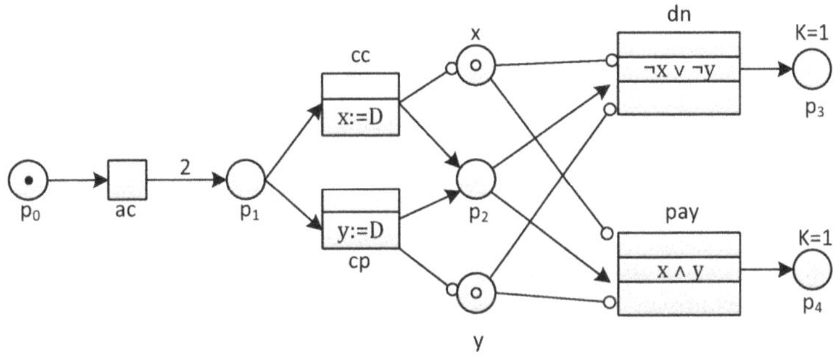

Fig. 11.3 Case semantics—C-net

Process logic + variables for resolving conflicts are case semantics, since data held by the variables come from case execution. Case semantics is the second layer above process logic.

The duality of process logic and management logic is the top layer.

Note that all S-elements in process logic, except the initial one and the end places, are synchronizers defined in Chap. 10. Transition rules around a synchronizer is also defined there. Correctness of a process logic and method for correctness of proof are also included there.

Recall that a net with variables as a new kind of S-elements is a C-net. Figure 11.3 below is the C-net for case semantics of insurance claim. The difference between C-net and C-net system is that the former is not initialized, while the latter has an

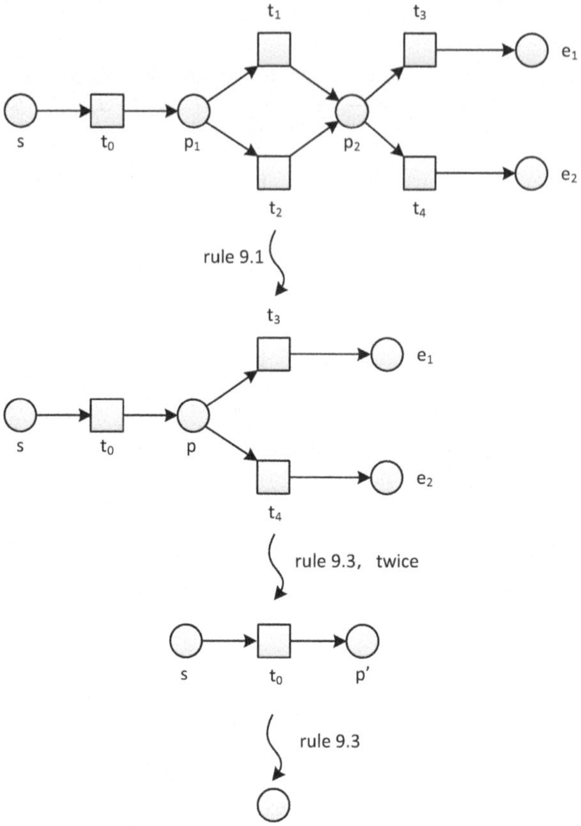

Fig. 11.4 To simplify process logic to harmony

initial marking. Case semantics is the middle layer in our three-layer model, of which Fig. 11.3 is an example.

Figure 11.4 gives a graphical proof for correctness of the process logic given in Fig. 11.2.

Figure 11.5 shows another simplification of process logic. This process logic is a bit more complicated than the insurance claim and explores a more complicated simplification. Apparently, process logic is not an EN-system; it is a P/T-system.

The correspondence relation between elements of business logic and elements of management logic is represented by arrows in Fig. 11.2. Note that the original arrows in business logic and management logic are replaced by dotted arrows, since tokens will flow from business logic to management logic and then back to process logic interactively. The function of case semantics in this interaction is to resolve conflicts existing in business logic.

Lemma 11.1 A process logic should contain no loop.

Before this lemma is verified, it must be made clear that there are two kinds of management. The first kind is itself a business task, called B-management, and it requires knowledge about the business item. The second kind belongs to

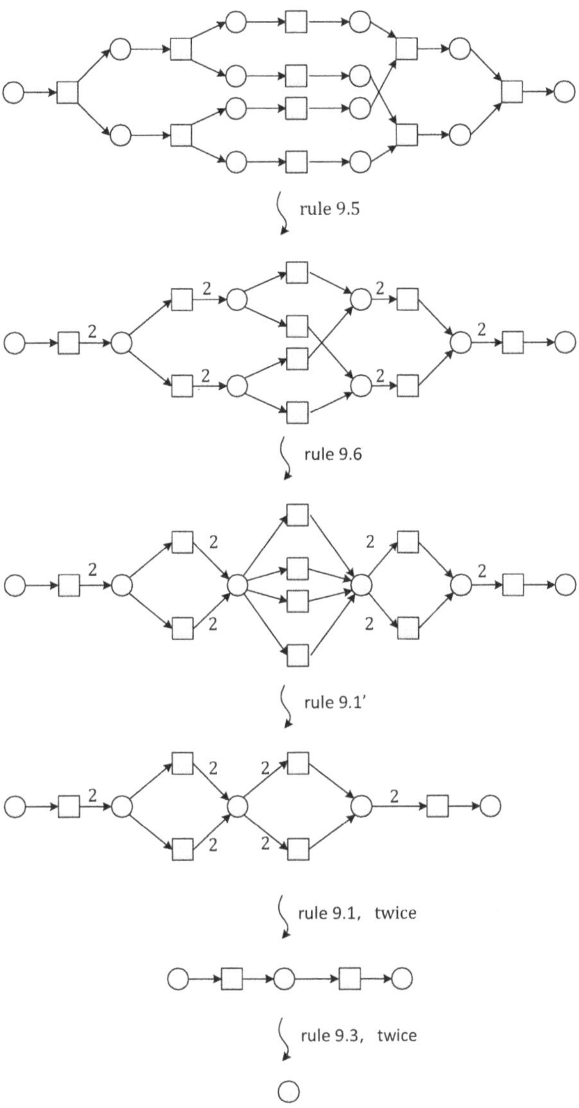

Fig. 11.5 To simplify a process logic

management logic, called M-management, and it requires no knowledge about the business item. An M-management follows management rules to carry out its duty, say to check whether the dual task complies with the duty task. If the duty is to draft a document, but a picture appears, then a wrong action is recorded and reported.

Loops may be needed to accomplish a business task, say to remove a pile of earth with a truck. It may require the truck to return several times. Such a loop is not necessary to appear explicitly as part of process logic, since tasks (transitions) are the smallest consisting objects of process logic, while loop is just the inner behavior of tasks. The missing of a loop structure from process logic is different. Although it is not avoidable that some business tasks must be done a second time if some errors are found, what the B-management task needs to do is just return the business form for correction. A loop is to repeat actions, not for correcting errors. Besides, a "return" action is case specific, while process logic covers all possible cases.

11.1.4 A Comparison Between WF-Net and the Three-Layer Model

1. WF-net is assumed to be at event/condition level; the three-layer model is at place/transition level.
2. WF-net does not distinguish a model for all cases and a model for individual cases. The three-layer model has it well separated.
3. WF-net has no idea how to deal with data for conflict resolution. The three-layer model has variables for data.
4. The insurance example leads WF-net into contradiction: Event cc (check claim) has to use two conditions c_1 and c_2 as its output for its decision to pay or to deny a claim. On the one hand, as output conditions of the same event, c_1 and c_2 would both receive a token when cc occurs by transition rules, but on the other hand, c_1 and c_2 cannot be true at the same time, since they are mutually exclusive.
5. It is a must to have a logic for all cases and a logic to exhibit cases individually. C-net is now the only net model capable of expressing case individuality. WF-net is even not a true Petri net.

Insurance claim is a simple example, but it leads to many important concepts.

Synchronizer is invented for constructing a BPM model. It is a key component for system design to implement a given way of synchronization between tasks.

For system analysis, different concepts are needed to measure the synchronization degree. This is what synchrony in general net theory is all about.

The universe has existed for hundreds of thousands of years in harmony (tiny local collisions are not avoidable). Is this another way of synchronization? A synchronizer specifies how two sets of transitions are synchronized, while the universe is not divided. It seems that every celestial body is synchronized with every other celestial body, though their synchronization is not strictly defined for tasks.

To end part 1, a summery is given below.

1. Visible and invisible nets exist everywhere, in nature, like a spider net, and in human society, like the internet of things. Petri net is but a human invented means with the difference being directed net (Petri net) or indirected net (spider net).
2. As a directed net, Petri net distinguishes two kinds of relations between resources and transitions (actions): consuming (input to transition) or producing (output from transition). Resources are static while transitions are dynamic. As an exception, catalyzer is just participating in a transition, but it is neither consumed

nor produced by the transition. Catalyzer makes a net impure. An impure net should be included by net theory.

3. Only countable resources are suitable for net applications. The unit for counting resources is abstracted as "token," and "residence" for tokens of the same kind is called a "place." This "place" is different from a geographic place; it does not have a fixed position and it occupies no area. A swimming pool is a place for sports while a water tank is a different "place" for storing drinking water. In the eye of net, these two places are different though water is their shared concrete resource. Tokens are abstractions of all countable resources that play a role in nets. A token represents neither concrete positions of resources nor what concrete objects they are. In case a concrete position of certain resources plays a role in an application, this position should appear as a place in net, just like a swimming pool or water tank. Positive integers, including zero, are sufficient for token counting.
4. With directed net as the underlying structure, net systems are invented for system design and system analysis. On top of a net, static elements, including place capacity, arc weight function, and marking, are defined. Transition rules define net dynamics.
5. Net systems are classified according to functions of their places. Positive integers, including zero, are the only allowed data for net systems, except C-net systems. The table below illustrates differences of S-elements for different net systems.

EN-system	P/T-system	Pr/T-system	Colour system	Self-control system	C-net system
condition (state) of individual token	Places, residence for tokens of the same kind	Predicate, individual tokens that makes it true	residence for multi-set of coloured tokens	Same as Pr/T-system, with flexible arc weights	Places or Variables of all data types

6. Occurrence nets are to record what has happened in a net system. It is comparable to a video recording. An occurrence net reflects correctly asynchronous concurrent behavior. Besides, it records how conflicts are resolved.
7. There are different ways to study properties of a net system. With focus being listed in the table below, together with properties related to the focus.

Transition sequence	Place	Transition and place	Incidence matrix	Reachable tree	Reachable graph
Recursive or not	Bounded or not	Process	Reachable marking	End node	Leaf node
Fairness	Trap	Process period	T-invariant	Dead transition	
Liveness	Siphon		S-invariant		

8. Nets are suitable for systems in which resource flow is the main character. Business process management is a good example. It is a digital business form that flows to record what has been done, what is to be done, etc. Resources include materials, human beings, and data.
9. The main contribution of Petri nets in information science is not limited to what is listed above. It is general net theory that makes a big difference.

Before approaching general net theory, a few words about differences between system design and system analysis. The three-layer model is an invention, constructed from scratch. It is also a simple example to exhibit the power of Petri nets. The first part of Petri nets, i.e., system theory, is mainly about system design.

General net theory is different. It is mainly about system properties and analysis methods.

Part II
General Net Theory

General Net Theory (GNT for short) consists of five branches, namely Concurrency axioms, Synchrony, Net topology, Enlogy (or net logic) and Information systems. Here in this part, all five branches will be introduced with different details.

Concurrency axioms are defined based on occurrence nets to describe structure characteristics. There are two kinds of occurrence nets, i.e., natural ones and artificial ones. The former is a recording of what happens in nature while the latter is a recording of what happens in a man designed system. For example, the system model of four seasons in Fig. 4.1a reflects people's common understanding, of which the occurrence net is given by Fig. 4.2a; the system model of four seasons in Fig. 4.1b reflects changes of four seasons in nature, of which occurrence net is given by Fig. 4.2b. Concurrency axioms are axioms on occurrence nets like Fig. 4.2b. There are many self-complete systems in nature, Fig. 4.2b is but one example. Concurrency axioms are applicable to all of such self-complete systems.

Synchrony is important for the understanding of BPM (business process management). It is the key to building a good system model for business process. Synchronizer is the only S-element to connect tasks (transitions) and to have tasks synchronized to form a correct (provable) business process. All concepts on BPM have been given in Chap. 11.

Net topology helps to extend the concept of continuity from real numbers to finite nets. Continuity has been defined in mathematics based on real numbers while nothing in the world conforms with it since things are consisting of articles. No matter how tiny an article is, the number of articles for any thing is bound to be finite.

Enlogy, or net logic, makes use of dead transitions for reasoning about system properties. A dead transition in a net system is something that never could occur. It seems that whenever system property is concerned, it refers to only those things that could happen. But in fact, both things that may happen and things that have no chance to happen are system properties. For example, no one in the world could jump over a horizontal bar 3 m high. This is a property of human beings so far.

Note that "something could never happen" is different from "something should never happen." The later might happen and leading to human disaster. A car should not run into another car, but traffic accident is heard every day.

The concept of information systems opens a new way to view computer CPU. An information system represented in terms of Petri nets may be decomposed into function blocks that are similar to CPU instructions. Reversible information system may lead to reversible CPU. Currently, CPU is not reversible.

Next is detailed description of the five branches.

Chapter 12
Synchrony

Abstract Synchrony is a branch of general net theory. The concept of synchronous distance provides a quantified way to specify how transitions are synchronized.

We have made a good use of synchronizers when BPM was discussed in Chap. 11. There, our focus was on application of nets. BPM has benefited from theory. Here, theory is the topic to be discussed. We must admit that some repetition is not avoidable.

Does "synchronized" mean "at the same time? Check it on the internet, "yes" is almost the only answer. This seems a well-accepted common understanding.

When we clap hands, the left hand and the right hand must touch each other to produce sound. Hands are synchronized. When we walk, both legs step forward one after another. Are the legs synchronized? The answer should be "no" since both legs cannot make a move "at the same time". But on the other hand, legs must be synchronized to make a normal walk. We have to say that this is another way of being synchronized, different from "at the same time."

The concept of synchronization should be cleared up for scientific research. It refers to the existence of regularity among action occurrences. What the internet tells is the simplest situation of synchronization.

First, what are synchronized? Hands? Legs? No, it is the actions of hands and legs that are synchronized. In terms of nets, it is transitions that are synchronized. For the BPM example introduced in Chap. 11, tasks are synchronized.

Second, "at the same time" is just one form of synchronization. Hand clap and leg walk are different forms of it.

What is the difference between the two? The former always involves the participation of both hands, while, for the latter, one leg step forward must be supported by the other stationary leg. As a quantified description, hand clap is 0, leg walk is 1, since, if you count the number of action occurrences, actions of the two hands are in fact inseparable, while one leg may make at the most 1 move more than the other leg. 0 and 1 are the respective measures of synchronization degree. 0 or 1, they are

C. Yuan, *Principle of Petri Nets*, https://doi.org/10.1007/978-981-97-7336-7_12

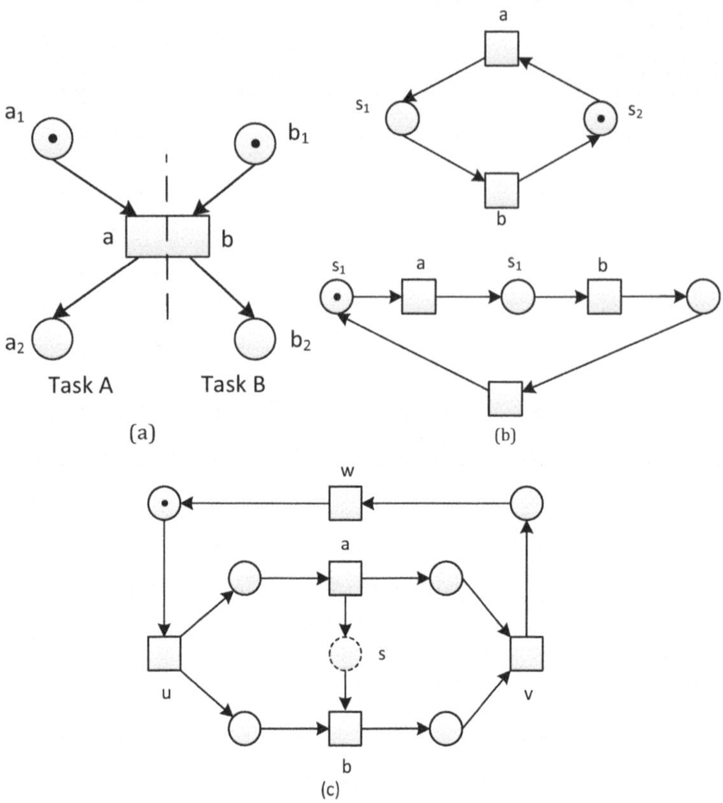

Fig. 12.1 Examples of synchronous distance $\sigma(a, b)$

"synchronous distance" between hand clapping and between leg walking. Figure 12.1 gives their corresponding net representation. This "ruler" for measuring the degree of synchronization is called "distance" since, as we will see, it satisfies distance axioms. Conventionally, synchronous distance between transition sets T_1 and T_2 is denoted by $\sigma(T_1, T_2)$, in which T_1 is called the positive side and T_2 is called the negative side. In case T_1 and T_2 are both singletons, say $T_1 = \{t\}$ and $T_2 = \{t'\}$, $\sigma(T_1, T_2)$ is written as $\sigma(t, t')$ instead of $\sigma(\{t\}, \{t'\})$.

The system to be discussed here in this chapter is the EN-system, that is the event/condition system. In case $W(t, p) > 1$ in a P/T-system, the token number in p does not correspond to the number of occurrences of t, and as such, it is much more complicated to define synchronous distances. It is more important to understand the concept of such distances than to compute. Letters T and t, instead of E and e, are used to denote a set of events and a single event respectively and the word "transition" is used instead of event. The reason for this is to emphasize the fact that concepts proposed here may well be applied for P/T systems and even high-level systems. The three-layer BPM model is a good example.

Back to synchronous distance. T_1 is the positive side, since each occurrence of a transition in T_1 is counted as +1; T_2 is the negative side, since each occurrence of a transition in T_2 is counted as −1. So, one move of left leg and one move of the right leg are respectively +1 and −1. A walk corresponds to a sequence of 1, −1, 1, −1, ⋯ or −1, 1, −1, ⋯ of which the sum is either 1 or 0. The difference 1 between 1 and 0 is the measure for the synchronization in normal walking.

The net in Fig. 12.1a can also be understand as a telephone call. Talking and listening are two sides of a call. This is synchronized information transfer. The two nets in Fig. 12.1b are asynchronized information transfers like the sending (transition a) and receiving (transition *b*) of a letter or telegram. The unnamed transition in (b) is the reply from the receiver.

Transition *a* and transition *b* in $\sigma(a,b)$ are treated as a singleton here. In case the positive side is a set of more than one transition, the occurrence of *a* represents an occurrence of any transition in the positive side. So is the negative side *b*.

Note that synchronous distance is symmetric, i.e., $\sigma(a,b) = \sigma(b,a)$. So, the adjectives "positive" and "negative" reflect nothing but the way occurrence times are counted in computing $\sigma(a,b)$.

It is easy to understand $\sigma(a,b) = 0$ in (a) and $\sigma(a,b) = 1$ in (b). To understand $\sigma(a,b) = 2$ in (c), just notice the fact that transition *a* (or *b*) may fire twice consecutively. There is a virtue place *p* in (c) denoted with a dotted circle. It is not a place of the net, but added to the underlying net by *S*-completion operation as an observing window. The distance 2 between *a* and *b* can be observed from this window in the same way mentioned above to find $\sigma(a,b) = 1$ from sequence 1, −1, 1, −1, ... Possible transition sequences seen on the net system in (c) from this window are as given below:

$$u\begin{cases} abvwu\begin{cases} abvwu \\ bavwu \end{cases} \\ bavwu\begin{cases} abvwu \\ bavwu \end{cases} \end{cases}\cdots$$

Taking *a* as the positive side, *b* as the negative side, and *u*, *v*, *w* as irrelevant, the corresponding sequences are:

$$\begin{aligned} &1,\ -1,\ 1.-1,\ \ldots \quad \text{sum} = 1 \text{ or sum} = 0 \\ &1,\ -1,\ -1,\ 1,\ \ldots \text{sum} = 1 \text{ or sum} = 0 \text{ or sum} = -1 \\ &-1,1,1,\ -1,\ \ldots \text{sum} = -1 \text{ or sum} = 0 \text{ or sum} = 1 \\ &-1,1,\ -1,1,\ \ldots \quad \text{sum} = -1 \text{ or sum} = 0 \end{aligned}$$

The difference between maximum and minimum of sums is 2. So, $\sigma(a,b) = 2$.

It is clear that only the maximum sum is observed from the window by one observation (first sequence), and only the minimum sum is observed from the window at another observation (last sequence). So, it requires complete observations to cover all possible transition sequences to find the maximum and the minimum.

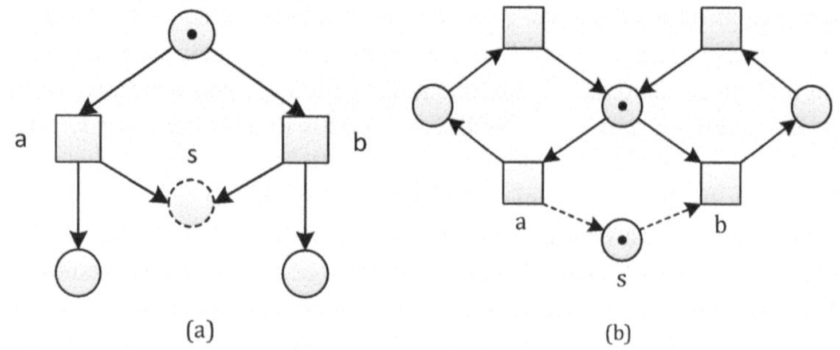

Fig. 12.2 Conflict and loop

With such observation windows on conflicts and loops as illustrated by Fig. 12.2 below, we have $\sigma(a, b) = 2$ for Fig. 12.2a and $\sigma(a, b) = \omega$ for Fig. 12.2b.

It is easy to see that $\sigma(a, b) = \omega$ in Fig. 12.2b, since transition a or transition b may fire an arbitrary number of times consecutively.

For a conflicting situation in Fig. 12.2a, transition a or transition b, each of them can fire just once, how to find $\sigma(a, b) = 2$? Assume that there are n tokens in the observation window, it becomes $n + 1$, if transition a occurs, and it becomes $n - 1$ if transition b occurs. So, the difference is $(n + 1) - (n - 1) = 2$. This is another way to observe, which is different from the positive side and the negative side. Note that $n + 1$ and $n - 1$ are reached in two different processes (though the so-called process consists of just one transition occurrence). This fact tells us, synchronous distance is a cross-process property of systems. Another way to compute $\sigma(a, b)$ is to make use of a special kind of transition sequence called deflection sequence. A deflection transition sequence contains transition firings as well as reverse transition firings like ab^{-1} in Fig. 12.2a. This reflects the cross-process property: a and b^{-1} belong to different process. The deflection transition sequence ab^{-1} yields $\sigma(a, b) = 2$, in which transition a is counted as 1 and transition b^{-1} is counted as 1 as well. Transition b is in the negative side, so the counting is negative, but its reverse leads to negative again for the second time. So the counting of b^{-1} is 1. The concept of deflection transition sequence is given by Definition 12.1 below.

It must be made clear that it is information systems that are focused in this chapter. Information system belongs to the EN-system in the net system hierarchy. When reverse transition firings are taken into account, an EN-system is extended to be a C/E-system. An EN-system is denoted as $(B, E; F, C_{\text{in}})$ and a C/E-system is denoted with $(B, E; F, C)$ where c_{in} is the initial case (state) while C is the complete set of cases reachable by transition firing sequences, including deflection transition sequences. As a complete set of cases, every case in C is reachable from any other case in C by a deflection transition sequence.

Definition 12.1 Deflection Transition Sequence Let each of $a_1, a_2, \ldots, a_n$ be an event firing or event reverse firing in C/E-system $\sum = (B, E; F, C)$, and $c_1, c_2, \ldots, c_n$, c_{n+1} be cases of $\sum$. If $c_i[a_i > c_{i+1}$ for all i, $i = 1, 2, \ldots, n$, then $a_1a_2, \ldots, a_n$ is a deflection transition sequence.

To prepare for formal definition of synchronous distance etc., two kinds of operations on nets are first introduced below.

12.1 Two Kinds of Operations on Nets

There are two kinds of operations on a net, namely, net completion and net complementation. Furthermore, completion operations include S-completion operation and T-completion, complementation operations include S-complementation and T-complementation.

First, an informal description on completion and complementation.

Let $N = (S, T; F)$ be a directed net. For two arbitrary subsets of T, say T_1 and T_2, $T_1 \cup T_2 \neq \varnothing$, an S-element s can be constructed with T_1 as preset and T_2 as post-set, i.e., ${}^{\cdot}s = T_1 \wedge s^{\cdot} = T_2$. The S-completion operation on N is to construct all such S-elements from given transition set T, and to add them into S. Let $S^{'}$ be the set so obtained, then $N^{'} = (S^{'}, T; F^{'})$ is a S-complete net in which $F^{'}$ is the arc set enriched from F in the course of S-completion.

Similarly, for two arbitrary subsets of S, say S_1 and S_2, $S_1 \cup S_2 \neq \varnothing$, a T-element t can be constructed with S_1 as preset and S_2 as post-set, i.e., ${}^{\cdot}t = S_1 \wedge t^{\cdot} = S_2$. The T-completion on N is to construct all such T-elements from a given place set S, and to add them into T. Let $T^{'}$ be the set so obtained. $N = (S, T^{'}; F^{'})$ is a T-complete net in which $F^{'}$ is the arc set enriched from F in the course of T-completion.

In definitions below, directed net $N = (S, T; F)$ is always assumed to be a simple net, i.e., every element of N is structurally unique.

Definition 12.2 Net Completion Directed net $N^{'} = (S^{'}, T; F^{'})$ is the S-completion of $N = (S, T; F)$, if for any subset pair (T_1, T_2) of T and $T_1 \cup T_2 \neq \varnothing$, there exists a unique element s in $S^{'}$, such that ${}^{\cdot}s = T_1 \wedge s^{\cdot} = T_2$. Elements in S are places, and elements in $S^{'} - S$ are called place items.

A place item will be used as an observation window on net systems. An observation window exposes firing regularity of transitions in its scope.

Directed net $N^{''} = (S, T^{'}; F^{'})$ is the T-completion of $N = (S, T; F)$, if for any subset pair (S_1, S_2) of S and $S_1 \cup S_2 \neq \varnothing$, there exists unique element t in $T^{'}$, such that ${}^{\cdot}t = S_1 \wedge t^{\cdot} = S_2$. Element in T are transitions, and elements in $T^{'} - T$ are called transition items.

For a given directed net N, S-completion and T-completion may be repeated to produce more and more new nets.

A net may be the underlying structure of an EN-system or a P/T-system. S-completion provides observation windows on both EN-system and P/T-systems while T-completion is important for an EN-system $(E, B; F, c_0)$, where a transition is called an event and a place is called a condition. When a condition is viewed as a Boolean variable, net logic is obtained for reasoning about system properties. This logic will be talked about in Chap. 13.

For EN-system $(E, B; F, c_0)$, let $\wp(B)$ be the power set of condition set B, i.e., the set of all subsets of B. $\wp(B)$ consists of two subsets C and N. C is the set of all cases

Fig. 12.3 Logic structure of a net system

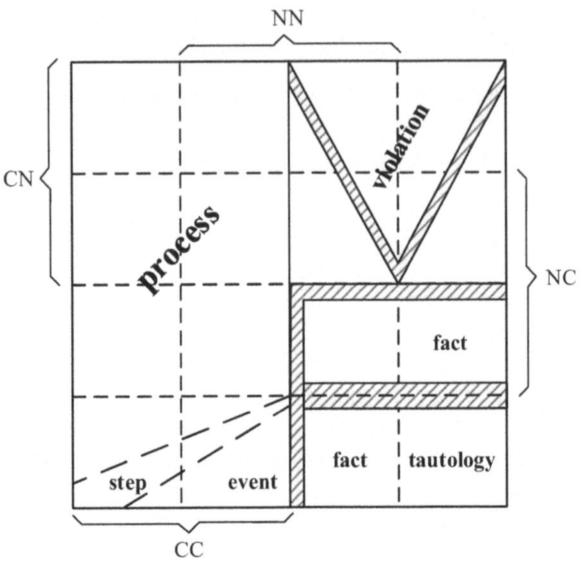

(subsets of B reachable from initial case c_0) and $N = \wp(B) - C$. Let $(E', B; F')$ be the EN-system obtained by T-completion operation on $(E, B; F)$. All elements in E' fall into 4 classes, i.e., CC, CN, NC, and NN according to their respective presets and post-sets: for a in E', $a \in CC$, if ${}^{\cdot}a \in C \wedge a^{\cdot} \in C$, $a \in CN$, if ${}^{\cdot}a \in C \wedge a^{\cdot} \in N$, $a \in NC$, if ${}^{\cdot}a \in N \wedge a^{\cdot} \in C$, $a \in NN$, if ${}^{\cdot}a \in N \wedge a^{\cdot} \in N$.

The picture in Fig. 12.3 is called net logic structure, that is, a detailed classification of E' elements, since a single transition form in E' may belong to more than one of the above four classes.

Formal definition of these classes will be given in Chap. 13 on net logic.

Definition 12.3 Net Complementation $N' = (S', T; F')$ is the S-complemented net of directed net $N = (S, T; F)$, if for all S-element s in S, there is a unique s' in S' such that ${}^{\cdot}s = s'^{\cdot} \wedge {}^{\cdot}s' = s^{\cdot}$. Place s and s' are said to be complemented with each other.

$N'' = (S, T'; F')$ is the T-complemented net of directed net $N = (S, T; F)$, if for all T-element t in T, there is a unique t' in T' such that ${}^{\cdot}t = t'^{\cdot} \wedge {}^{\cdot}t' = t^{\cdot}$. Transition t' and transition t are reverse with each other.

A token held by s and a token held by its complementation s' are resources of reverse property, like a car and a parking space.

If a net system has a T-complemented net as its structure, then the token flow would "miss direction," since t and its reverse t' would make tokens flow in reverse directions. If "forward" is reachable from u to v, then "backward" is also reachable from u to v, since $M[t > M' \leftrightarrow M[-t' > M'$, in which $-t'$ is the backward firing of t'.

If a net system has a S-complemented net as its structure, and for every complemented pair (s, s'), $M_0(s)$, + $M_0(s') = K(s)$, then for every reachable marking M, $M(s) + M(s') = K(s)$. This is the property of a parking lot: the occupied spaces + the unoccupied spaces = capacity of the lot.

Lemma 12.1 *S*-complemented Net System Is Contact Free A contact situation denotes the possibility of token overflow. $M(s) + M(s') = K(s)$ implies $M(s) \leq K(s)$, overflow is impossible.

The *S*-completion operation on the underlying net structure of a net system gives rise to the key concept of synchronous distance.

12.2 Synchronous Distance

Let s be an *S*-element added by *S*-completion on P/T-system $\sum = (S, T; F, K, W, M_0)$ and $s = (T_1, T_2)$ as shown in Fig. 12.4 in which $T_1 = \{t_{11}, t_{12}, \ldots, t_{1n}\}$ and $T_2 = \{t_{21}, t_{22}, \ldots, t_{2m}\}$. With s as an observation window, the concept of synchronous distance is given by Definition 12.4 below.

As said above, the way to observe is: to put a token into s when a transition in T_1 occurs, to remove a token from s when a transition in T_2 occurs. To ensure the observation to go on smoothly, assume that many tokens had been put into s before observation. In case the token number in s has a peak and a valley, the difference between the peak and the valley is defined as the synchronous distance between T_1 and T_2. It represents some regularity of transition firings. In case there is no up bound or no bottom, the synchronous distance is ω (infinity).

An observation window s may happen to be a *S*-element of the system under observation. If so, transition rules and the initial marking decide the variance of token numbers in s. This variance is also understood as the synchronous distance. Thus, the synchronous distance between the preset and the post-set of a condition in an EN-system is always 1.

For P/T-system $\sum = (S, T; F, K, W, M_0)$ and a *S*-completed element (observation window) $s = (T_1, T_2)$, $T_1 = \{t_{11}, t_{12}, \ldots, t_{1n}\}$ and $T_2 = \{t_{21}, t_{22}, \ldots, t_{2m}\}$. Let $S' = S \cup \{s\}$ and $F' = F \cup \{(t_{1i}, s) | i = 1, 2, \ldots, n\} \cup \{(s, t_{2j}) | j = 1, 2, \ldots, m\}$, and . $\sum' = (S', T; F', K', W', M'_0)$, in which $K'(s) = \omega$ and $K'(p) = K(p)$ for all p in S; $W'(x, s) = 1$ and $W'(s, y) = 1$, where $x \in T_1$ and $y \in T_2$; $M'_0(p) = M_0(p)$ for all p in S. $M'_0(s) = L$, i.e., s holds L tokens initially that is great enough for the observation.

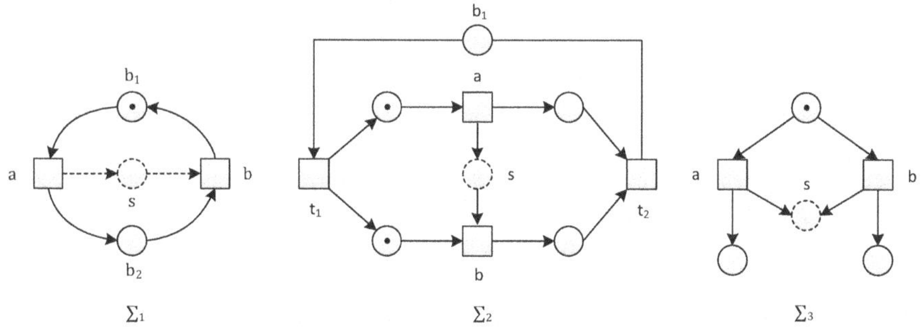

Fig. 12.4 Three windows for observation

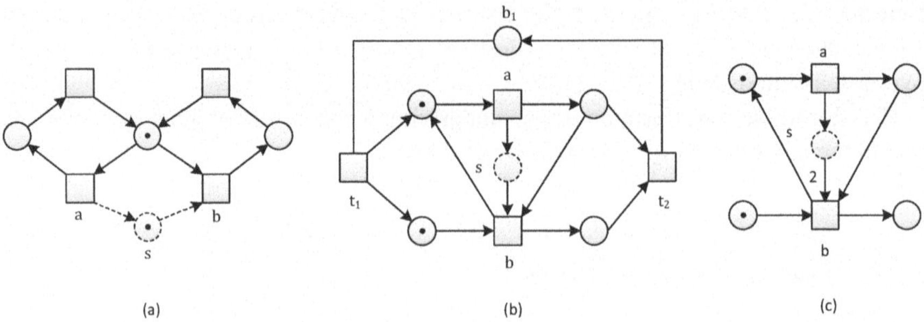

Fig. 12.5 Infinite synchronous distance

Definition 12.4 Synchronous Distance For P/T-system $\sum = (S, T; F, K, W, M_0)$, $s = (T_1, T_2)$, and $\sum' = (S', T; F', K', W', M_0')$ is constructed as given above, then $\sum'$ is called the synchronous observation system for (T_1, T_2).

The synchronous distance $\sigma(T_1, T_2)$ is the drop height of tokens at s in net system $\sum'$:

$$\sigma(T_1, T_2) = \begin{cases} \omega & \exists M' \in [M_0' > : M'(s) = \omega \\ \max\{M'(s) | M' \in [M_0' >\} - \min\{M'(s) | M' \in [M_0' >\} \end{cases}$$

Note that "the drop height is infinite" is the same as $\exists M' \in [M_0' > : M'(s) = \omega$. Other drop height is given by $\max\{M'(s) | M' \in [M_0' >\} - \min\{M'(s) | M' \in [M_0' >\}$.

Figure 12.5 below are examples of infinite distances, in which Fig. 12.5a consists of two circles that are not connected. As we have claimed earlier, it makes no sense to put disconnected nets into one system, since their behaviors are independent. The infinite synchronous distance is but a quantified description of independent dynamics. Figure 12.5b is another kind of infinite distance. Transitions a and b belong to the same system and their firings are closely related with regularity, i.e., repetition of t_1abat_2. Transition a occurs one more time than transition b in one loop. This difference would accumulate to infinite so that $\sigma(a, b) = \omega$.

The infinite distance in Fig. 12.5b comes from a fact that $a : b = 2 : 1$. This observation leads to the concept of weighted synchronous distance.

In preparation for defining the concept of synchronous distance above, a net system $\sum' = (S', T; F', K', W', M_0')$ was constructed from $\sum = (S, T; F, K, W, M_0)$, in which $W'(x, s) = 1$ and $W'(s, y) = 1$, where $x \in T_1$ and $y \in T_2$. As said above, the token drop height at s in $\sum'$ gives out $\sigma(T_1, T_2)$.

Though $\sigma(T_1, T_2) = \omega$ for Fig. 12.5b, there exists some regularity between transition firings of T_1 and T_2. To describe such regularity, we need another net system $\sum''$, $\sum'' = (S', T; F', K', W'', M_0')$, which is almost the same as $\sum'$ except W''. If there exist positive integers u_i and v_j, $i = 1, 2, \ldots, n$ and $j = 1, 2, \ldots, m$, such that $W''(t_{1i}, s) = u_i$ and $W''(s, t_{1j}) = v_j$ would lead $\sum''$ to have a finite token drop height at

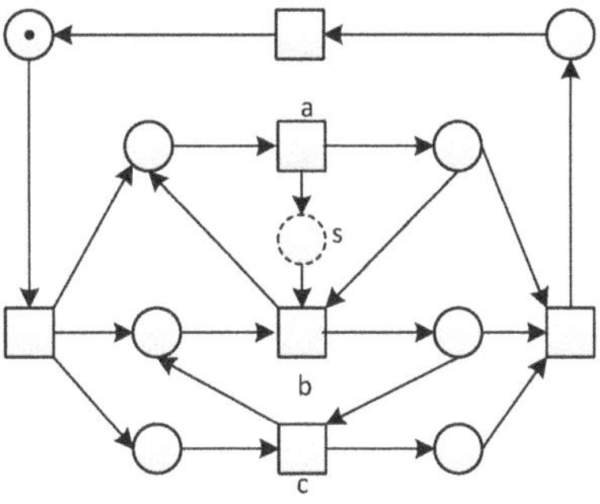

Fig. 12.6 $\sigma(a, b) = \omega$ and $\sigma(a, 3b) = 3$

$s = (T_1, T_2)$, then this drop height is the weighted synchronous distance between T_1 and T_2.

Definition 12.5 Weighted Synchronous Distance For P/T-system $\sum = (S, T; F, K, W, M_0)$, $s = (T_1, T_2)$, and $\sum'' = \left(S', T; F', K', W'', M_0'\right)$ is constructed as given above, then the weighted synchronous distance $\sigma(T_1, T_2)$ is the drop height of tokens at s in net system $\sum''$. All the positive integers u_i and v_j, $i = 1, 2, \ldots, n$ and $j = 1, 2, \ldots, m$ are respective weights on due transitions.

Figure 12.6 below is an example of infinite distance and finite weighted distance where $\sigma(a, b) = \omega$ and $\sigma(a, 3b) = 3$. Note that 3 is the weight on b.

Note that $\sigma(a, c) = \omega$, $\sigma(2a, 3bc) = 6$, $\sigma(c, b) = \omega$ and $\sigma(b, 2c) = 2$ and $\sigma(a, 3b) = 3$ for the net system in Fig. 12.6. In fact, to keep the figure simple and easy to read, observation $a : c : b = 3 : 2 : 1$ windows for $\sigma(a, c)$ and $\sigma(c, b)$ are not included in the figure.

The general form of weighted synchronous distance is $\sigma\left(T_1', T_2'\right)$, where T_1' and T_2' are multi sets:

$$T_1' = u_1 t_{11} + u_2 t_{12} + \cdots + u_n t_{1n} = \sum_{i=1}^{n} u_i t_{1i}$$

$$T_2' = v_1 t_{21} + v_2 t_{22} + \cdots + v_m t_{2m} = \sum_{j=1}^{m} v_j t_{2j}$$

To show that $\sigma(a, b)$ is indeed a distance, we have the lemma below.

Lemma 12.2 $\sigma(a, b)$ Satisfies Distance Axioms

1. $\sigma(a, b) = 0 \leftrightarrow a = b$,
2. $\sigma(a, b) \geq 0$,
3. $\sigma(a, b) = \sigma(b, a)$,
4. $\sigma(a, b) + \sigma(b, c) \geq \sigma(a, c)$,
5. $\sigma(a, b) = \sigma(a - b, b - a)$,
6. $\sigma(a \cup b, c \cup d) \leq \sigma(a, c) + \sigma(b, d) + \sigma(a \cap b, c \cap d)$.

Proof The first three properties are directed consequences of the definition of $\sigma(a, b)$. Note that a and b in $\sigma(a, b)$ is not necessarily a singleton. To write it this way is just to avoid a complicated formula.

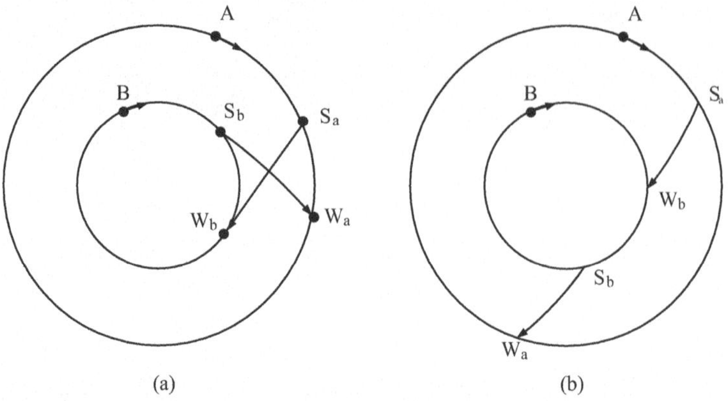

Fig. 12.7 Signal synchronization

To prove $\sigma(a, b) + \sigma(b, c) \geq \sigma(a, c)$, it is assumed that all these distances are finite since only finite distances are realistic in real applications. Let τ_1 be the transition sequence that leads the token number at observation window (a, c) from M_0 to maximum, and let τ_2 be the transition sequence that leads the token number at observation window (a, c) from M_0 to minimum. Then, $\tau_1^{-1}\tau_2$ is a deflection transition sequence that changes the token number at observation window (a, c) from maximum to minimum. Let l_1, l_2, l_3 be the firing times of transitions a, b and c in $\tau_1^{-1}\tau_2$, then we have ,$\sigma(a, c) = |l_1 - l_3|$ (absolute value). On the other hand however, $\sigma(a, b)$ is the drop height at observation window (a, b), $\sigma(a, b) \geq |l_1 - l_2|$. Similarly we have $\sigma(b, c) \geq |l_2 - l_3|$. Now,

$$\sigma(a, b) + \sigma(b, c) \geq |l_1 - l_2| + |l_2 - l_3| \geq |l_1 - l_3| = \sigma(a, c).$$

Similarly, the other properties can be proved.

Note that $\tau_1^{-1}\tau_2$ is reasonable, since synchronous distance is a cross-process concept, the maximum and the minimum may be reached in different processes.

Example 12.1 Signal Transfer Figure 12.7 below (a) is a mechanism to get signal A and signal B synchronized by signal splitting (s_a and s_b) and waiting (w_a and w_b). Once this was a used mechanism, but later it was given up for it was erroneous. The goal for this synchronization is to keep $\sigma(s_a, s_b) = 1$. In case signal A goes much faster than signal B, then s_a may occur twice consecutively to make $\sigma(s_a, s_b) > 1$. Figure 12.7b is the right solution.

Figure 12.8 is the net systems corresponding to Fig. 12.7. It easy to find that transition s_a and transition s_b in Fig. 12.7a are concurrent while s_a and transition s_b in Fig. 12.7b are sequential, i.e., $\sigma(s_a, s_b) > 1$ in Fig. 12.7a and $\sigma(s_a, s_b) = 1$ in Fig. 12.7b.

Example 12.2 Deflection Sequence and Conflict It has been made clear above that $\sigma(a, b) = 2$ for conflicting a and b. Figure 12.9 below is a net system in which

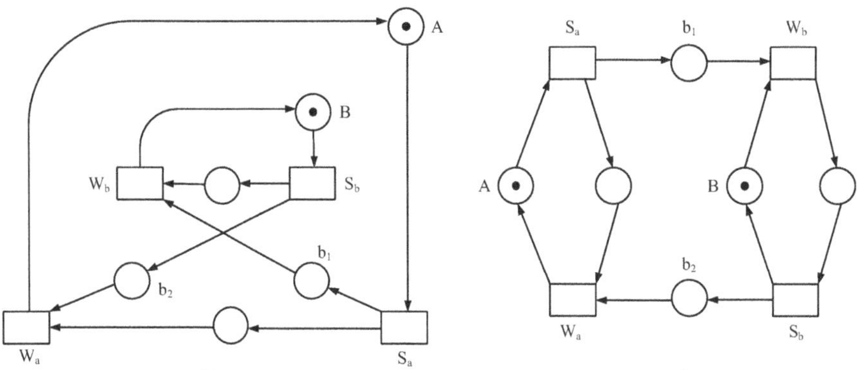

Fig. 12.8 Net system for signal synchronization

Fig. 12.9 Transition c and $\sigma(a, b) = 2$

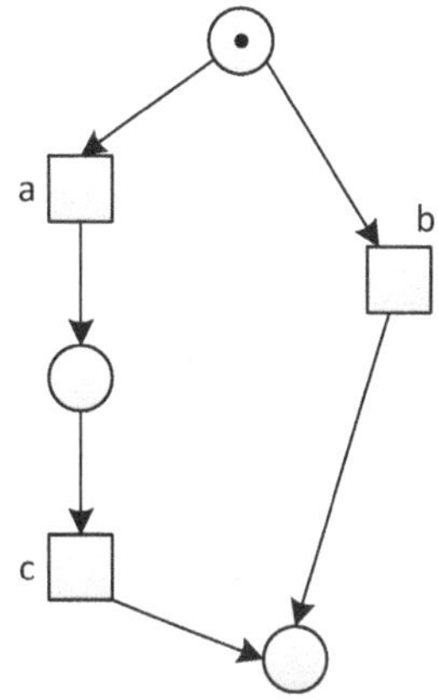

a transition c is added to conflicting a and b. Now, acb^{-1} is a deflection sequence and $acb^{-1}acb^{-1}$ is also a deflection sequence. Is it reasonable to conclude, from $acb^{-1}acb^{-1}$, that $\sigma(a, b) = 4$ or $\sigma(a, b) = \omega$?

This confusing question had raised another question years ago: is synchronous distance meaningful? Now, the answer is definitely "yes!" There should be no doubt about it since the concept of synchronizer has played the key role in BPM as described in Chap. 11.

The regularity of the occurrences of transitions a and b is fully displayed by deflection sequence acb^{-1}, and $acb^{-1}acb^{-1}$ does not tell any more. Thus, it remains that $\sigma(a, b) = 2$.

The concepts of synchronous distances and weighted synchronous distances are useful in system analysis. But for system design, the reverse of computing synchronous distances is even more useful. The way to do this is to list how actions are synchronized in terms of synchronous distances, and check whether these given distances satisfy distance axioms. As long as the listed distances comply with

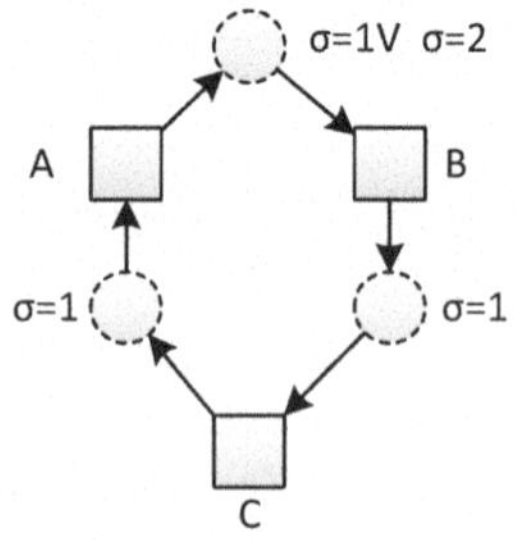

Fig. 12.10 A program for church wedding

distance axioms, then add details to implement each of these distances separately. Figure 12.10 is a program of a church wedding. There are three main actions for it, namely, interaction between the host and the bride (action A), interaction between the host and the bridegroom (action B), and interchange of rings between the bride and the bridegroom (action C). As a blueprint, $\sigma(A, C) = 1$ and $\sigma(B, C) = 1$ is a must, since A and B must be before C and occurring exactly once each. As for A and B, both $\sigma(A, B) = 1$ and $\sigma(A, B) = 2\sigma$ are acceptable according to distance axioms. $\sigma(A, B) = 1$ tells that first A than B, or first B then A. Once this order is decided, it would be fixed. $\sigma(A, B) = 2$ tells that A and B are in conflict since the host is shared by the wedding couple. The host is free to talk to the bride first or to talk to the bridegroom first.

Note that synchronous distance is symmetric, and so $\sigma(C, A) = \sigma(A, C) = 1$. For the above wedding program, equation $\sigma(C, A) = 1$ is not the same as shown by the dotted circle in Fig. 12.10, since the circle has a given positive side A and a given negative side C.

It is easy to add details to make Fig. 12.10 a complete design as given in Fig. 1.2a.

12.3 Synchronous Distance and System Property

The S-completion operation on a net will bring many place items into a given net. In fact, the total number of S-elements and place items for $|T| = n$ is $2^{2n} - 1$ in which $(\varnothing, \varnothing)$is not included. With place items as observation windows, condition items (synchronous distance 1) would be figured out. Figure 12.11b is the net system obtained from the simplest four-season system in Figure 12.11a by S-completion in which all condition items are included. The concept of condition items is relative: Conditions are given as part of a system, and condition items are found by S-completion and synchronous distance computing. Different condition sets correspond to different sets of condition items.

The net system in Fig. 12.11b is said to be most complete, since it contains all conditions related to season alternating. Note that the inner most condition is $\bar{p_7}$ and the out big circle is p_7. All these conditions are pairwise complemented denoted by p and $\bar{p}$. Say, p is "flower blooming" and $\bar{p}$ is "flower falling", or "swallow coming" and "swallow leaving," etc.

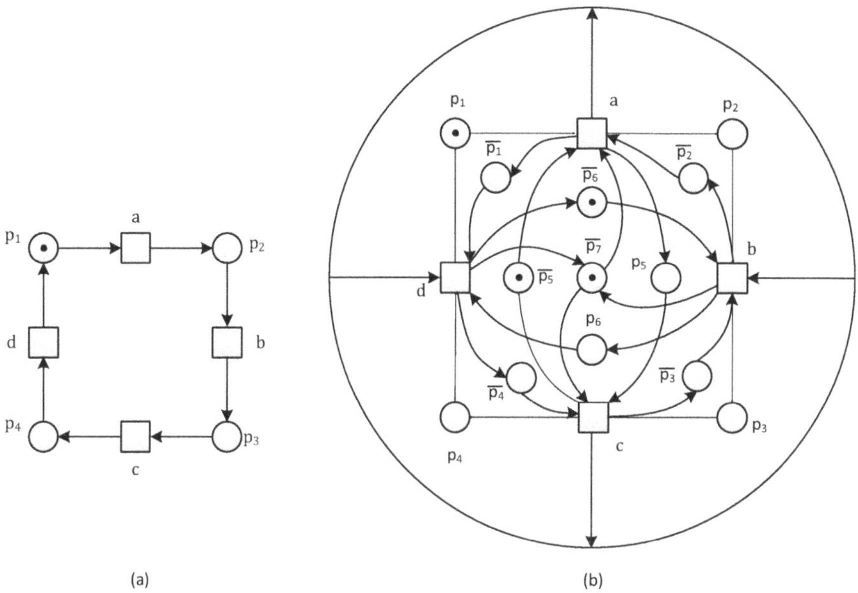

Fig. 12.11 Four-season system: the simplest and the most complete

Definition 12.6 Basic Set The set of all conditions and all condition items of system $\sum = (S, T; F, c_{in})$ and system $\sum' = (S, T; F, C)$ is called the basic set of $\sum$ and $\sum'$ respectively.

Note that $\sum$ and $\sum'$ are respectively an EN-system and a C/E-system.

The basic set for a given system $\sum$ is unique, but the same basic set may be shared by more than one system. For example, the four-season system has four events a, b, c, and d that occur in above appearing order, and another system with the same event set $\{a, b, c, d\}$ and the firing order is b, d, c, a, they share the same basic set.

The basic set contains too many conditions and condition items to be applicable in reality. One way to simplify it is to delete one condition item from each complement pair; another way is to keep only all accompany conditions of transitions. The four-season system with eight conditions is a good example for the latter.

We have gone over a complete process on the four-season net system via S-completion operation, from the simplest one to the condition complete one, from the basic set to accompany conditions only. This process may be applied in real applications to figure out a system model that is most suitable to the problem in question.

In case the number of elements is important, Figure 12.12 suggests a net system that has three conditions only.

Lemma synchronous distance between a and b

1. If $\sigma(a, b) = 1$, then $[a \rightarrow b>$,
2. If $[a \rightarrow b>$, then $\sigma(a, b) \geq 1$,
3. If $[a | b>$ or $[a \parallel b>$, then $\sigma(a, b) \geq 2$.

Fig. 12.12 Four-season system: the simplest one

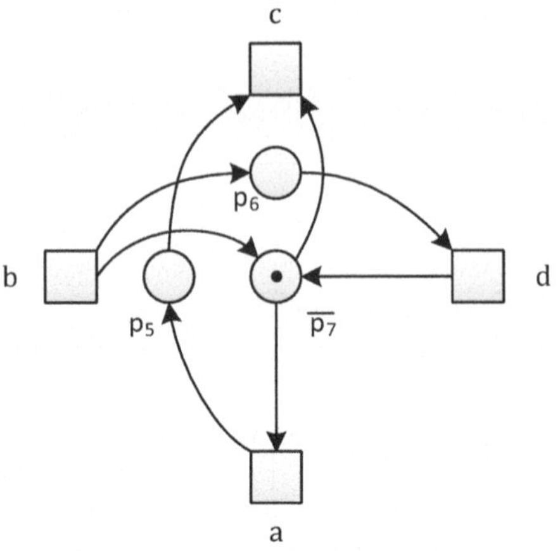

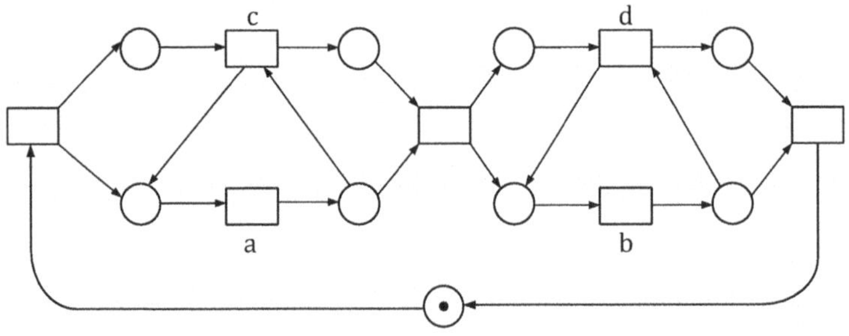

Fig. 12.13 $[a \rightarrow b>$ and $\sigma(a, b) \geq 1$

Remarks To put the lemma in words

If $\sigma(a, b) = 1$, then a and b must be sequential, but the reverse is not necessarily true. Figure 12.13 is an anti-example: $\sigma(a, b) = 2$ while a must before b.

In case a and b are in conflict or parallel, then $\sigma(a, b) \geq 1$.

12.4 Computing Synchronous Distance

The concept of synchronous distances is important for system analysis. It is more important to compute these distances in real application. But synchronous distances as well as weighted synchronous distances are defined based on the set of reachable markings, i.e., $[M_0>$. $[M_0>$ might be infinite. Here in this section, we will hunt for applicable methods for the distance computing.

Theorem 12.1 About Recursive Process Let R be a recursive process of C/E-system $\sum = (S, T; F, C)$ and T_1, T_2 be subsets of S and $T_1 \cap T_2 = \varnothing$, then

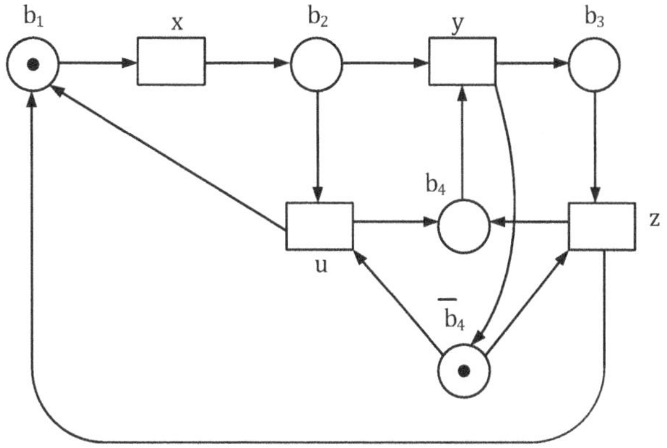

Fig. 12.14 A system with recursive processes

$$Occ(T_1,R) \neq Occ(T_2,R) \rightarrow \sigma(T_1,T_2) = \omega,$$

in which $Occ(T_1,R)$ and $Occ(T_2,R)$ are respectively the number of transition occurrences of T_1 and T_2 in R.

Proof Since $Occ(T_1,R) \neq Occ(T_2,R)$, then the difference would accumulate to infinity to make $\sigma(T_1,T_2) = \omega$.

The rebellious theorem is true:

Theorem 12.2 Recursive Process For recursive process R,

$$\sigma(T_1,T_2) < \omega \rightarrow Occ(T_1,R) = Occ(T_2,R).$$

Remarks $\sigma(T_1,T_2)$ is meaningful only if $T_1 \neq \varnothing \wedge T_2 \neq \varnothing$ since synchronous distance is a ruler measuring the degree of dependence between the positive side and the negative side.

It is reasonable to have $T_1 \cap T_2 = \varnothing$, since $\sigma(T_1,T_2) = \sigma(T_1 - T_2, T_2 - T_1)$.

Theorem 12.3 Recursive Process If $Occ(T_1,R) = Occ(T_2,R)$ is true for all recursive process R of $\sum = (S,T;F,C)$, then the counting of $\sigma(T_1,T_2)$ can be carried out on those processes that do not contain any complete recursive process.

This theorem is true since the counting of the difference between $Occ(T_1,R)$ and $Occ(T_2,R)$ on any complete recursive process R results in 0.

Figure 12.14 below is a net system containing recursive processes. Transition x may fire at the initial marking to enable transition u. Transitions x, y, z will fire recursively after x and u.

All processes of the system in Fig. 12.14 may be given by $xu(xyz)*$. Transition u fires only once and x, y, z may fire arbitrary many times So, $\sigma(u,x) = \omega$, $\sigma(u, y) = \omega$, $\sigma(u,z) = \omega$.

There are two ways to deal with the prefix xu of $xu(xyz)*$. One way is to take $xuxyzxyz\ldots$ as process formula to have $\sigma(y,z) = 1$, $\sigma(x,y) = 2$ and $\sigma(x,z) = 2$.

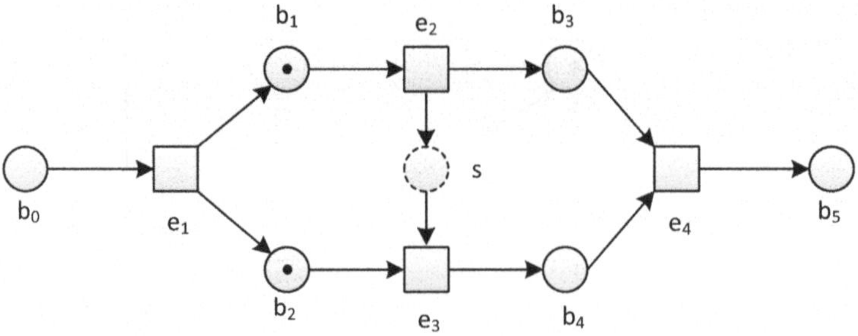

Fig. 12.15 $\sigma(e_2, e_3) = 2$

Another way is to ignore xu, so to have $\sigma(y, z) = 1, \sigma(x, y) = 1$ and $\sigma(x, z) = 1$. In fact, the regularity among occurrences of x, y, and z is reflected by $(xyz)*$.

The structure and the initial state (marking or case) decide system property, including synchronous distances between actions (transitions or events). The net system $\sum$ in Fig. 12.15 is an EN-system as well as a C/E-system. With this system as an example, introduced next is an algebraic method for synchronous distance computing.

For the C/E-system $\sum = (B, E; F, C)$ in Fig. 12.15, $E = \{e_1, e_2, e_3, e_4\}$. The observation window s may be represented by vector $(0, 1, -1, 0)$ for its positive side is $\{e_2\}$ and its negative side is $\{e_3\}$. In the same way, we have:

$$b_1 = (1, -1, 0, 0), \bar{b_1} = (-1, 1, 0, 0),$$

$$b_2 = (1, 0, -1, 0), \bar{b_2} = (-1, 0, 1, 0),$$

$$b_3 = (0, 1, 0, -1), \bar{b_3} = (0, -1, 0, 1),$$

$$b_4 = (0, 0, 1, -1), \bar{b_4} = (0, 0, -1, 1),$$

Note that the focus now is $\sigma\{e_2, e_3\}$, and conditions b_0 and b_5 are irrelevant.

$\bar{b_i}$ above is the reverse vector of b_i for i = 1, 2, 3, 4. As S-element, $\bar{b_i}$ is the complement: $b_i \bigoplus \bar{b_i}$ is true.

$\sum$, as a C/E-system, its complete set of cases is $C = \{c_0, c_1, c_2, c_3, c_4, c_5\}$ in which $c_0 = \{b_0\}, c_1 = \{b_1, b_2\}, c_2 = \{b_1, b_4\}, c_3 = \{b_2, b_3\}, c_4 = \{b_3, b_4\}, c_5 = \{b_5\}$. To add complement conditions to these cases, we have:

$$c_0' = \{b_0, \overline{b_1}, \overline{b_2}, \overline{b_3}, \overline{b_4}, \overline{b_5}\},$$

$$c_1' = \{\overline{b_0}, b_1, b_2, \overline{b_3}, \overline{b_4}, \overline{b_5}\},$$

$$c_2' = \{\overline{b_0}, b_1, \overline{b_2}, \overline{b_3}, b_4, \overline{b_5}\},$$

$$c_3' = \{\overline{b_0}, \overline{b_1}, b_2, b_3, \overline{b_4}, \overline{b_5}\},$$

$$c_4' = \{\overline{b_0}, \overline{b_1}, \overline{b_2}, b_3, b_4, \overline{b_5}\},$$

$$c_5' = \{\overline{b_0}, \overline{b_1}, \overline{b_2}, \overline{b_3}, \overline{b_4}, b_5\}.$$

So, $\max_{i=0}^{5}\{|c_i' \cap \{b_3, \overline{b_4}\}|\} = |\, c_3' \cap \{b_3, \overline{b_4}\}\,| = 2,$

$$\min_{i=0}^{5}\{|c_i' \cap \{b_3, \overline{b_4}\}|\} = |\, c_2' \cap \{b_3, \overline{b_4}\}\,| = 0.$$

$\{b_3, \bar{b_4}\}$ denotes the firing of e and no e_3 firing. So $\max_{i=0}^{5}\{|c_i' \cap \{b_3, \overline{b_4}\}|\} = 2$ indicates that e_2 may fire twice consecutively.

$\min_{i=0}^{5}\{|c_i' \cap \{b_3, \overline{b_4}\}|\} = 0$ indicates that e_2 may observe no firing. The difference between the maximum and the minimum leads to $\sigma\{e_2, e_3\} = 2$.

The observation window may take e_3 as the positive side and e_2 as the negative side to obtain $\sigma\{e_3, e_2\} = 2$.

The above discussion has focused on a concrete example, in which vectors are the main means for distance computation. The method is obviously beyond human ability in case the net system in question is complicated. The only way is to develop auto tools for it. This example provides a basis for the tool.

12.5 Synchronous Distance Application

Example 12.3 Contract Design Two parties A and B are negotiating over a cooperation contract. The following conditions are agreed upon by both sides:

1. To provide service for each other,
2. No one bears the obligation to provide service first,
3. Nothing relies on trust, everything must be clearly written on the contract,
4. No third party has the right as the judge to rule over them.

The last condition is necessary since both parties wish to keep it secret. The contract should be symmetric to A and B, since they should be equally treated.

Let a and b be services provided by party A and party B. $\sigma(a, b)$ is a ruler to measure the potential price to pay. The smaller $\sigma(a, b)$ is, the better the contract is, since both A and B want to keep loses as tiny as possible in case one party quits.

$\sigma(a, b) = 1$ is not acceptable, since either party has to serve the other side first.

To keep the candidate system as tiny as possible, we have the three net systems in Fig. 12.16. The net in Fig. 12.16a is symmetric, a and b are equally positioned. But, no matter how to place a token to make it a system, $\sigma(a, b) = 1$ is true. Figure 12.16b, c are efforts in order to enrich Fig. 12.16a to make it a contract.

$\sigma(a, b) = 2$ is the best possible choice. The problem is how to design the contract to make $\sigma(a, b) = 2$ true.

If a and b are in conflict, $\sigma(a, b) = 2$ is true, but the same as $\sigma(a, b) = 1$. One party has to serve the other party first.

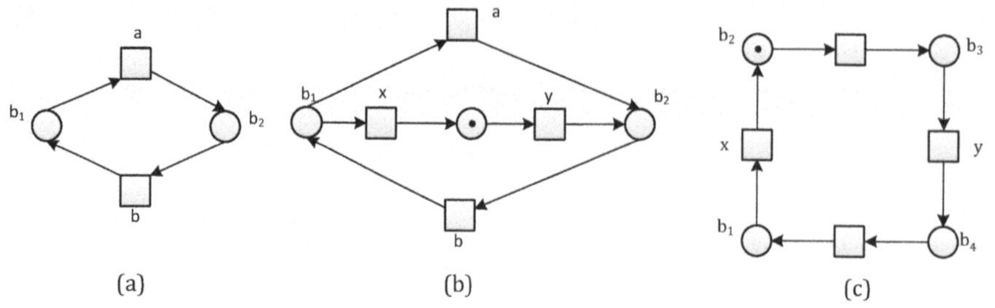

Fig. 12.16 Contract to be ruled out

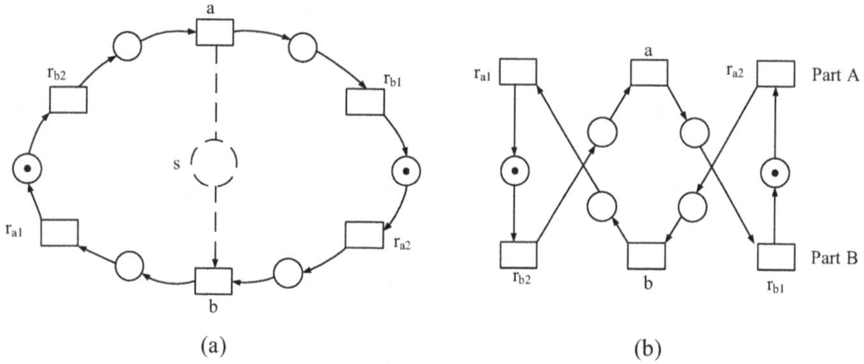

Fig. 12.17 Acceptable contract

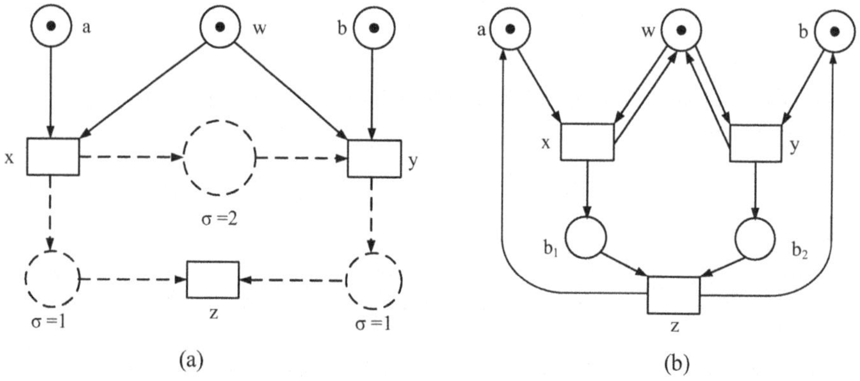

Fig. 12.18 Draft design with synchronous distances

There are different situations, except conflict, that make $\sigma(a,b) = 2$ true. Figure 12.17 provides an acceptable contract. It is acceptable since A and B are equal in the contract and $\sigma(a,b) = 2$. $\sigma(a,b) = 2$ tells that the maximum loss is $2a$ or $2b$, i.e., either party may provide service for the second time without being served by the other side.

Synchronous distance is a quantified measure to help contract design. System Figure 12.17a and system Figure 12.17b in the figure are the same system drawn differently. The dotted circle in Figure 12.17a is an observation window.

Example 12.4 Similar to church wedding, a worker (w) is doing three things: first *a* and *b*, then *c*. *a* and *b* are in conflict since both are carried out by *w*. With synchronous distances to specify how *a*, *b*, and *c* are related, we have the draft design shown in Fig. 12.18a. Figure 12.18b is a primary design in which detailed implementations of transitions *x* and *y* are to be added.

It is the *S*-complete operation on the underlying pure net structure of a finite C/E-system that brings to us this branch of general net theory, namely synchrony. The next chapter introduces net logic (Enlogy).

Chapter 13
Net Logic (Enlogy)

Abstract Enlogy is another branch of general nnet theory, that connects a dead transition in a net system with system properties. A transition is dead if and only if it has not even one chance to occur. Dead transitions form a logic system for system property analysis.

This chapter introduces the way to reason about system properties with dead event items.

To start with, the systems in question are C/E-systems consisting of conditions and events. An event e has its preset $^{\cdot}e$ and its post-set $e^{\cdot}$. Let $^{\cdot}e = \{b_{11}, b_{12}, \cdots, b_{1n}\}$ and $e^{\cdot} = \{b_{21}, b_{22}, \cdots, b_{2m}\}$, then e is enabled if $(b_{11} \wedge b_{12} \wedge \cdots \wedge b_{1n}) \wedge \neg (b_{21} \vee b_{22} \vee \cdots \vee b_{2m})$. So, e is dead if and only if

$$\begin{aligned}&\neg((b_{11} \wedge b_{12} \wedge \cdots \wedge b_{1n}) \wedge \neg(b_{21} \vee b_{22} \vee \cdots \vee b_{2m}))\\ &\equiv \neg(b_{11} \wedge b_{12} \wedge \cdots \wedge b_{1n}) \vee (b_{21} \vee b_{22} \vee \cdots \vee b_{2m})\\ &\equiv (b_{11} \wedge b_{12} \wedge \cdots \wedge b_{1n}) \rightarrow b_{21} \vee b_{22} \vee \cdots \vee b_{2m}.\end{aligned}$$

Definition 13.1 Dead Transition If $b_{11} \wedge b_{12} \wedge \cdots \wedge b_{1n} \rightarrow b_{21} \vee b_{22} \vee \cdots \vee b_{2m}$ is true for all cases of C/E-system $\sum = (B, E; F, C)$, then e is dead. A dead event is also called a dead transition.

The formula $b_{11} \wedge b_{12} \wedge \cdots \wedge b_{1n} \rightarrow b_{21} \vee b_{22} \vee \cdots \vee b_{2m}$ is a true proposition or effective proposition on $\sum$.

Graphically, a true proposition (dead transition) is represented by a box with "sleeping T" inside, as shown in Fig. 13.1.

As a common practice, dead transitions are, generally speaking, not included by a system model, no matter real application or scientific research. It is obtained by T-completion operation applied on the underlying net of a system. The added events are called event items. These event items may be classified according to their characteristics specified below.

C. Yuan, *Principle of Petri Nets*, https://doi.org/10.1007/978-981-97-7336-7_13

Fig. 13.1 Dead transition and proposition

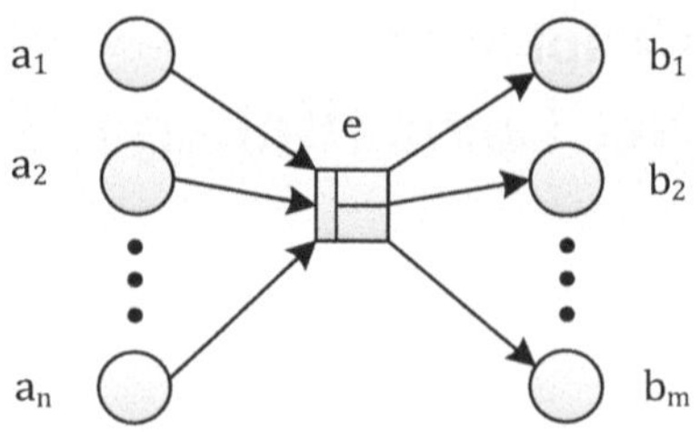

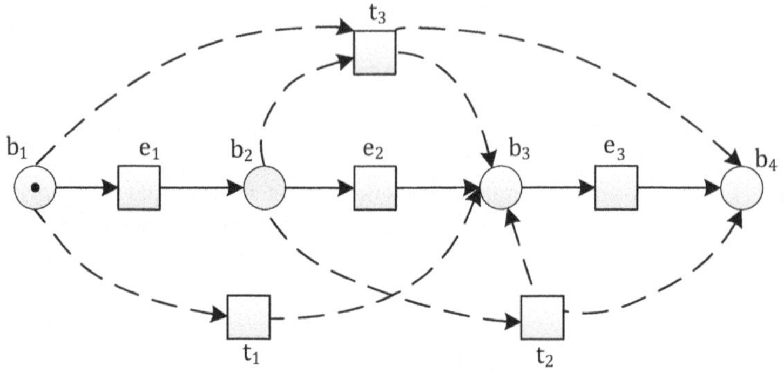

Fig. 13.2 Examples of *CC*, *CN*, *NC*, *NN*

13.1 Classification of Event Items

For C/E-system $\sum = (B, E; F, C)$, *NC* is its set of cases. Let *N* be the set of all those subsets of conditions that are not cases.

Definition 13.2 Classes of Events and Event Items Events and event items may be classified into 4 classes, namely *CC*, *CN*, *NC* and *NN*. Let *t* be an event or event item,

1. $CC = \{t | \exists c, c' \in C : c[t > c'\}$,
2. $CN = \{t | \exists c \in C \wedge c' \in N : c[t > c'\}$,
3. $NC = \{t | \exists c \in N \wedge c' \in C : c[t > c'\}$,
4. $NN = \{t | \exists c \in N \wedge c' \in N : c[t > c'\}$.

Figure 13.2 gives three examples of event items, represented by dotted arrows and dotted boxes. The system has four conditions and four cases. $B = \{b_1, b_2, b_3, b_4\}$, $C = \{\{b_1\}, \{b_2\}, \{b_3\}, \{b_4\}\}$ and $N = \wp(B) - C$, where $\wp(B)$ is the power set of *B*, i.e., the set of all subsets of *B*.

It is clear that

$t_1 \in CC \cap NN$: $\{b_1\}[t_1 > \{b_3\}$ and $\{b_1, b_2\}[t_1 > \{b_2, b_3\}$.

$t_1 \in CN \cap NN$: $\{b_2\}[t_2 > \{b_3, b_4\}$ and $\{b_1, b_2\}[t_2 > \{b_1, b_3, b_4\}$.

$t_3 \in NN$: $\{b_1, b_2\}[t_2 > \{c_3, b_4\}$.

$t_2^{-1} \in NC \cap NN$: $\{b_3, b_4\}[t_2^{-1} > \{b_2\}$ and $\{b_1, b_3, b_4\}[t_2^{-1} > \{b_1, b_2\}$.

For event item $t_4 = (\{b_3\}, \{b_3\})$, which is not included in Fig. 13.2, it does not belong to any one of *CC*, *CN*, *NC*, *NN*.

Definition 13.3
1. Process $= \{t|t \in CC\}$,
2. Violence $= \{t|t \in CN - CC\}$,
3. Fact $= \{t|t \in \overline{CC \cup CN}\}$,
4. Tautology $= \{t|t \in \overline{CC \cup CN \cup NC \cup NN}\}$.

The over bar on top of $CC \cup CN$ is the complement operation: $\overline{CC \cup CN} = T - CC \cup CN$, where T is the set of all events and all event items. So is $\overline{CC \cup CN \cup NC \cup NN}$.

A process consists of the occurrences of one or more event. A violence is the occurrence of an event item that leads a normal case to a non-case, so the system might run into chaos. A fact is an event item that never has a chance to occur at all cases. A tautology is an event item that never has a chance to occur.

13.2 Facts, Proposition, and Reasoning Rules

Facts, or dead event items, are the basis for net logic. As defined by Definition 13.2, dead event item t, ${}^{\cdot}t = \{b_{11}, b_{12}, \cdots, b_{1n}\}$ and $t^{\cdot} = \{b_{21}, b_{22}, \cdots, b_{2m}\}$, gives rise to a true proposition on the underlying C/E-system:

$$b_{11} \wedge b_{12} \wedge \cdots \wedge b_{1n} \rightarrow b_{21} \vee b_{22} \vee \cdots \vee b_{2m}$$

as shown graphically by Fig. 13.1 above. Net logic makes it possible to reason about propositions with graphics.

As a preparation, a graphic presentation of contradiction is needed.

Since

$$\begin{aligned} & b_{11} \wedge b_{12} \wedge \cdots \wedge b_{1n} \rightarrow b_{21} \vee b_{22} \vee \cdots \vee b_{2m} \\ & \equiv \text{true} \wedge b_{11} \wedge b_{12} \wedge \cdots \wedge b_{1n} \rightarrow \text{false} \vee b_{21} \vee b_{22} \vee \cdots \vee b_{2m} \end{aligned}$$

If $n = 0 \wedge m = 0$ in the proposition above:

$$\text{True} \rightarrow \text{False}.$$

So, the graphic representation of contradiction is *a* pure box with a sleeping T inside, since True $\rightarrow$ False $\equiv$ contradiction. The reasoning method to be used is proof by contradiction.

First, some reasoning rules with examples below:

Example 13.1 Reduction

Logic reasoning : $(a \wedge b \rightarrow x) \wedge (x \rightarrow c \vee d) \rightarrow (a \wedge b \rightarrow c \vee d)$.

Graphic reasoning is presented in Fig. 13.3:

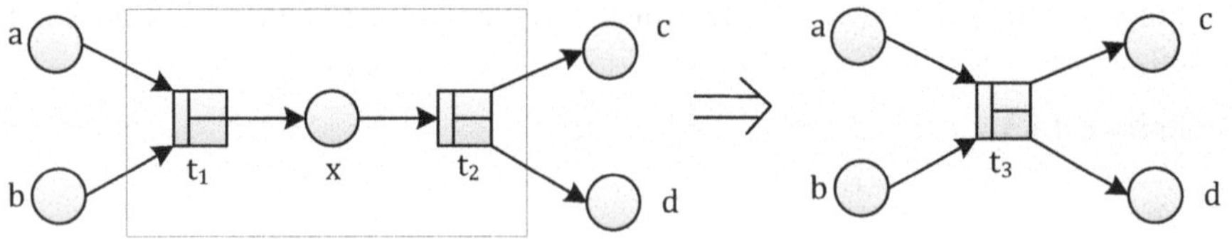

Fig. 13.3 Logic reasoning

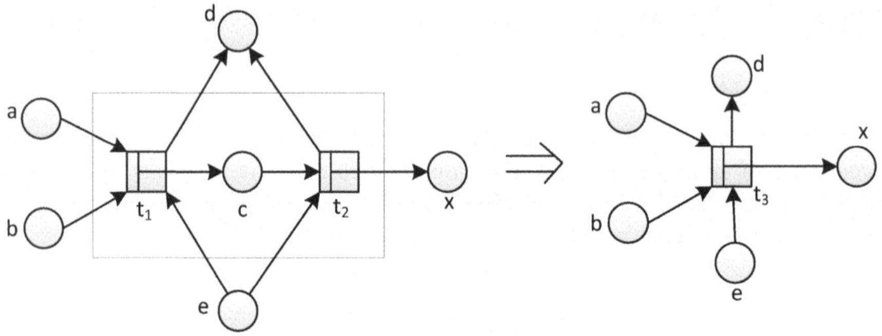

Fig. 13.4 Logic reasoning with shared factor

The special situation of above reduction is $(a \rightarrow b) \wedge (b \rightarrow a) \rightarrow (a \rightarrow a)$ by graphic reasoning. Such reasoning is ineffective since $(a \wedge b \wedge d \rightarrow c \vee e) \wedge (c \wedge d \rightarrow e \vee x) \rightarrow$ is always true. In fact $(a \rightarrow b) \wedge (b \rightarrow a) \equiv a = b$ is a given rule, or given axiom.

Example 13.2 Reduction with Shared Factors Logic reasoning: (d and e are shared by p and q in $p \rightarrow q$)

$$(a \wedge b \wedge d \rightarrow c \vee e) \wedge (c \wedge d \rightarrow e \vee x) \rightarrow (a \wedge b \wedge d \rightarrow e \vee x)$$

Graphic reasoning is given in Fig. 13.4:

Rule 13.1 Resolution Rule
For t_1, $t_2 \in$ Fact and $\{a\} = t_1^{\cdot} \cap {}^{\cdot}t_2$, and t_3 is defined by

$${}^{\cdot}t_3 = {}^{\cdot}t_1 \cup {}^{\cdot}t_2 - \{a\}, t_3^{\cdot} = t_1^{\cdot} \cup t_2^{\cdot} - \{a\}$$

then $t_3 \in$ Fact.

Note that if $\{a\} \subset t_1^{\cdot} \cap {}^{\cdot}t_2$ and $\{a\} \neq t_1^{\cdot} \cap {}^{\cdot}t_2$, then above defined ${}^{\cdot}t_3$ would be impure, i.e., a tautology.

Rule 13.2 Extension
For $t \in$ Fact and $B_1, B_2 \subseteq B$, if t_1 is defined by

$$^{\cdot}t_1 = {}^{\cdot}t \cup B_1 \wedge t_1{}^{\cdot} = t^{\cdot} \cup B_2,$$

Then $t_1 \in$ Fact.
In case $B_1 \cap B_2 \neq \emptyset$, t_1 is impure.

The next sections will talk about how facts are related with various logics.

13.3 Net System and Propositional Logic

It is clear now that every dead event item of C/E-system $\sum$ is a fact about its conditions, and a fact is a true proposition. A true proposition is a property of $\sum$.

Is it possible to have every proposition represented by facts? The answer is definite. The way to do it is in two steps. First to rewrite it into a proposition consisting of logic operators $\wedge$ and $\neg$ only; then to represent it with dead event items.

Let p be a proposition composed of conditions and logic operators $\wedge, \vee, \neg, \rightarrow$ (imply), and $\leftrightarrow$ (equivalent).

$$\begin{aligned} a \vee b &\equiv \neg(\neg a \wedge \neg b), \\ a \rightarrow b &\equiv \neg a \vee b \equiv \neg(a \wedge \neg b), \\ a \leftrightarrow b &\equiv (a \rightarrow b) \wedge (b \rightarrow a) \\ &\equiv \neg(a \wedge \neg b) \wedge \neg(b \wedge \neg a). \end{aligned}$$

So, it is possible to represent a proposition with $\wedge$ and $\neg$.

Let T be the set of events and event items of $\sum$. Event items are obtained by T-completion operation applied on $\sum = (B, E; F, C)$. $T = \{(B_1, B_2) | B_1, B_2 \subseteq B \wedge B_1 \cup B_2 \neq \emptyset\}$. For a given t, $t \in T$, we write $t = (B_1{}', B_2{}')$ if ${}^{\cdot}t = B_1{}'$ and $t^{\cdot} = B_2{}'$.

Theorem 13.1 Facts and Propositions For $t = (B_1{}', B_2{}')$, $t \in$ Fact is equivalent to

$$\neg\left(\left(\wedge_{x \in B_1{}'} x\right) \wedge \left(\wedge_{y \in B_2{}'} \neg y\right)\right) \equiv \text{true}.$$

Proof is not necessary since $t \in$ Fact requires that either at least one condition in its preset $B_1{}'$ is untrue, i.e., $\neg\left(\wedge_{x \in B_1{}'} x\right)$, or at least one condition in its post-set $B_2{}'$ is true, i.e., $\neg\left(\wedge_{y \in B_2{}'} \neg y\right)$. So, $t \in$ Fact and $\neg\left(\left(\wedge_{x \in B_1{}'} x\right) \wedge \left(\wedge_{y \in B_2{}'} \neg y\right)\right) \equiv$ true are two ways to say that t is a dead event item.

Theorem 13.2

1. True proposition of C/E-system $\sum$ can be represented with a set of facts.
2. Tautology of C/E-system $\sum$ is equivalent to impure event item.

Before the proof of the theorem, next is a concrete example.

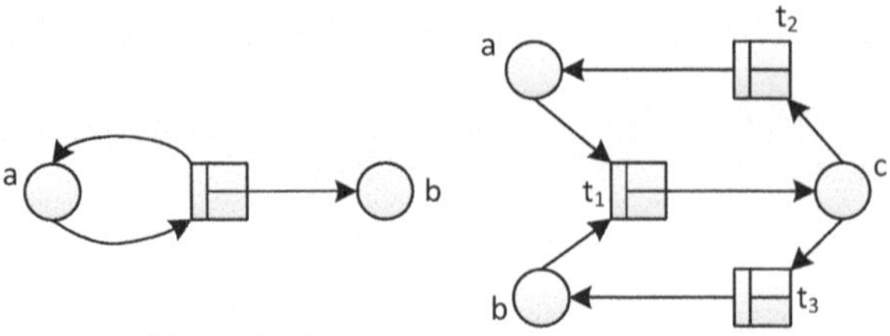

(a) $a \to (b \vee a)$ (b) $(a \wedge b) \leftrightarrow c$

Fig. 13.5 (**a**) Tautology; (**b**) equivalence

Figure 13.5 below includes net presentations. One is a tautology, and the other is an equivalent relation between two propositions.

The dead event item t in (a) is equivalent to $a \to (b \vee a) \equiv$ true; it is a tautology. The net is impure.

The dead event items t_1, t_2 and t_3 are respectively equivalent to $(a \wedge b) \to c$, $c \to a$, $c \to b$. Put them together,

$$t_1 \wedge t_2 \wedge t_3 \quad \equiv (a \wedge b) \to c \wedge c \to a \wedge c \to b$$
$$\equiv a \wedge b \leftrightarrow c$$

Now, to prove the theorem.

Let p be a proposition consisting of conditions and operators $\wedge$ and $\neg$. First, "p is a given true proposition" is graphically equivalent to .

1. If $p \in B$, i.e., p is a condition, then  is a fact;
2. If $p \notin B$ and $p = \neg q$, then ;
3. If $p \notin B$ and $p = q_1 \wedge q_2$, then q_1 and q_2 are both true propositions.

Above steps (2) and (3) are, respectively, given graphically by Fig. 13.6; (a) is for (2) and (b) is for (3).

All dotted lines and circles denote the rest part of facts being processed. To verify that (2) and (3) are effective and correct, two points need to be proved: (3) must terminate and all converting on $\wedge$ and $\neg$ should be correct. Correctness is guaranteed by logical proofs. Termination is definitely true, since every step removes an operator and p contains a finite number of operators only.

Example 13.3 From $p = a \wedge b \leftrightarrow c$ to Facts First step: to rewrite $a \wedge b \leftrightarrow c$ with $\wedge$ and $\neg$.

$$a \wedge b \leftrightarrow c \equiv \neg(a \wedge b \wedge \neg c) \wedge \neg(\neg(a \wedge b) \wedge c) \equiv \neg q_1 \wedge \neg q_2,$$

in which $q_1 = a \wedge b \wedge \neg c$, $q_2 = \neg (a \wedge b) \wedge c$. So, $p = \neg q_1 \wedge \neg q_2$.

Second step:

From 

Third step: to apply operations shown in Fig. 13.6 until only conditions and facts are left. Figure 13.7 is what is so obtained from 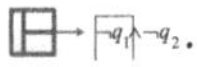.

Finally, to denote the same condition with one circle so as to obtain the fact representation of equivalence relation in Fig. 13.5b.

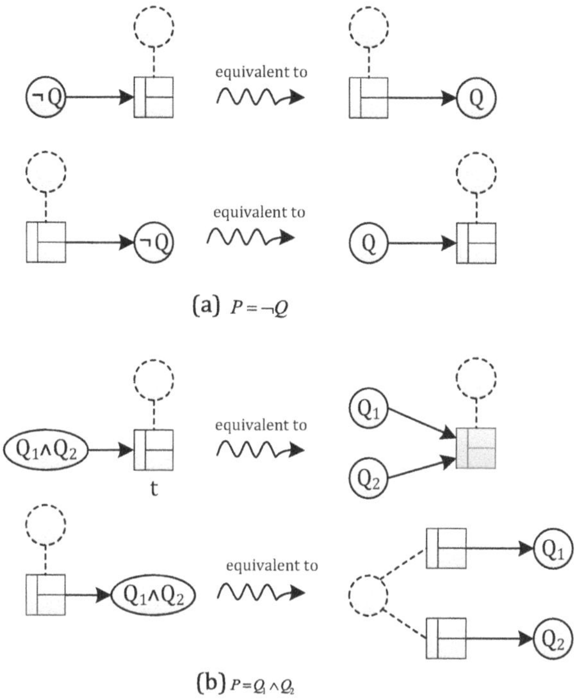

Fig. 13.6 From true proposition to facts

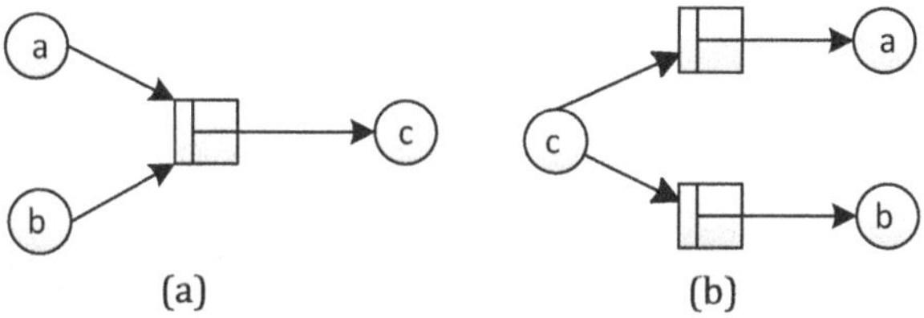

Fig. 13.7 3 facts from $a \wedge b \leftrightarrow c$

Figure 13.8 shows the details of the third step.

It is worthy to mention how to graphically represent propositions $a \vee b \rightarrow c$ and $\neg(a \rightarrow c)$. This is given in Fig. 13.9.

Theorem 13.3 Propositional Calculus in Net The reasoning rule and the extension rule composes a complete consistent propositional calculus in net.

It is complete since all true propositions can be represented with facts, and all new propositions obtainable by propositional calculus in logic can also be obtained by reasoning rule and extension rule, i.e., by proposition calculus in net.

The way to prove q from given p is to prove that $\neg q \wedge p$ leads to contradiction. For example, to prove $\neg(a \rightarrow c) \wedge ((a \wedge b) \rightarrow c)$ leads to contradiction in order to prove $a \rightarrow c$ (a implies c) from $(a \wedge b) \rightarrow c$. Next is the proof, but not by graphical reasoning, since graphical representation of facts and graphical reasoning are not suitable for automatic treatment (AI). Algebraic formulas are better.

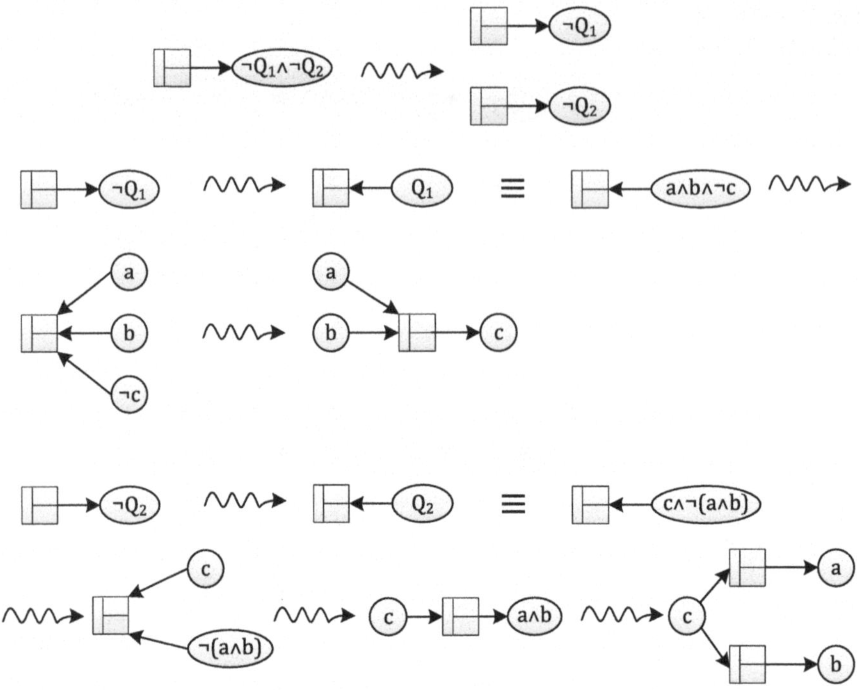

Fig. 13.8 Details of the third step

Fig. 13.9 (**a**) $a \vee b \rightarrow c \equiv a \rightarrow c \wedge b \rightarrow c$, (**b**) $\neg(a \rightarrow c) \equiv a \wedge \neg c$

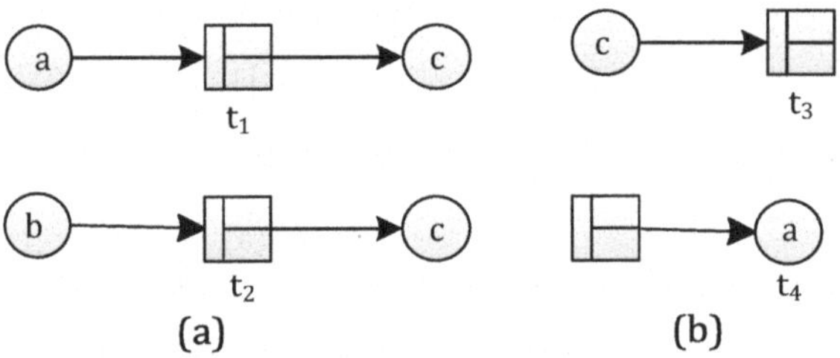

Assume that proposition p is to be proved.

First step: rewrite p until it contains conditions and operators $\neg$ and $\wedge$ in the same way as above.

Second step: Write $l \equiv (p, 1)$ in which I is a matrix and p is the row index.

Third step: if there is a matrix row index that is not a condition, then name this row with x and the element in column i is $l(x, i)$.

1. If $x = \neg q$, then change $\neg q$ to q and $l(x, i) := -1 \times l(x, i)$ for all i, i.e., for all columns.
2. If $x = q_1 \wedge q_2$, then add two rows with q_1 and q_2 as their respective row indexes, and for all i, $l(q_1, i) = 0$ and $l(q_2, i) = 0$. If $l(x, i) = -1$, then $l(x, i) := 0$, $l(q_1, i) := -1$ and $l(q_2, i) := -1$; If $l(x, i) = 1$, then $l(x, i) := 0$, and add a new column

j that is exactly the same as column i, except $l(q_1, i) = 0$, $l(q_1, j) = 1$ and $l(q_2, i) = 1$, $l(q_2, j) = 0$. In case all elements of row x becomes 0, delete row x.

Repeat step (2) until all indexes are conditions in B.

3. Combine all rows with the same index to one new row y. For column j, if all the combined rows has 0 as their elements in column j, then $l(y, j) = 0$. If all rows being combined have 1 as its element at column j, then the new row has 1 as its element at column j. If all rows being combined have -1 as their element at column j, then the new row has -1 as its element at column j. If both 1 and -1 are elements at column j of rows being combined, then the initial p is a tautology, and nothing further is required.

Example 13.4 Find the Matrix for $a \to (b \to a)$ First step: $a \to (b \to a) \equiv \neg (a \wedge b \wedge \neg a)$,

Second step: $l = (\neg(a \wedge b \wedge \neg a), 1)$,

Third step:

$$l = (\neg(a \wedge b \wedge \neg a), 1) \Rightarrow ((a \wedge b \wedge \neg a), -1) \Rightarrow$$

$$\begin{pmatrix} a \wedge b, & -1 \\ & \\ \neg a, & -1 \end{pmatrix} \Rightarrow \begin{pmatrix} a, & -1 \\ b, & -1 \\ \neg a, & -1 \end{pmatrix} \Rightarrow \begin{pmatrix} a, & -1 \\ b, & -1 \\ a, & 1 \end{pmatrix}$$

If there exist 1 and -1 in the same column, it is a tautology.

Example 13.5 Find the Matrix for $a \wedge b \leftrightarrow c$. First step: $a \wedge b \leftrightarrow c = \neg (a \wedge b \wedge \neg c) \wedge \neg (\neg(a \wedge b) \wedge c)$

Second step: $l = (\neg(a \wedge b \wedge \neg c) \wedge \neg (\neg(a \wedge b) \wedge c), 1)$

Third step:

$$l \Rightarrow \begin{pmatrix} \neg(a \wedge b \wedge \neg c) & 0 & 1 \\ \neg(\neg(a \wedge b) \wedge c) & 1 & 0 \end{pmatrix} \Rightarrow \begin{pmatrix} a \wedge b \wedge \neg c & 0 & 1 \\ \neg(a \wedge b) \wedge c & 1 & 0 \end{pmatrix}$$

$$\Rightarrow \begin{pmatrix} a & 0 & -1 \\ b & 0 & -1 \\ \neg c & 0 & -1 \\ c & -1 & 0 \\ \neg(a \wedge b) & -1 & 0 \end{pmatrix} \Rightarrow \begin{pmatrix} a & 0 & -1 \\ b & 0 & -1 \\ c & 0 & 1 \\ c & -1 & 0 \\ a \wedge b & 1 & 0 \end{pmatrix} \Rightarrow \begin{pmatrix} a & 0 & 0 & -1 \\ b & 0 & 0 & -1 \\ c & 0 & 0 & 1 \\ c & -1 & -1 & 0 \\ a & 1 & 0 & 0 \\ b & 0 & 1 & 0 \end{pmatrix}$$

Fourth step: combine the same condition into one row:

$$l \Rightarrow \begin{pmatrix} a & 1 & 0 & -1 \\ b & 0 & 1 & -1 \\ c & -1 & -1 & 1 \end{pmatrix}$$

Careful readers may have noticed that the last three columns of matrix I are exactly the vector representations of the three facts in Fig. 13.5b.

It is not difficult to write a program to do the above steps.

Now, to represent reasoning rules with vectors.

Extension rule:

As a fact of system $\sum$, column vector $(a_1, a_2, \cdots, a_n)^T$ allows arbitrary substitution for 0 in $a_1, a_2, \cdots, a_n$ with 1 or -1 to remain as a fact. Superscript T is the transpose operation.

Resolution rule

For different facts $(\alpha_1, \alpha_2, \cdots, \alpha_n)^T$ and $(\beta_1, \beta_2, \cdots, \beta_n)^T$, if there exists a unique k, $1 \le k \le n$, such that $\alpha_k = -\beta_k \ne 0$, then $(\gamma_1, \gamma_2, \cdots, \gamma_n)^T$ is also a fact, in which $\gamma_k = 0$, and for $i \ne k$,

$$\gamma_i = \begin{cases} \alpha_i \text{ if } a_i = \beta_i \vee \beta_i = 0 \\ \beta_i \text{ if } \beta_i = a_i \vee a_i = 0 \end{cases}$$

Remarks on resolution rule:

In case $\alpha_i \ne 0 \wedge \beta_i \ne 0 \wedge i \ne k$, $\alpha_i = \beta_i$ must be true, since $\alpha_k = -\beta_k \ne 0$ is unique. So, $(\gamma_1, \gamma_2, \cdots, \gamma_n)^T$ is well defined and unique. The uniqueness insures $(\gamma_1, \gamma_2, \cdots, \gamma_n)^T$ not to be a tautology.

Rules given with vectors are suitable for AI to apply.

Theorem 13.4 Effective Reasoning If zero vector is obtained from $p \wedge \neg q$ by above resolution rule and extension rule, then q is a true proposition as long as p is a true proposition.

Proof is simple, since the zero vector means $\neg(p \wedge \neg q)$, and $\neg(p \wedge \neg q) = \neg p \vee q$, so $p \wedge \neg (p \wedge \neg q) = p \wedge (\neg p \vee q) = q$.

As an example, let $p = a \vee b \to c$ and $q = a \to c$. It is not difficult to have

$$p \wedge \neg q = \begin{pmatrix} a, & -1 & 0 & 0 & 1 \\ b, & 0 & -1 & 0 & 0 \\ c, & 1 & 1 & -1 & 0 \end{pmatrix}$$

The matrix from column 2 to column 4 is called the matrix of $p \wedge \neg q$, i.e., the matrix of $(a \vee b \to c) \wedge \neg (a \to c)$. From columns 2 and 4, a new column $(-1, 0, 0)^T$ is obtained by resolution. Add this column to the rear of the matrix as shown below.

$$p \wedge \neg q \Rightarrow \begin{pmatrix} a, & -1 & 0 & 0 & 1 & -1 \\ b, & 0 & -1 & 0 & 0 & 0 \\ c, & 1 & 1 & -1 & 0 & 0 \end{pmatrix}$$

It is easy to notice that the last two columns may be resolved to zero column, and so $q = a \to c$ is proved.

The above vector reasoning is in fact a matrix multiplication, as shown below, to obtain zero vector, in which matrix $(1, 0, 1, 1)^T$ denotes that columns 1, 3, and 4 are each used once in the resolution.

$$\begin{pmatrix} -1 & 0 & 0 & 1 \\ 0 & -1 & 0 & 0 \\ 1 & 1 & -1 & 0 \end{pmatrix} \begin{pmatrix} 1 \\ 0 \\ 1 \\ 1 \end{pmatrix} = \begin{pmatrix} 0 \\ 0 \\ 0 \end{pmatrix}$$

A straight way to find $(1, 0, 1, 1)^T$ from the matrix for $(a \vee b \rightarrow c) \wedge \neg (a \rightarrow c)$ is to solve the quadratic linear equation below:

$$\begin{pmatrix} -1 & 0 & 0 & 1 \\ 0 & -1 & 0 & 0 \\ 1 & 1 & -1 & 0 \end{pmatrix} \begin{pmatrix} x_1 \\ x_2 \\ x_3 \\ x_4 \end{pmatrix} = \begin{pmatrix} 0 \\ 0 \\ 0 \end{pmatrix}$$

Theorem 13.5 Solution Zero Zero vector is derivable from $p \wedge \neg q$ if the linear equation with the matrix of $p \wedge \neg q$ as coefficient has positive integer non-zero solution.

Example 13.6 From $p = (a \rightarrow b) \wedge (b \rightarrow c) \wedge (b \rightarrow d)$, $q = a \rightarrow c \wedge d$ is easy to prove. Next is the vector way to do so.

Let l_1 be the matrix for $\neg q$, $\neg q = \neg (a \rightarrow c \wedge d) = a \wedge \neg (c \wedge d)$.

$$l_1 = (a \wedge \neg(c \wedge d), 1) \Rightarrow \begin{pmatrix} a & 1 & 0 \\ \neg(c \wedge d) & 0 & 1 \end{pmatrix}$$

$$\Rightarrow \begin{pmatrix} a & 1 & 0 \\ c \wedge d & 0 & -1 \end{pmatrix} \Rightarrow \begin{pmatrix} a & 1 & 0 \\ c & 0 & -1 \\ d & 0 & -1 \end{pmatrix}$$

Similarly, l_2 as the matrix of $p = (a \rightarrow b) \wedge (b \rightarrow c) \wedge (b \rightarrow d)$,

$$l_2 = ((a \rightarrow b) \wedge (b \rightarrow c) \wedge (b \rightarrow d), 1) \Rightarrow$$

$$\begin{pmatrix} a & -1 & 0 & 0 \\ b & 1 & -1 & -1 \\ c & 0 & 0 & 1 \\ d & 0 & 1 & 0 \end{pmatrix}$$

To combine l_1 and l_2, obtained is the matrix l for $p \wedge \neg q$.

$$l = (p \wedge \neg q, 1) \Rightarrow \begin{pmatrix} p & 0 & 1 \\ \neg q & 1 & 0 \end{pmatrix} \Rightarrow$$

$$\begin{pmatrix} a & 1 & 0 & -1 & 0 & 0 \\ b & 0 & 0 & 1 & -1 & -1 \\ c & 0 & -1 & 0 & 0 & 1 \\ d & 0 & -1 & 0 & 1 & 0 \end{pmatrix}$$

The second and third columns are the matrix of l_1 and the last three columns are the matrix of l_2. With above matrix (excluding the first column of condition names) as coefficient, the linear equation system with five unknown variables is given below, of which the nonzero positive integer solutions suggest how to resolve to zero vector (contradiction).

$$\begin{pmatrix} a & 1 & 0 & -1 & 0 & 0 \\ b & 0 & 0 & 1 & -1 & -1 \\ c & 0 & -1 & 0 & 0 & 1 \\ d & 0 & -1 & 0 & 1 & 0 \end{pmatrix}\begin{pmatrix} x_1 \\ x_2 \\ x_3 \\ x_4 \\ x_5 \end{pmatrix} = \begin{pmatrix} 0 \\ 0 \\ 0 \\ 0 \end{pmatrix}$$

It's easy to check that $x_1 = x_3 = 2$ and $x_2 = x_4 = x_5 = 1$ is a positive integer solution. Name the five facts represented by the five columns of the matrix with t_1, t_2, t_3, t_4 and t_5, then $x_1 = x_3 = 2$ and $x_2 = x_4 = x_5 = 1$ denotes times of t_1, t_2, t_3, t_4 and t_5 being used in the resolution. The resolution process is: t_1 and t_3 resolve to a fact t_6, t_6 and t_4, t_5 resolve to t_7, t_8, t_2 and t_7, t_8 resolve to $(0, 0, 0, 0)^T$.

Remarks on this section.

1. Every fact corresponds to a nonzero unique vector, as long as it is not a tautology.
2. Every proposition corresponds to one or more facts, as long as it is not a tautology. These facts correspond to a matrix.
3. The first column of the fact matrix is the index column consisting of conditions. This column is necessary, since conditions are not formally ordered (conditions may be named freely to require an explicit ordering).

The concept of dead transitions of C/E-systems may be extended to P/T-systems. Let $\sum = (S, T; F, K, W, M_0)$ be a P/T-system and t a dead transition item. Assume that the preset of t consists of n places and these places contain a_1, a_2, $\cdots$, a_n tokens respectively; The post-set of t consists of m places and these places contain b_1, b_2, $\cdots$, b_m tokens respectively. Besides, the weights on the input arcs of t are u_1, u_2, $\cdots$, u_n, and the weights on the output arcs are v_1, v_2, $\cdots$, v_m. The capacities of the output places are k_1, k_2, $\cdots$, k_m. As such, "t is a dead transition item" is equivalent to a true proposition

$$\neg\big((\forall i : 1 \le i \le n : a_i \ge u_i) \wedge (\forall j : 1 \le j \le m : v_j + b_j \le k_j)\big)$$

Or,

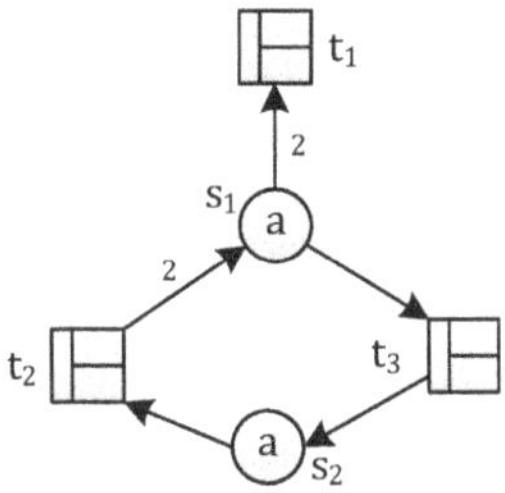

Fig. 13.10 $k(s_1) = 2$, $k(s_2) = 2$, $M(s_1) = a$, $M(s_2) = b$

$$\exists i : 1 \le i \le n : (a_i < u_i) \vee \exists j : 1 \le j \le m : v_j + b_j > k_j.$$

Figure 13.10 has three dead transition items where $k(s_1) = 2$, $k(s_2) = 2$ and $M(s_1) = a, M(s_2) = b$. The three facts tell respectively that $t_1 : a < 2, t_2 : b < 1 \vee a + 2 > 2$ and $t_3 : a < 1 \vee b + 1 > 2$. These three facts may be reduced to $(a = b = 0) \vee (a = 1 \wedge b = 2)$. This may be reduced to $2a = b \wedge a \le 2 \wedge b \le 2$, since $k(s_1) = 2$, $k(s_2) = 2$.

The true proposition $2a = b \wedge a \le 2 \wedge b \le 2$ corresponds to the three facts in Fig. 13.10.

In case the capacity function is a constant $K - 1$, then the token number for every place is in the set $\{0, 1, \cdots, K - 1\}$. Facts of such a P/T-system form a K-value logic. Interested readers may try it.

13.4 Nets and First-Order Predicate Logic

Facts in a Pr/T-system correspond closely to predicate logic.

Predicates are incomplete propositions. The default part is usually the subject. For example, "John is a boy" is a proposition and "is a boy" is a predicate. This predicate is usually written as "x is a boy," where x is a variable. The missing subject comes from a given domain D, so the universal quantifier $\forall$ and the existence quantifier $\exists$ apply. For example, let D be all students in the same class, then$\forall x \in D : boy(x)$, or $\forall x : x \in D \rightarrow boy(x)$, $\exists x \in D : boy(x)$, or $\exists x : x \in D \rightarrow boy(x)$ are all predicates.

Some predicates may have more than one subject missing, that are binary predicates, trilogy predicates, etc. The domains for binary and trilogy predicates are D^2 and D^3, respectively.

Let P, Q be unary predicates, R be a binary predicate and a, b be objects in D. For variables x, y on the domain, transition t_1 with P, Q as input and R as output is dead, if proposition $\neg P(g(x)) \vee \neg Q(b) \vee \neg R(x, b)$ is true, where $g(x)$ is a function from D to D. Dead transition t_2 with R as input and no output is the fact $\neg R(a, y)$. Figure 13.11 is the graphical presentation of instance proposition t_1 and t_2. The two presentations are easy to understand, but they are not conventional Pr/T-system facts.

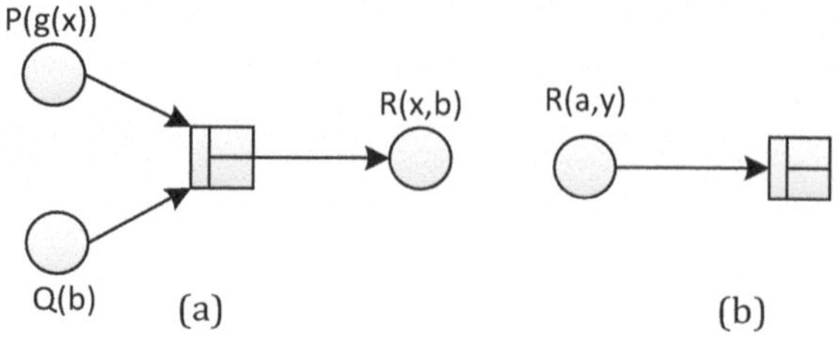

Fig. 13.11 (**a**) $\neg P(g(x)) \vee \neg Q(b) \vee \neg R(x, b)$, (**b**) $\neg R(a, y)$

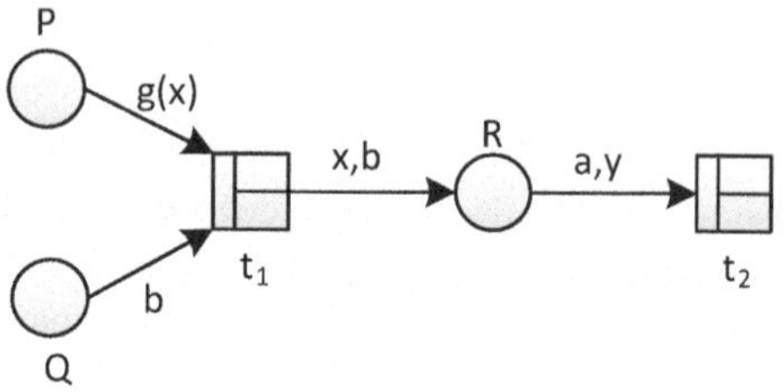

Fig. 13.12 Dead transitions in terms of Pr/T-system

For a Pr/T-system, a place is a dynamic predicate while a transition is a static one. The above instance propositions t_1 and t_2 are represented in terms of Pr/T-system as shown in Fig. 13.12, where symbolic sums on arcs have been written a bit informally to avoid "+" and "<>", so as to simplify the figure. Complete formalism is good for AI, not so good for human readers.

The scope of variables on the arcs of a Pr/T-system is in fact the whole domain of the objects in question, or in other words, they are implicitly confined by universal quantifier "for all x." So the above fact $\neg P(g(x)) \vee \neg Q(b) \vee \neg R(x, b)$ means that $\forall x \in D : (\neg P(g(x)) \vee \neg Q(b) \vee \neg R(x, b))$ is true at all states of the Pr/T-system in question.

Example 13.7 Properties Expressed in Facts The relation "<" has two properties: non-reflexivity and transitivity. The universal quantifier used below is confined to the domain on which "<" is defined.

1. $\forall u : \neg (u < u)$, or $\forall x, y : \neg (x < y) \wedge x = y$
2. $\forall x, y, z : (x < y \wedge y < z) \rightarrow x < z$

In terms of Pr/T-system facts, Fig. 13.13 (a) expresses non-reflectivity, (b) is transitivity, and (c) is a combination of (a) and (b).

The universal quantifier is not necessary to appear for graphically represented facts since variables on arcs are conventionally understood as "for all." The existence quantifier requires the use of a Skolem function. For example, the density of "<" is given by

$$\forall x \forall y : (x \neq y \rightarrow \exists z : (x < z \wedge z < y) \vee (y < z \wedge z < x)).$$

Its paradigm is

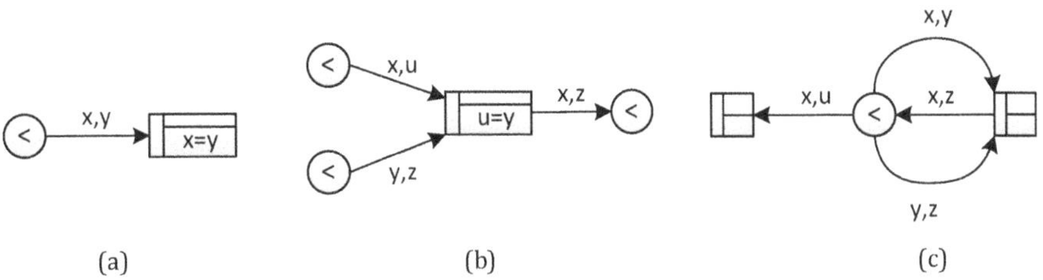

Fig. 13.13 (**a**) Non-reflectivity, (**b**) Transitivity, (**c**) A combination

Fig. 13.14 Density of "<" and $\check{z} = \check{z}(x, y)$

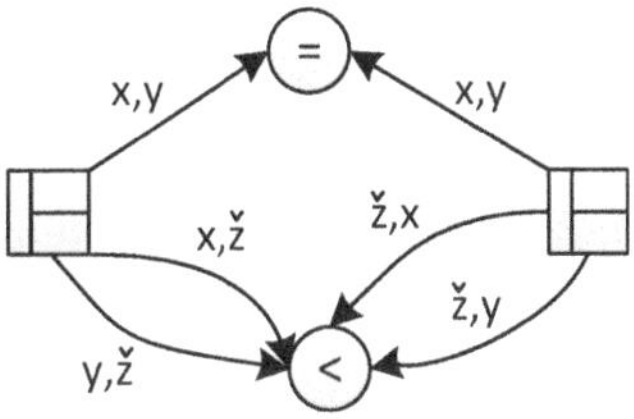

$$\forall x \forall y \forall z : ((x = y \vee x < z \vee y < z) \wedge (x = y \vee z < x \vee z < y)).$$

With Skolem function to remove "∃":

$\forall x \forall y \quad : ((x = y \vee x < \check{z}(x, y) \vee y < \check{z}(x, y))$
$\wedge (x = y \vee \check{z}(x, y) < x \vee \check{z}(x, y) < y)$, in which $\check{z}(x, y)$ is the Skolem function of z. Figure 13.14 is the density of "<" expressed with Pr/T-system facts. So, facts may be used to express knowledge. With rules given below for Pr/T-systems, reasoning about knowledge is feasible.

The resolution rule and extension rule applies to Pr/T-system facts for reasoning.

Extension rule:

An arbitrary predicate may be added to a given Pr/T-system fact as input or output. So obtained is also a fact.

Resolution rule:

Two given facts may be resolved to a new fact if they are respectively in the preset and in the post-set of a unique predicate, and the arc weights are the same.

The same as for proposition logic, if the uniqueness is not true, then the two facts would be resolved to tautology.

Arc weights may require some changes in order to see whether they are the same as required by the resolution rule. Thus, substitution rule is needed.

Substitution rule:

For individuals on an object domain, variables $x_1, x_2, \cdots, x_n$ on an arc may be substituted with objects $e_1, e_2, \cdots, e_n$ at the same time to gain an equivalent fact.

This substitution rule is feasible since arc weights are implicitly confined by the universal quantifier by convention. All appearances of the same name on all input

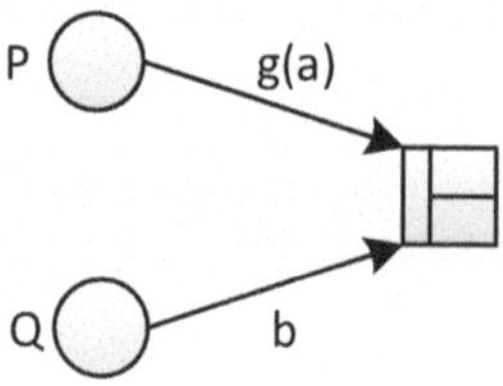

Fig. 13.15 Substitution followed by resolution

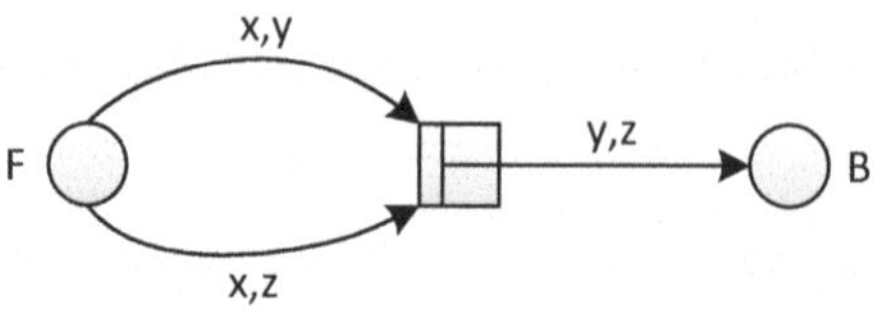

Fig. 13.16 Fact and common sense

and output arcs of the same transition represent either the same object or the same variable. Substitution rule must respect this principle.

Substitution must be applied on weights of all arcs of the same fact, for example, variable x on arcs of fact t_1 in Fig. 13.12 may be substituted with object a. If variable y is on the input arc of fact t_2 in the same figure, then t_1 and t_2 can be resolved to the fact in Fig. 13.15.

The next figure is an abstract fact in which predicates F, B and variables x, y, z may be explained differently. For example, F may be understood as binary predicate "father(u, v)" and B as binary predicate "brother(u, v)". If so, this fact tells that x is the father of y and z (not father-in-law), then y and z must be brothers (Fig. 13.16).

Here, if F in the figure is an asymmetric binary relation and B is a symmetric binary relation, then the fact would tell how these two relations are related. For example, P/T-systems are at a lower level than Pr/T-systems at the net system hierarchy, and they are also at a lower level than the color systems, while Pr/T-systems and color systems are at the same level. That is:

One-level-lower $(A, B) \wedge$ One-level-lower $(A, C) \rightarrow$ At-same-level (B, C).

Facts, or dead transitions, have led to a whole branch of general net theory, i.e., Enlogy. So, it is important not to underestimate things that have no chance to occur. They have their reasons.

The author is not familiar with the logic to be introduced next starting from Sect. 13.5. The purpose to include them in this book is just to show connections between Nets and logic. In case errors (even conceptual errors) are found, please let me know.

13.5 Nets and Modal Logic/Deontic Logic

Model logic (ML) is obtained from proposition logic (PL) by adding two modal prefixes Δ and □. to it. For proposition p, Δp and □.p denote possible p and inevitable p, respectively. Δ and □. follow the next rules:

1. $p \rightarrow \Delta p$
2. $\Delta(p \vee q) \leftrightarrow (\Delta p \vee \Delta q)$
3. $\neg\Delta(p \wedge \neg q)$
4. $[]\cdot p \leftrightarrow \neg \Delta \neg p$
5. $[]\cdot p \rightarrow \Delta p$

The first 4 rules may be considered axioms for modal logic. The fast rule is implied by the first four as given below.

$$\neg p \vee p \xrightarrow{1} \Delta(\neg p \vee p) \xrightarrow{2} \Delta\neg p \vee \Delta p \rightarrow$$
$$\neg\neg\Delta\neg p \vee \Delta p \xrightarrow{4} \neg[]\cdot\ p \vee \Delta p \rightarrow ([]\cdot\ p \rightarrow \Delta p)$$

The digits on top of arrows are above rules applied at that step. PL rules are applied at other steps.

The rule $[]\cdot\ (p \rightarrow q)$ in modal logic is called "strongly implies", denoted by $p \Rightarrow$ (or = $> >$)q.

Theorem 13.6 For C/E-system $\sum = (B, E; F, C)$ and its full reachability relation R on $C \times C$, then (C, R) is a structure frame that satisfies the above rule.

A true proposition p of $\sum$ is inevitable, i.e., $[]\cdot p$, while for $b \in B$, $[]\cdot(\Delta b \wedge \Delta \neg b)$ is true.

Relation R divides the power set of B into two parts: C, the set of all reachable cases, and N, the set of unreachable states. This division brings modal logic to C/E-systems.

Among all cases in C, some are good and some are not so good (bad, or to be avoided). Such a finer division leads to deontic logic (DL). With two prefix operators "!" (must) and "δ" (allowed), axioms are, in addition to ML axioms, given below:

1. $!p \leftrightarrow \neg \delta \neg p$
2. $\delta p \vee \delta \neg p$
3. $\delta(p \vee q) \leftrightarrow \delta p \vee \delta q$
4. $!p \rightarrow \Delta p$
5. $\Delta \neg *$

"$*$" is a deontic constant, denoting a bad case. So, the last axiom tells that a case is possibly not bad, or that not all cases are bad.

With deontic constant $*$, "!" and "δ" may be defined as below:

$$\delta p \leftrightarrow (\Delta p \wedge \neg *)$$
$$!p \leftrightarrow []\cdot\ (\neg p \rightarrow *)$$

It's easy to check that so defined "!" and "δ" satisfy DL axioms.

The meaning of "δp is true at case k, $k \in C$" is that there exists k', $k' \in C$, and $k R k'$ such that p is true at k' and k' is a good case. The meaning of "$!p$ is true at k" is that for all $k' \in C$, if p is not true at k', then k' is not a good case.

The above tells us how nets are related to ML and DL. ML, DL and other logics to be introduced below are not topics to be discussed in this book.

13.6 Nets and Temporal Logic (TL)

Temporal logic is also built up from proposition logic. The added operators are closely related to time progress like "first ⋯ then ⋯".

Note that "first ⋯ then ⋯" is meaningless for C/E-systems with loop structure. Thus, it is assumed that every event and every condition appears in system processes at most once.

Definition 13.4 Information Transfer C/E-system $\sum$ is an information transfer if it has the following properties:

1. $\exists c_1 \in C: \uparrow c_1 = \varnothing \wedge {}^{\cdot}c_1 = \varnothing$
2. $\exists c_2 \in C: \downarrow c_2 = \varnothing \wedge c_2{}^{\cdot} = \varnothing$,

in which $\uparrow c_1 = \{t | t \in E \wedge <t]c_1\}$, i.e., the set of events that are reversely enabled and $\downarrow c_2 = \{t | t \in E \wedge c_2[t>\}$, i.e., the set of events that are enabled by c_2. Note that ${}^{\cdot}c_1$ is the preset of c_1 and $c_2{}^{\cdot}$ is the post-set of c_2. This definition tells that an information transfer has an initial case c_1 and a final case c_2. Figure 13.17 contains two examples of information transfer, where (b) is a transfer with conflict.

$a \vee b \vee c \vee d \vee e \vee f$ is a true proposition of $\sum_2$. With temporal operator "/", their occurring order may be described as: $a/(b/d) \vee (c/e)/f$. There is only one of b and c that may occur no matter how the conflict is resolved. So, $(b/d) \vee (c/e)$ is different from $p \vee q$ in proposition logic, since propositions q and q may both be true. $\triangledown$ is used here in TL as such one-from-two operator:$(b/d) \triangledown (c/e)$. Figure 13.17 provides a visual picture to help understand. / and $\triangledown$ are formally defined in TL by the following axioms.

1. $p \rightarrow (p \triangledown q)$
2. $q \rightarrow (p \triangledown q)$
3. $(p \triangledown q) \rightarrow (p/q) \wedge (q/p)$

Note that p/q does not require q or q to be true. What it says is that if q is true, then it cannot become untrue before q is true.

There are other axioms for TL. They are not listed here since TL is not among our focus.

Let a and b be conditions. With $\wedge$, $\triangledown$ and /, many propositions may be constructed from a and b. Figure 13.18 shows ten equivalent classes of these propositions. In the figure, symbols "$\vdash$" and "$\dashv$" denote "false" and "true", p "$|=$"q tells that p is the logical consequence.

It is hard to understand $(a/b) \wedge (b/a)$ if a/b means "first a, then b". "First a, then b" and "first b, then a" cannot be true at the same time. Is it correct to understand $(a/b) \wedge (b/a)$ as $a \triangledown b$, as suggested by axiom (3) above? Figure 13.19 tells the difference between the two, where $(a/b) \wedge (b/a)$ and $a \triangledown b$ are both true for the first two cases, but $a \triangledown b$ is not true at the third situation. $a \triangledown b$ does not allow both a and b to be true at the same time.

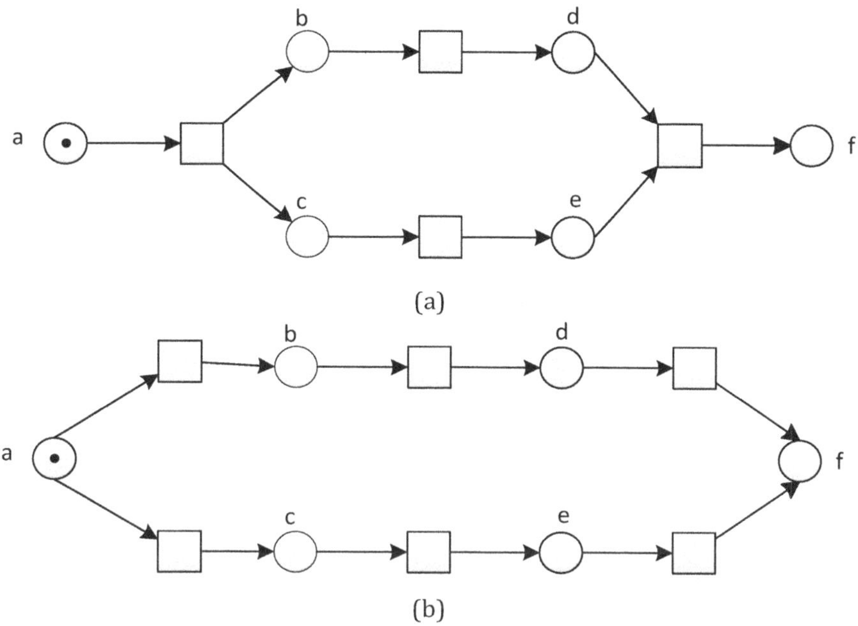

Fig. 13.17 Information transfers

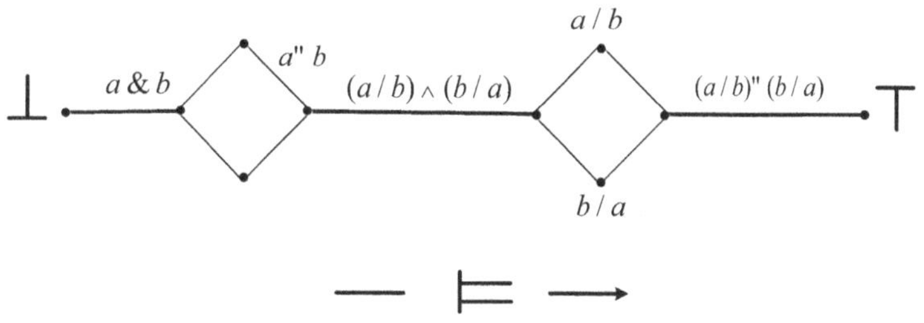

Fig. 13.18 Logical relation of propositions: a lattice

The concept of dual relation is important in Nets. Propositions represent system properties, of that the atomic (smallest) elements are conditions like *a*, *b*, etc. The dual of conditions are atomic changes or atomic plans (to be used for constructing greater plans). Figure 13.18 is a lattice of atomic propositions, and Fig. 13.20 is the dual lattice constructed from atomic plans. Atomic plans *a* and *b* are connected with structure operators /, &, and ∇ to be used by plan designers to tell the plan-executors their duties and their limits of authorities.

For atomic plans *a* and *b*, *a*/*b*: first *a*, then *b*, probably $a \nabla b$: *a* or *b*, the executor has the choice *a* & *b*: *a* and *b*, in parallel $p \supset q$: completion of *p* implies completion of *q* ⊢: a task that can never be done ⊣: trivial task, easier than any *a* or *b*

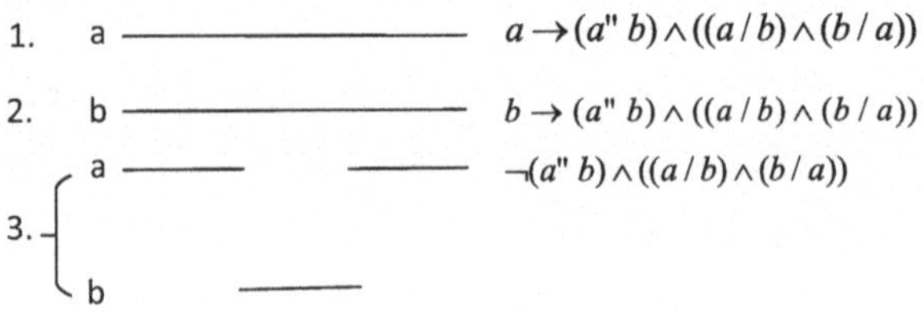

Fig. 13.19 Difference between (*a*/*b*) ∧ (*b*/*a*) and *a* ▽ *b*

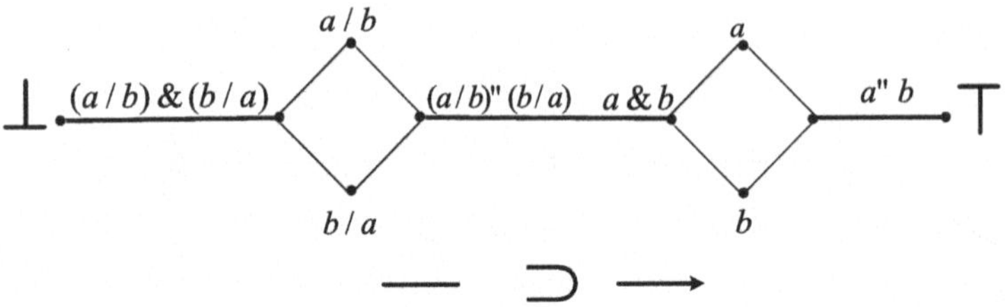

Fig. 13.20 Dual lattice of the proposition lattice

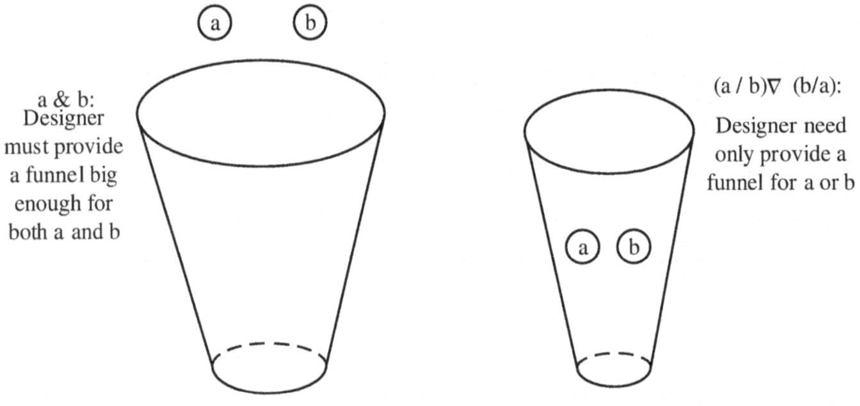

Fig. 13.21 *a* & *b* and (*a*/*b*) ▽ (*b*/*a*)

It would be hard to understand (*a*/*b*) & (*b*/*a*) if *a*/*b* is simply explained as "first *a*, then *b*". "/" does not only set an order between *a* and *b*, it includes certain rights for executor. For example, the executor should be paid after the completion of plan a. The resources needed for plan b must be provided, and so on so forth. If "/" is understood as such, then (*a*/*b*) & (*b*/*a*) is more difficult than *a*/*b*, since (*a*/*b*) & (*b*/*a*) does not have the above rights for "/".

The symbol "– ⊃ →" in Fig. 13.20 indicates the hardness for the plan executor, from being difficult to being easy. From impossible ⊢ to very hard (*a*/*b*) & (*b*/*a*), to easy *a* and *b*, to trivial T. Why (*a*/*b*) ▽ (*b*/*a*) is more difficult than *a* & *b*? The plan designer need only to provide resources for *a* or *b* for (*a*/*b*) ▽ (*b*/*a*), but resources needed by *a* and *b* must be made available for the executor. As indicated by Fig. 13.21, (*a*/*b*) ▽ (*b*/*a*) may run into a deadlock for lack of resources.

What has been described above belongs to the completion theory, the dual of temporal logic. For C/E-systems, events and conditions are dual to each other, thus, the completion theory may be modeled by information transfers (C/E-systems without repeated conditions or repeated events). With the help of C/E-systems, the completion theory may be better understood. Fundamental concepts about decisions and actions might be the basis for pragmatics.

Chapter 14
Information Flow Structure

Abstract A bit of information has three states: being true, false or being absent. This chapter introduces basic information structures that specify how information flows in a closed information system, or how to get into/out. The key point is how to build an information system with basic information structures. Basic structures include P function, Q function and arrow functions.

Information flow structure does not have rich content yet for the time being, hence not qualified to be a branch of general net theory.

By information we mean the value held by a Boolean variable, 1 (true) or 0 (false).

It is assumed that information does not come from nothing and it does not vanish. It comes from some source and it goes into some sink. Information is conservative. A system that is globally conservative must be locally conservative. In terms of nets, every transition or event in an information system must be conservative.

Conflict in a net is an entry point or source since it requires a bit of information from outside. A reverse conflict is an information sink, since it is where missing information goes. Let $\sum = (B, E; F, C)$ be a C/E-system, and $Env(\sum)$ is the environment of $\sum$. Then, information comes from $Env(\sum)$ to $\sum$ at a conflict point and goes out to $Env(\sum)$ at a reverse conflict point.

Conventionally, there are arrow functions to describe how information interacts with each other while it is flowing. These functions are called information flow graph.

Figure 14.1 is an example of information flow in which the net provides a flow structure and an individual token represents a bit of information. In order to make the tokens in s_1 and s_2 flow, conflicts between t_1 and t_2, t_3 and t_4 must be resolved. In case these two conflicts are resolved in favor of transitions t_1 and t_3, then t_{10} and t_{11} would finally be enabled. At this point, it is still possible to trace back how conflicts were resolved. In other words, the two bits of information coming through the source still remain in the net. When conditions s_{10} and s_{11} receive a token each after the firings of t_{10} and t_{11}, the two out-coming bits have vanished. It is impossible to trace back how tokens reached s_{10} and s_{11}.

C. Yuan, *Principle of Petri Nets*, https://doi.org/10.1007/978-981-97-7336-7_14

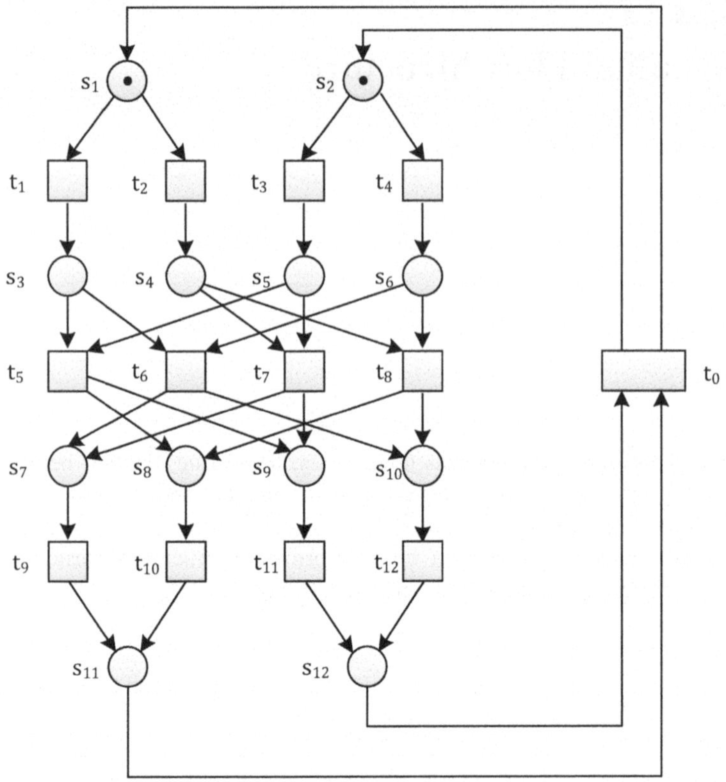

Fig. 14.1 Information flows on a C/E-system

The C/E-system in the figure helps to understand how information flows between $\sum$ and *Env*($\sum$).

14.1 Information Flow Graphs

Information flow graphs tell how information interacts with each other. There are three kinds of basic flow graphs: the first arrow function P_1, the second flow function P_2, and the condition exchange function Q.

Conventionally, P_1 is denoted with $.\!\rightarrow$, P_2 is denoted with $. - . \rightarrow$, and Q is denoted with $\leftarrow \bigoplus \rightarrow$. The meaning of these arrow functions are given by Fig. 14.2 below, in which a, b and c are three one-bit information and arrows are flow directions. Formulas for u compute to the final information after interaction. Information a (P_1), or a and b (P_2 and Q), does not change.

P_1, P_2, and Q are also called information transfers. P_1 has a and b as its input and a and $b \bigoplus a$ as output. P_2 has a, b, and c as input and a, b, and $c \bigoplus a \cdot b$ as output. Q has a, b and c as input and $Q(a, b, c)$, b, and $Q(c, b, a)$ as output. Definitions of

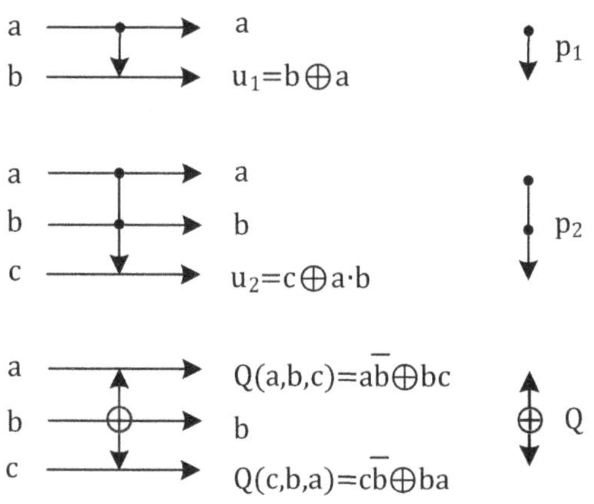

Fig. 14.2 Basic information flow graphs P_1, P_2, and Q

$Q(a, b, c)$, b, and $Q(c, b, a)$ are given in Fig. 14.2. The operator $\oplus$ is exclusive OR, defined by

$$a \oplus b = \begin{cases} 1 \text{ if } a \neq b \\ 0 \text{ if } a = b \end{cases}$$

Proposition 14.1 ***ID*** **= identity**

1. ${P_1}^2 = ID$
2. ${P_2}^2 = ID$
3. $Q^2 = ID$

As an information transfer, *ID* has its input as output; ${P_1}^2$ denotes that information interaction P_1 repeats itself. So are ${P_2}^2$ and Q^2.

The output of P_1 is a and $b \oplus a$. This is taken as the input of the second P_1. So, the output of ${P_1}^2$ is a and $b \oplus a \oplus a = b$.

The output of P_2 is a, b, and $c \oplus a \cdot b$ where a, b, and c are its inputs. So, the output of ${P_2}^2$ is a, b, and $(c \oplus a \cdot b) \oplus a \cdot b = c$. The multiplication operator "·" between a and b will be omitted below. Note that $aa = a$, $\bar{a}\bar{a} = \bar{a}$ and $a\bar{a} = 0$.

The function of Q is to exchange the values in a and c when $b = 1$. So, to exchange twice is the same as no change.

$$Q(a, b, c) = a\bar{b} \vee bc, Q(c, b, a) = c\bar{b} \vee ba,$$
$$Q^2(a, b, c) = Q(Q(a, b, c), b, Q(c, b, a)) = Q(a, b, c)\bar{b} \vee bQ(c, b, a)$$
$$= (a\bar{b} \vee bc)\bar{b} \vee b(c\bar{b} \vee ba) = a\bar{b}\bar{b} \vee bba = a(\bar{b}\bar{b} \vee bb) = a.$$

$$Q^2(c, b, a) = Q(Q(c, b, a), b, Q(a, b, c)) = Q(c, b, a)\bar{b} \vee bQ(a, b, c)$$
$$= (c\bar{b} \vee ba)\bar{b} \vee b(a\bar{b} \vee bc) = c\bar{b}\bar{b} \vee bbc = c(\bar{b}\bar{b} \vee bb) = c.$$

$Q^2 = ID$ is represented as shown in Fig. 14.3.

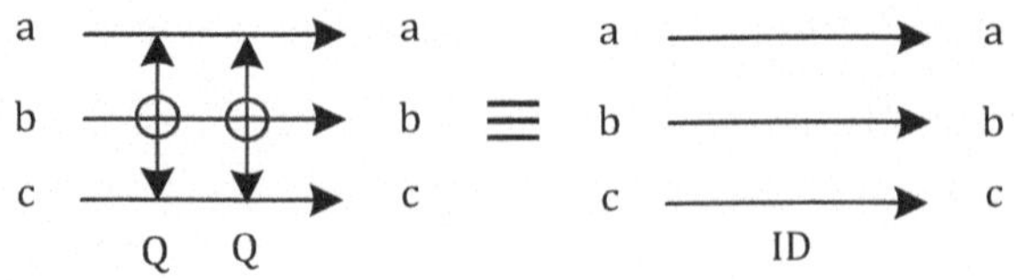

Fig. 14.3 $Q^2 = ID$

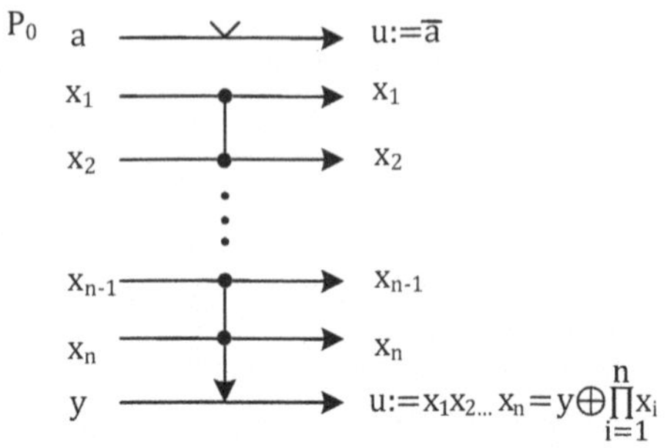

Fig. 14.4 Definition for P_n $(n \geq 0)$

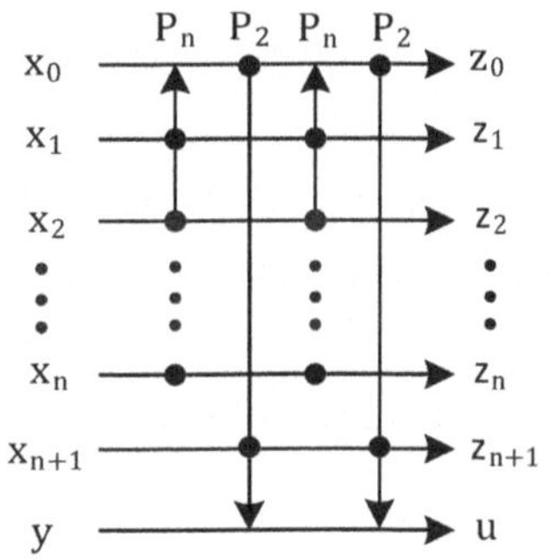

Fig. 14.5 Constructing P_{n+1} from P_2 and P_n

For any positive integer n, $n \geq 0$, the n(th) arrow function is defined as given by Fig. 14.4.

The definition of P_0 in Fig. 14.4 seems not consistent with P_n $(n \geq 0)$. But they are consistent since the output is $u = \overline{a} = a \bigoplus 1$, in which 1 may be understood as $\prod_{i=1}^{0} x_i$.

The next theorem explains why P_1, P_2, and Q are said to be the fundamental information flow graph.

Theorem 14.1 Arrow functions

1. $P_n^{-1} = P_n$
2. P_n may be constructed from P_n and P_2 for $n > 2$.
3. All logic functions $f : 2^n \rightarrow 2^m$ may be constructed from arrow functions.

Proof

1. $P_n^{-1} = P_n$ is equal to $P_n^2 = ID$.
2. Figure 14.5 explains how to construct P_{n+1} from P_2 and P_n.

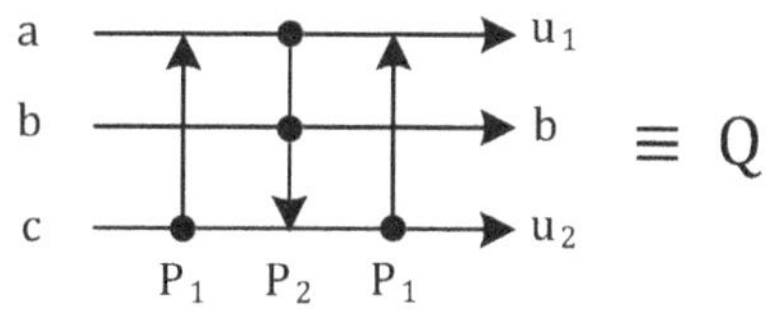

Fig. 14.6 Constructing Q with P_1 and P_2

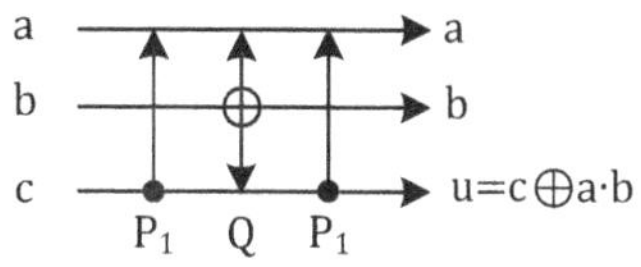

Fig. 14.7 Constructing P_2 with P_1 and Q

This is a recursive construction. The flow line of x_0 has been acted upon twice by P_n, and it finally remains unchanged. Lines for x_i, $i = 1, 2, \cdots, n + 1$ remain unchanged as well since no information has acted on them. So $z_i = x_i$, $i = 1, 2, \cdots, n + 1$. Line y has been acted upon twice by P_2. For the first time, $x_0 \bigoplus \prod_{i=1}^{n} x_i$ on line x_0 and information x_{n+1} act on y, so the information on line y becomes

$$y \bigoplus \left(x_0 \bigoplus \prod\nolimits_{i=1}^{n} x_i\right) x_{n+1} = y \bigoplus x_0 x_{n+1} \bigoplus \prod\nolimits_{i=1}^{n+1} x_i$$

After the first-time action, information on line x_0 has been back to x_0. So, it is x_0 and x_{n+1} that act on line y. The output u on line y is

$$U = \left(y \bigoplus x_0 x_{n+1} \bigoplus \prod\nolimits_{i=1}^{n+1} x_i\right) \bigoplus x_0 x_{n+1} = y \bigoplus \prod\nolimits_{i=1}^{n+1} x_i$$

This is exactly the function of P_{n+1}. The recursive construction of P_{n+1} in Fig. 14.5 is correct.

The proof of the third part of the theorem is a bit too complicated to fill in here. The proof of "all logic functions $f : 2^n \to 2^m$ may be constructed from arrow functions" may be done in two steps: first consider $n = m$, then, for $n \neq m$, to insert f into $f' : 2^k \to 2^k$, $k = \text{maximum}(n, m)$. Information split and information merge may play an important role in doing so. Note that the concept of constant information (i.e., 1 or 0) is important. Lines of 0 or 1 are information carriers needed for information flow.

Figures 14.6 and 14.7 are examples of constructing logic functions with arrow functions. Function Q is constructed in Fig. 14.6 with P_1 and P_2.

Line a in Fig. 14.6 is acted upon twice by P_1. The final information after the first P_1 is $u_1 = a \bigoplus c$. Final information on line c is u_2 and input information to P_2 is $a \bigoplus c$ from line a and b from line b, respectively. So $u_2 = c \bigoplus (a \bigoplus c)b = c \bigoplus ac \bigoplus cb = c(1 + b) \bigoplus ab = c\bar{b} \bigoplus ab = Q(c, b, a)$. This is the final information on line c. This information acts (second time of P_1) with $a \bigoplus c$ on line a to obtain

$$
\begin{aligned}
u_1 &= Q(c,b,a) \bigoplus \left(a \bigoplus c\right) = \left(c\bar{b} \bigoplus ab\right) \bigoplus \left(a \bigoplus c\right) \\
&= c\left(\bar{b}+1\right) \bigoplus a(1+b) = cb \bigoplus a\bar{b} \\
&= Q(a,b,c)
\end{aligned}
$$

With $u_1 = Q(a,b,c)$ and $u_2 = Q(c,b,a)$, Fig. 14.6 is correct. As such, Q may be excluded from being a fundamental information flow function. But it provides convenience to keep it as a fundamental function. Besides, P_2 may be constructed from P_1 and Q as shown in Fig. 14.7. So, another choice is to exclude P_2 from being fundamental.

The proof of correctness of Fig. 14.7 is similar to the proof of Fig. 14.6. It is not repeated here. Readers may try it, if interested.

This section talked about functions of P_1, P_2, and Q. The next section is about how to implement them with nets.

14.2 Net Representation of Information Flow Functions

What is needed is to construct P_1 and Q with nets since P_2 may be implemented with them. As P_0, it is equivalent to "$\neg$". Since $\neg a = 1 \bigoplus a$, P_0 may be constructed from p_1 with constant information 1 and information a as inputs.

P_1 is equivalent to modulo two addition. Figure 14.8 is a rough design of P_1, just to notify that P_1 is a transition with a and b as inputs and $a \bigoplus b$ as the wanted output.

It is critical how a one-bit information is expressed. Is it true that information a is just a condition in C/E-net: a token denotes value 1, and no token denotes value 0. But this is untrue. A hardware bit is either 1 or 0, but an information bit has three states: apart from being 1 or 0, no value is also a possible state. So, one-bit information must be expressed with two conditions: a token in one condition denotes 1 and a token in the other condition denotes 0. If there is no token in both of them, then there is no information. These two conditions as a whole are called an information station. A station has a fact as its property $\neg(a = 1 \wedge a = 0)$ for station a.

Now, the inputs to P_1 are two pairs of conditions: $a = 1$ or $a = 0$, $b = 1$ or $b = 0$. There 4 possible interactions form these two pairs to decompose P_1 into 4 transitions. The complete net structure for P_1 is given by Fig. 14.9.

The net structure of P_1 consists of input slice (Z slice) and output slice (Q slice) as shown in Fig. 14.10. The input slice is the fore half (4 input conditions plus

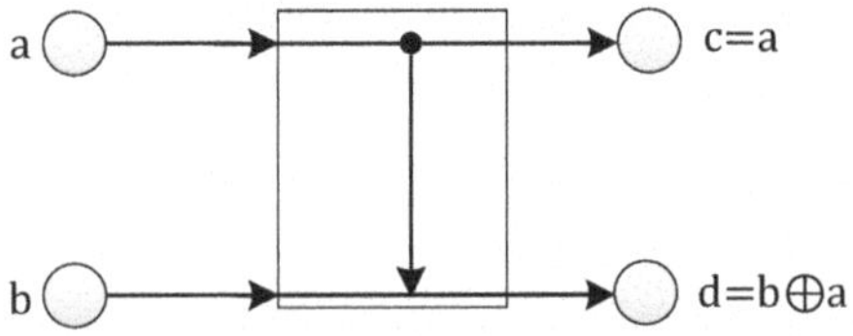

Fig. 14.8 P_1 is a transition

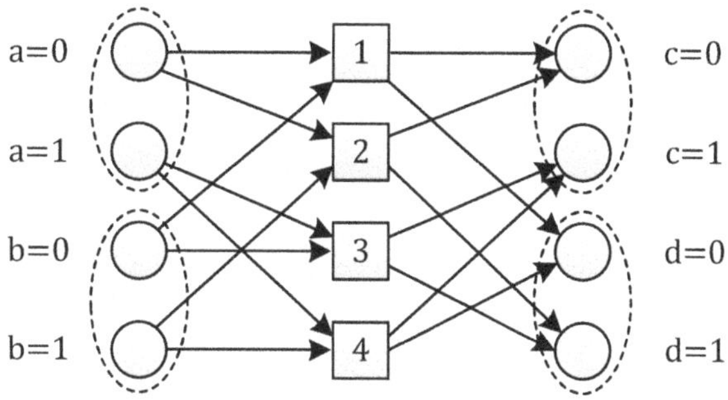

Fig. 14.9 The net structure of P_1

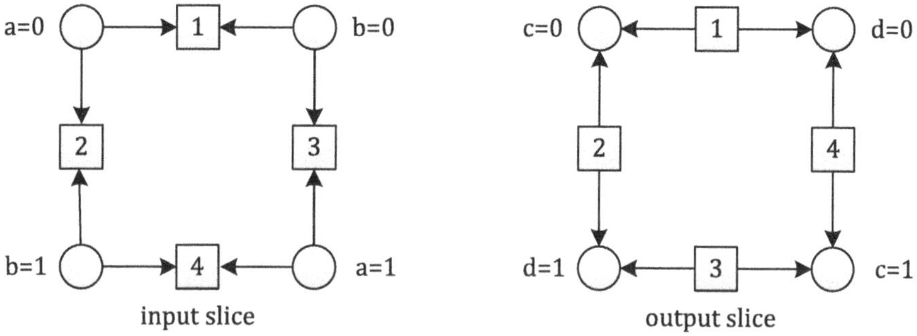

Fig. 14.10 Input slice and output slice

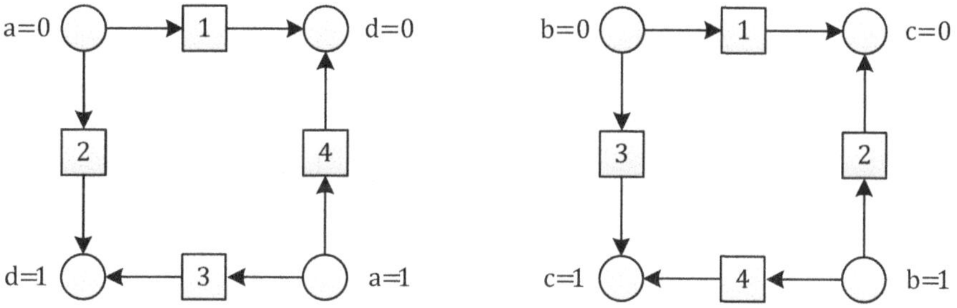

Fig. 14.11 One-bit noise channel

4 transition), while the output slice is the post half (4 transitions plus 4 output conditions).

Another way to decompose the net structure of P_1 is to let each part contain one input station and one output station as shown by Fig. 14.10. These two parts are called one-bit noise channel (Fig. 14.11).

Figure 14.12 is the net structure of Q function, in which a, b, c are input, d, e, f are output, and $d = Q(a, b, c), f = Q(c, b, a)$. Condition b' and e' are two names of the same condition; they consist of a close ring in the net.

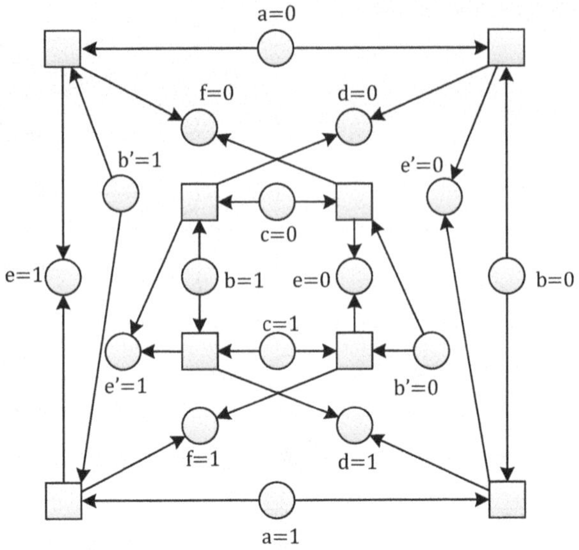

Fig. 14.12 Net structure of Q

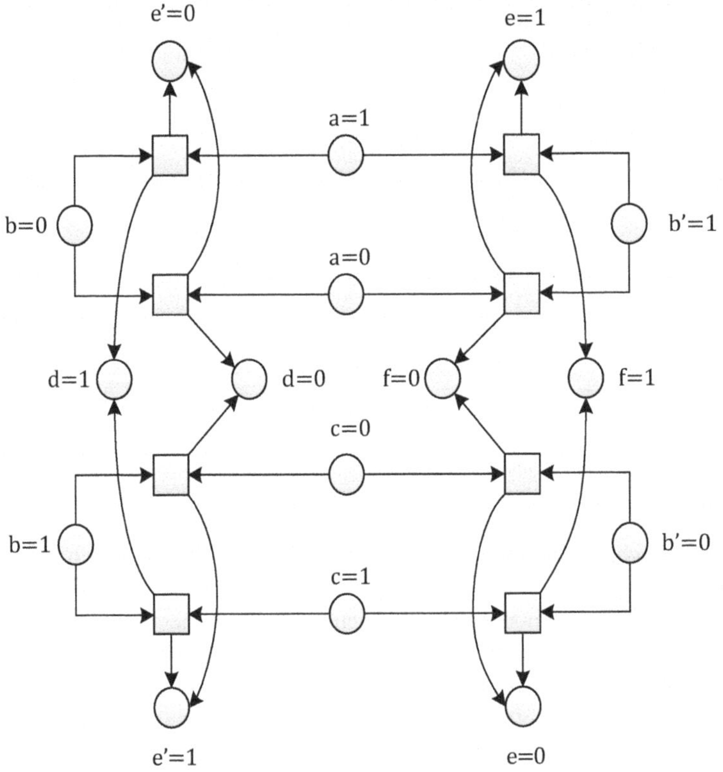

Fig. 14.13 Every saddle is a noise channel

Fig. 14.14 Information station

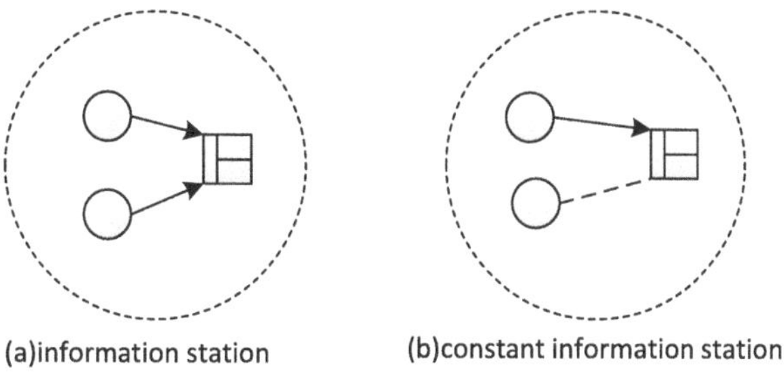

The net structure of Q may be decomposed into 4 one-bit noise channels. In order to see the decomposition clearly, the net of Q is drawn differently in Fig. 14.13, in which every saddle shaped part is a noise channel.

The following proposition is true since both P_1 and Q may be constructed from noise channels.

Proposition 14.2 Noise channel and logic operation

All bit computing (logic operation) may be expressed with noise channels.

This proposition suggests that it is possible to take noise channel as the unique function unit for building computer systems. For such computer systems, software migration would be easy, since it is done by net morphism (to be introduced in the chapter on net topology).

Figure 14.14 shows the inner structure of an information station with the help of dead transitions.

Nets for information flow graph are called information flow nets. They provide interface between net theory and other disciplines.

14.3 Examples

Concepts of formation flow and information interaction provide a way of systematic thinking and to find solutions to some problems that are seemingly difficult.

Example 14.1 Given that prisoner P is detained alone in a room. The room has two exits guarded by soldier A and soldier B. One of the exit leads to freedom and the other exit leads to being hanged. One of A and B is a truth teller to yes/no questions while the other one is a liar. Now, P is allowed to ask A or B just one yes/no question, and based on the answer from the soldier, he may choose an exit to leave. Certain questions are not allowed. For example, to ask B the question "if I ask A 'the exit behind you leads to freedom, yes or no?', what would be the answer from A?"

Readers may try it, if interested. Just don't take it as a puzzle.

There are two bits of information here: the exit and the guard. Let T and F be the information of the guard to be asked, L and D be the information of the exit behind this guard. The only possible interaction between these two bits of information has

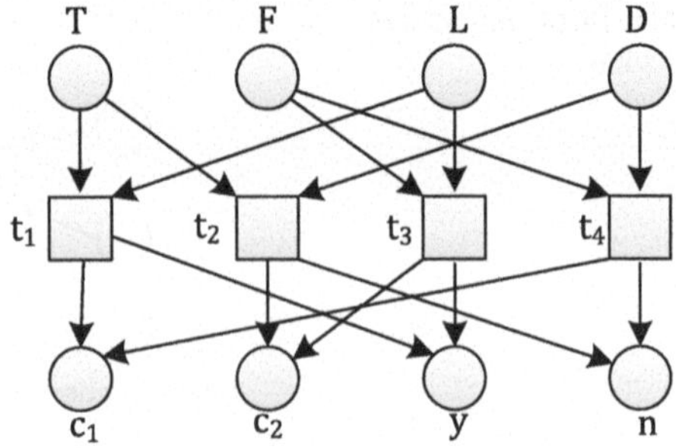

Fig. 14.15 The only way of information interaction

been analyzed and given in Fig. 14.9. Figure 14.15 is the same net explained differently. It provides hints to us: condition c_1 comes from (T, L) or (F, D), c_2 from (T, D) or (F, L). Thus, conditions c_1 and c_2 represent only two physical combinations between exit and guard: either T is guarding exit L and F guarding D, or, If A is asked whether (F, D) is true, the answer would be:

$$\begin{cases} \text{yes if } A = T \text{ and } (T, D), \text{the free exit is behind him} \\ \text{no if } A = F \text{ and } (T, D), \text{the free exit is behind B} \end{cases}$$

$$\begin{cases} \text{no if } A = T \text{ and } (T, L), \text{the free exit is behind } B \\ \text{yes if } A = F \text{ and } (T, L), \text{the free is exit behind him} \end{cases}$$

So, if the answer is yes, go out from the exit behind him, if the answer is no, go out from the exit behind B.

There are 4 questions to be asked: (T, D) ? (T, L) ? (F, D) ? (F, L)?

It is the idea of information flow nets that helps.

Example 14.2 Dinning Table Three friends are sitting at a round table in a restaurant. Given that one of them is a liar, one is a true teller and the last one is a normal person, sometimes tells the truth, sometimes tells a lie. How to figure out who is who with three yes/no questions?

This problem seems to have nothing to do with Example 14.1. But they are closely related. Here is just some hint.

"A is sitting on the left of B" is comparable to "A is guarding t exit B". An eater (person) may play the role of an exit.

Chapter 15
Net Topology

Abstract Topology on a set is defined, in conventional mathmetics, with axioms that require the set to have as many elements as real numbers. Net topology is defined by modified axioms to let a finite set enjoy continuity. A system model for real application is often finite.

The topological structure of a space is the basis to distinguish continuity and discrete. Conventionally, the cardinality of a continuous space must be $\aleph$, that is the number of elements in the set $\{u | 0 < u < 1\}$. Net systems in real applications are usually finite. Net topology is a modified topology aiming at introducing the concept of continuity into nets. And as such, continuous math and discrete math are no longer so far apart.

As said earlier in this book, all physical objects, including the human body, are, on the one hand, composed from a finite number of articles or cells, and on the other hand, continuous. Thus, being finite and being continuous are more reasonable than continuity $=> \aleph$.

15.1 Conventional Topology

Let X be a space of points, $P(X)$ be the power set of X. The power set of X consists of all subsets of X.

Definition 15.1 Axioms of Topological Space The ordered pair (X, θ) is a topological space, if

1. $\theta \subseteq P(X)$, i.e., θ is a set of subsets of X.
2. $\varnothing \in \theta \wedge X \in \theta$,
3. $\forall A \in P(X) : (\cup_{a \in A} a) \in \theta$, that is, the union of an arbitrary number of elements in θ (A is a subset of θ) is also an element of θ,

C. Yuan, *Principle of Petri Nets*, https://doi.org/10.1007/978-981-97-7336-7_15

4. $\forall A \in P(\theta) : (|A| < \infty \rightarrow (\cap_{a \in A} a) \in \theta)$, that is, the intersection of a finite element in θ is also an element of θ.

An element of θ is called an open set of (X, θ), or simply an open set of X.

Different θ (set of open sets) of X are different topologies. For example, $\theta_1 = \{\varnothing, X\}$ and $\theta_2 = P(X)$ are two topologies (assuming $|X| > 1$). A meaningful topology is between the two.

In the definition below, $a \in P(X)$ and $\overline{a} = X - a$. $B = \{b | b \in \theta \wedge a \cap b = \varnothing\}$ is the complementary set of a.

Definition 15.2 Basic Concepts

1. Set a is an open set if and only if $a \in \theta$.
2. Set a is close set if and only if $\overline{a} \in \theta$.
3. $cl(a) = X - \cup_{b \in B} b$, in which $B = \{b | b \in \theta \wedge a \cap b = \varnothing\}$ is the closure of a. It is the complementary set of the union of all open sets that do not intersect with a. Or in other words, it is the smallest close set that contains a.
4. If $a \in \theta \wedge \overline{a} \in \theta$, then a is said to be isolated.
5. If $y \in cl(a)$, y is an aggregate point of a.
6. Denote $\{x\}$ with $\dot{x}$, if $y \in cl(\dot{x})$, then y at x. Note that "*at*" is a binary relation: $at \subseteq X \times X$.
7. Points x and y are isotopes if and only if no open set contains x or y alone.
8. For topological spaces (X, θ) and (X', θ'), mapping $f : X \rightarrow X'$ is continuous if and only if $a' \in \theta' \rightarrow f^{-1}(a') \in \theta$, in which $f^{-1}(a') = \{x | f(x) \in a'\}$, that is the set of reverted images of elements in a'.

The above two definitions are based on number axis. As such, the following properties are implied.

1. Total order: number axis is a totally ordered set.
2. Density: For points x and y on the axis, $x \neq y \rightarrow \exists z : x < z < y$.
3. The cardinality of number axis is $\aleph$.
4. Every singleton is a close set.

These properties are a bit apart from application. More useful concepts refer to partial order and finite sets. The following are properties required for real applications.

1. Partial order or cyclic partial order, not total order.
2. Not dense by Dedekind cut.
3. Finite cardinality or countable infinity.
4. Not all singletons are close sets; otherwise, there would be no difference between close sets and open sets.

Net topology must consider the above 4 properties.

15.2 Net Topology

Let X be a set of points, (X, θ) is a net topology if

1. $\theta \subseteq P(X)$,
2. $\varnothing \in \theta \wedge X \in \theta$,
3. $\forall A \in P(\theta) : (\cup_{a \in A} a) \in \theta$,
4. $\forall A \in P(\theta) : (\cap_{a \in A} a) \in \theta$,
5. $\forall x \in X : \dot{x} \in \theta \bigoplus \bar{\dot{x}} \in \theta$.

The main difference between conventional topology and net topology is the above fourth property. Net topology allows the union of an arbitrary number of open sets to be open set. While for conventional topology, only the union of a finite number of open sets is open set. The last property tells that a singleton $\dot{x}$ may be either an open set, or a close set, but not to be open and close at the same time.

By the way, a topology that fulfils conditions 1 to 4 is called an elementary topology, and a topology that fulfils conditions 1, 2, 3, and 5 is called a primitive topology.

A net is directed. Remove all arrowheads, and a net becomes an indirect net. The above-defined topology is named net topology since such a topological structure is equivalent to the structure of indirect net. Net topology is also called Petri topology.

Definition 15.3 Indirect Net (X, P) is an indirect net if

1. $X \neq \varnothing$,
2. $P \subseteq X \times X$,
3. $dom(P) \cup cod(P) = X$,
4. $dom(P) \cap cod(P) = \varnothing$,

In which $dom(P) = \{x | \exists y : (x, y) \in P\}$ and $cod(P) = \{y | \exists x : (x, y) \in P\}$.

Proposition 15.1 From Direct Net to Indirect Net For direct net $(S, T; F)$, let be $X = S \cup T$ and $P = \{(x, y) | (x, y) \in F \cup F^{-1} \wedge x \in S\}$, then (X, P) is an indirect net.

Proof Since $x \in S$, $dom(P) = S$ and $cod(P) = T$. The equality comes from the fact that a net has no isolated element. By definition of net, the last two conditions of Definition 15.3 are true.

Proposition 15.2 Indirect Net and Net Topology

1. For indirect net (X, P), let be $\theta = \{a | a \in P(X) \wedge a = P^{-1}(a) \cup a\}$, then (X, θ) is a net topology, in which $P^{-1}(a) = \{x | \exists y \in a : (x, y) \in P\}$.
2. For net topology (X, θ), let be $P = \{(x, y) | \dot{x} \in \theta \wedge \bar{\dot{y}} \in \theta \wedge \forall a \in \theta : y \in a \rightarrow x \in a\}$, then (X, P) is an indirect net.

Proof First to prove the first conclusion. From the definition of indirect net, $dom(P) \cap cod(P) = \varnothing$. Let be $S = dom(P)$ and $T = cod(P)$. From the definition of P^{-1}, $P^{-1}(a)$ contains only S-elements. If all elements in a are S-elements, then $P^{-1}(a) = \varnothing$. If there is T-element t, $t \in a$, then $P^{-1}(a)$ contains all T-elements being connected to t. With these hints, it is easy to conclude that the set θ defined with P^{-1} satisfies the definition of net topology.

Next to prove the second conclusion. What is required to be proved is that $dom(P) \cup cod(P) = X$ and $dom(P) \cap cod(P) = \varnothing$.

From the definition of P and condition 5 in the definition of net topology, $dom(P) \cap cod(P) = \varnothing$ is a direct conclusion.

Assume that $dom(P) \cup cod(P) = X$ is not true, then there is $x, x \notin dom(P) \cup cod(P)$. From condition 5 of net topology, $\dot{x} \in \theta$ or $\bar{x} \in \theta$.

If $\dot{x} \in \theta$, then for all $y \in X$ and $y \neq x$, let be

$$a(y) = \begin{cases} \dot{y} & \text{if } \underline{\dot{y}} \in \theta \\ a & \text{if } \dot{y} \in \theta \end{cases}$$

From $\bar{y} \in \theta$ and the definition of P, there exists $a \in \theta$ such that $y \in a \wedge x \notin a$. This a is the a in the definition of $a(y)$ above. So, from condition 3 of net topology, $(\cup_{y \neq x} a(y)) \in \theta$. But $x \notin a(y)$, so $\bar{x} = \cup_{y \neq x} a(y)$, that is $\bar{x} \in \theta$. This contradicts $\dot{x} \in \theta$.

Similarly, contradiction may be derived from $\bar{x} \in \theta$ and $x \notin dom(P) \cup cod(P)$.

So, $dom(P) \cup cod(P) = X$ is true by reduction to absurdity.

Proposition 15.2 tells that indirect net and net topology are equivalent. An indirect net implies a net topology and a net topology leads to a structure of indirect net.

As said before, a net must have at least two elements. Otherwise, $\dot{x} \in \theta \oplus \bar{x} \in \theta$ would be impossible.

15.3 Net Morphism

The focus in this section is net topology. Whenever indirect net is mentioned, it is the indirect net structure constructed from net topology as given by Proposition 15.2.

Lemma 15.1 Continuous Mapping For net topology (X, θ) and (X', θ'), mapping $f: X \to X'$ is continuous if for any $a \in P(X)$, $x \in X$ is an aggregate point of a, then $f(x)$ is the aggregate point of $f(x)$. That is

$$x \in cl(a) \to f(x) \in cl(f(a)),$$

in which $f(a) = \{x' \mid \exists x \in a : f(x) = x'\}$.

Proof Mapping f is continuous, so $\forall a' \in \theta' : f^{-1}(a') \in \theta$. For x, an aggregate point of a, if $f(x)$ is not an aggregate point of $f(a)$, then, by definition, $\exists a' \in \theta' : a' \cap f(a) = \varnothing \wedge f($-$a' \in \theta' : a' \cap f(a) = \varnothing \wedge f(x) \in a'$. *Since* f *is continuous,* $f^{-1}(a') \in \theta$, *and since* $f(x) \in a'$, $x \in f^{-1}(a')$. *From* $f(f^{-1}(a')) = a'$, *we have* $a \cap f^{-1}(a') = \varnothing$, *since otherwise* $f(x) \cap a' \neq \varnothing$, *contradicting the property of* a. *Now,* $x \in f^{-1}(a')$, $f^{-1}(a') \in \theta$, *and* $a \cap f^{-1}(a') = \varnothing$. *These contradict the given condition that* x *is an aggregate point of* a. *So,* f(x) *must be an aggregate point of* f(a).

Proofs will not be given for propositions and theorems below, since this book is aimed mainly at practitioners. There are simple methods to check, from graphical

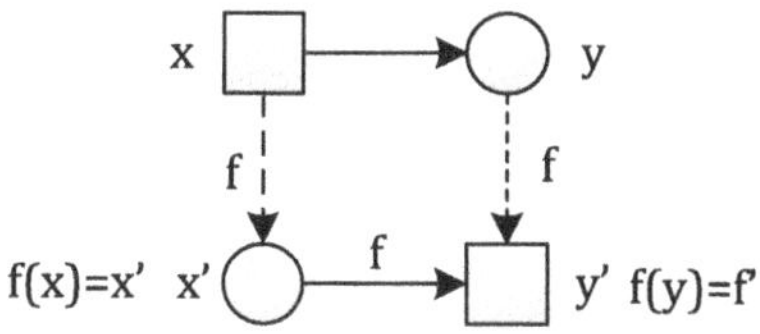

Fig. 15.1 $F \cup ID$ is preserved, $P \cup ID$ is not

representations of nets, whether a mapping is continuous. The methods will be given after necessary definitions.

Lemma 14.2 Closure

$\forall x \in X : cl(\dot{x}) = \{y|(x, y) \in P\} \cup \dot{x}$,

in which $cl(\dot{x})$ is the closure of $\dot{x}$, or, the set of all aggregate points of $\{x\}$.

This lemma is the basis for the proof of the next theorem. In what follows, ID is the identity mapping for all space.

Theorem 15.1 $P \cup ID$ preserved For continuous mapping $f : X \rightarrow X'$ from (X, θ) to (X', θ'),

$$\forall x, y \in X : (x = y \vee (x, y) \in P \rightarrow (f(x) = f(y) \vee (f(x), f(y)) \in P'))$$

Theorem 15.2 Necessary and Sufficient Condition The necessary and sufficient condition for mapping $f : X \rightarrow X'$ to be continuous is that $P \cup ID$ is preserved by f.

Definition 15.4 Net Morphism For direct nets $(S, T; F)$ and $(S', T'; F')$, mapping $f : S \cup T \rightarrow S' \cup T'$ is a net morphsim if and only if f is continuous, and $P \cup ID$ is preserved. That is, $(x, y) \in F \cup ID \rightarrow (f(x), f(y)) \in F' \cup ID$.

Proposition 15.3 Mapping $f : S \cup T \rightarrow S' \cup T'$ is a net porphsim if and only if f preserves both $P \cup ID$ and $F \cup ID$.

It is true that for direct net, $\forall x' : x' \in X' \rightarrow \exists x \in X : f(x) = x'$ is uniquely defined by F. But the reverse is not true. Many direct nets may share the same P. Figure 15.1 is an example to show the difference between preserving $P \cup ID$ and preserving $F \cup ID$. There are two simplest nets with $\{x, y\}$ and $\{x', y'\}$ as their respective element sets, and they are dual with each other. The dotted vertical lines define the mapping f. It is easy o see that $(y, x) \in P$, $(f(x), f(y)) = (x', y') \in P'$, but $(f(y), f(x)) = (y', x') \notin P'$. $F \cup ID$ is preserved while $P \cup ID$ is not.

Next, the simplest methods to check whether a mapping is a net morphism.

Proposition 15.4 Local Morphsim For direct nets $(S, T; F)$ and $(S', T'; F')$, mapping $f : S \cup T \rightarrow S' \cup T'$ is a net morphsim if and only if f has the dotted arrows as its consisting part as shown in Fig. 15.2.

To make it more precise, if the solid arrows with "f" attached are given part of mapping f, then the dotted arrows with "f" attached must be consisting part of "f". Otherwise, f is not a net morphsim. A net morphsim has three situations (a), (b), and (c). If only situation (a) is found from mapping f, the f is called a folding.

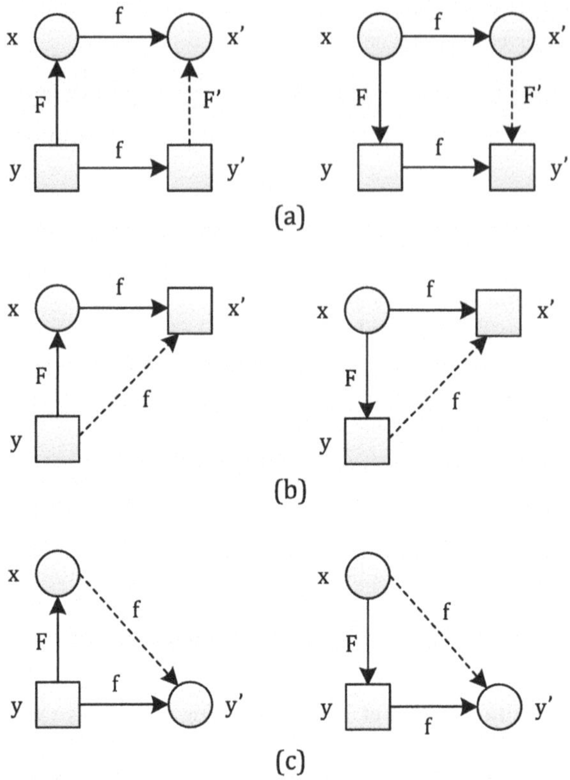

Fig. 15.2 Local situations of net morphsim

Definition 15.5 Folding Mapping *f* is a folding if and only if *f* has *F* and *P* reserved. That is, $(x, y) \in F \rightarrow (f(x), f(y)) \in F$, $(x, y) \in P \rightarrow (f(x), f(y)) \in P$.

A folding does not allow the start and the head of the same arrow to be mapped to the same point. So, (b) and (c) in Fig. 15.2 are not folding.

There are several kinds of net morphisms in net theory. For direct nets $(S, T; F)$ and $(S', T'; F')$, mapping $f: S \cup T \rightarrow S' \cup T'$ is classified as below:

1. If $\forall x' : x' \in X' \rightarrow \exists x \in X : f(x) = x'$, then *f* is an onto-morphism,
2. If $\forall x, y \in X : x \neq y \rightarrow f(x) \neq f(y)$, then *f* is an injection,
3. $\forall a \in \theta : f(a) \in \theta'$, then *f* is an open morphism, $\forall a \in \theta : f(X - a) \in \theta \rightarrow (X' - f(a)) \in \theta'$, then *f* is a close morphism,
4. If $f(S) \subseteq S', f(T) \subseteq T', f(F) \subseteq F'$ and $f(P) \subseteq P'$, then *f* is an isoporphism. If f is an onto morphism and is also an injection, then *f* is an isomophism.
5. If the image of *f* and $(S, T; F)$ are isomorphic, then *f* is a sub-net injection.

The function of Net topology is to have the concept of continuity extended to finite space, so the gap between pure math and applied math vanishes.

There are still other concepts in net topology. Interested readers may find them in the literature.

Chapter 16
Concurrency

Abstract Concurrency is not the same as being at the same time. Concurrency is not transitive while being at the same time is. Examples are given here to show cases where two points are concurrent with the same point while they are themselves ordered.

Readers who are not interested in theory are suggested to skip this chapter. The only important point is: concurrency is not transitive. It is not the same as "at the same time."

It is no exaggeration to say that there would be no computer science without concurrency, let alone billions of computers, high-performance computing, etc.

Concurrency is very important, but many do not really understand it. A widely accepted saying is "two events, say a and b, are concurrent (or parallel) if their occurring order does not change the consequence."

For a black box, the relation between its input and output is considered as included as part of consequence. For a scientific computation like solving a differential equation, solution is the consequence. But, for many other applications, the concept of "consequence" is not so simple and clear.

First, what is an event? Is it an atomic action? If not, and $a \neq b$, then there exist different intermediate states for a and b. Is "consequence" related to these intermediate states? Even if a and b are atomic actions, the difference between an event and event occurrence should be clearly distinguished. The same event may occur more than once. There are examples earlier in this book that different occurrences of a and b are ordered as well as in parallel at different times.

Second, concurrency is a relation without transitivity. Examples can also be found in this book.

Axioms to be presented below was proposed by Prof. Petri in the year 1979 first, and then revised in the year 1986. Concurrency axioms are axioms on occurrence nets. Let $(B, E; F)$ be an occurrence net, and $X = B \cup E$. Let "$<$" be the ordering relation among elements in X. $x < y$ denotes that x and y are connected by arrows.

C. Yuan, *Principle of Petri Nets*, https://doi.org/10.1007/978-981-97-7336-7_16

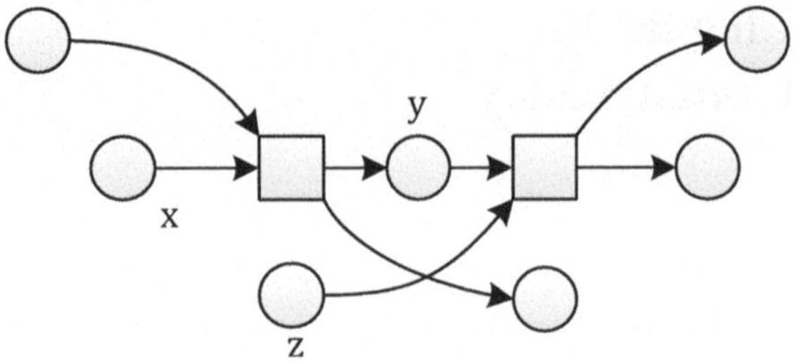

Fig. 16.1 *co* is not transitive

"<" is a strict partial order, transitive but not reflexive. That is $(< \subseteq X \times X) \wedge (< \cap Id = \varnothing) \wedge (<^2 \subseteq <)$.

To better understand axioms on concurrency, just keep in mind a concrete occurrence net, so all axioms are no longer just formulas.

For strict partial order relation, an unordered relation co is implied as given by Definition 16.1.

Definition 16.1 Unordered Relation

$$x \; co \; y :\Leftrightarrow x, y \in X \wedge \neg(x < y) \wedge \neg(y < x),$$

or equivalently, $co : < \bar{\cup} >$.

Note that ":⇔" reads as "defined by" and ":=" reads as "identically equal." The over bar is the operator for complement operation: $< \bar{\cup} > = X \times X - (< \cup >)$.

Relation co is a reflexive symmetric relation as given by the first three axioms below.

$$|X| > 1 \quad \text{Nontrivial} \tag{16.1}$$

$$Id \subseteq co \quad \text{Reflexive} \tag{16.2}$$

$$co = co^{-1} \quad \text{Symmetric} \tag{16.3}$$

where $co^{-1} = \{(x, y) | (y, x) \in co\}$. co^{-1} is a similarity relation.

Definition 16.2 Order-relation

$$li := < \cup Id \cup >$$

"*li*" is called the order-relation deduced from <. It may be defined by $li = \overline{co} \cup Id$. The *li* defined totally ordered set is called a line. The relation *co* on a line is transitive since it is degenerated to Id.

Relation *li* is also a similar relation, and

$Id \subseteq li$, $li = li^{-1}$, $li \cap co = Id$, $li \cup co = X \times X$.

It is not possible that *X* is a line, since a line would degenerate to a single point. As said earlier in this book, *co* is not transitive, that is $co^2 \subseteq co$ is not true. $co^2 - co \neq \varnothing$.

Let points x and y be on the same line, i.e., $(x, y) \in li$, and *z* is a point on a different line. Then it is possible that $(x, z) \in co$ and $(y, z) \in co$ as shown by Fig. 16.1.

Relation *co* is a bit similar to "not distinguishable" in daily life. For example, as far as height is concerned, students A and B are not distinguishable, and students B and C are also not distinguishable, but A and C may be apparently different.

There are properties of *co* that are transitive.

Let be $Co(x) = \{y|\,(x, y) \in co\}$. *Co* is the set of points that are in relation *co* with *x*. If $x \neq y$, but $Co(x) = Co(y)$, then *x* and *y* are not distinguishable by *co*. Such a relation is denoted with "$\tilde{co}$", so, $x\ \tilde{co}\ y :\Leftrightarrow Co(x) = Co(y)$. $\tilde{co}$ is the transitive kernel of *co*. In the study of *co*, all points that are not distinguishable from *x* are considered as the same point of *x*. That is $Co(x) = Co(y) \rightarrow x = y$. Put as an axiom, we have

$$\tilde{co} = Id, \tag{16.4}$$

$$\tilde{li} = Id, \tag{16.5}$$

$$\tilde{co} = \tilde{li}. \tag{16.6}$$

This is the axiom of irreducibility.

In which $\tilde{li}$ is similar to $\tilde{co}$. $Li(x) = \{y|\,(x, y) \in li\}$, $x\ \tilde{li}\ y :\Leftrightarrow Li(x) = Li(y)$.

These axioms ensure $|X| > 1$. Note that Axioms (16.4) and (16.5) are implied by (16.6). Axioms are not Independent with each other, so that axioms can be better understood. If *X* consists of lines that do not intersect, then each of the lines would degenerate to a point each by (16.4), these points then would degenerate to one point by (16.5). So, *X* must be lines that intersect.

Let be $co^* = co^0 \cup co^1 \cup co^2 \cup \cdots = \cup_{n=0}^{\infty} co^n$, where $co^0 = Id$.

Similarly, $li^* = li^0 \cup li^1 \cup li^2 \cup \cdots = \cup_{n=0}^{\infty} li^n$, where $li^0 = Id$.

$$co^* = X \times X, \tag{16.7}$$

$$li^* = X \times X, \tag{16.8}$$

$$co^* = li^*, \tag{16.9}$$

This is the coherent axiom.

For an arbitrary pair $(x, y) \in X \times X$, one of $x\ co^*\ y$ and $x\ li^*\ y$ must be true. From (16.9), the other must also be true. (16.7) tells that (X, co) is continuous: any two points are "connected" by invisible "*co*" lines.

Figure 16.2 shows the smallest structure that fulfils axioms (16.1) to (16.9).

The structure in Fig. 16.2 cannot be further simplified. Besides, the order relation from *li* to $<$ is decided by the order between just one pair. For example, from $x < y$, it must be that $v < y$ and $v < u$, since otherwise relation *li* and *co* would be altered. Such an order relation is called natural order, and the corresponding *co* is called natural disorder.

$$(X, co) \text{ is a natural disorder.} \tag{16.10}$$

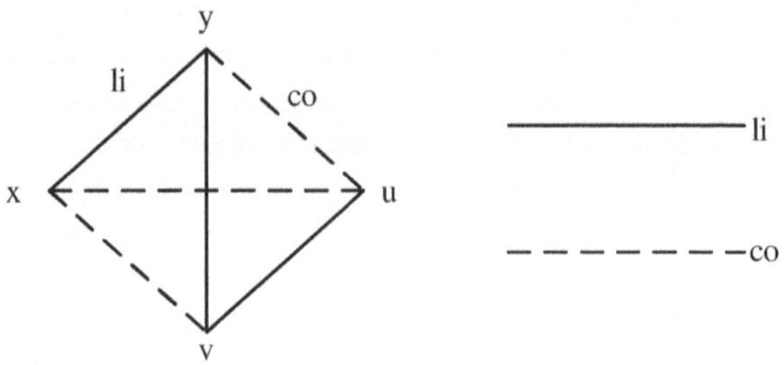

Fig. 16.2 Smallest structure for (16.1) to (16.9)

The order relation $\bar{co}$ is uniquely decided by the order of any two different points. Thus, *co* is very fundamental.

Let *r* be a binary relation on *X*, that is $r \subseteq X \times X$, $a \subseteq X$.

$$Ken(a, r) :\Leftrightarrow \left(\forall x, y \in a : (x, y) \in r \cup r^{-1} \cup Id\right) \\ \wedge \left(\forall x \notin a \exists y \in a : (x, y) \notin r \cup r^{-1} \cup Id\right)$$

So, *Ken*(*a*, *r*) is true if and only if a is the maximum set whose element pairs are in relation *r*. Let *Kens*(*r*) be the set of all sets whose element pairs are in relation $r : Kens(r) \coloneqq \{a | Ken(a, r)\}$.

To substitute *r* with *co* and *li*, the concepts *cut* and *line* are defined.

Definition 16.3 ***cut* and *line***

$$cut(c) :\Leftrightarrow Ken(c, co),$$

$$line(l) :\Leftrightarrow Ken(l, li).$$

If *cut*(*c*) is true, *c* is called a cut on *X*; If *line*(*l*) is true, *l* is a line on *X*. A line is the trace left by a token (signal or a bit of information) in the process recorded by this occurrence net, while a cut is a snapshot in the course of the process. Every line and every cut must intersect, otherwise the snapshot is not complete. So, $cut(c) \wedge line(l) \rightarrow c \cap l \neq \emptyset$. This a kind of density of (*X*, *co*), called K-density, is denoted by $K-$ dense (*X*, *co*).

Definition 16.4 K-dense

$$K - \text{dense}(X, co) :\Leftrightarrow \text{cut}(c) \wedge \text{line}(l) \rightarrow c \cap l \neq \emptyset. \\ K - \text{dense}(X, co). \quad (16.11)$$

The structure in Fig. 16.2 is not dense(*X*, *co*), since $\{x, u\}$ and $\{y, v\}$ are respectively a cut and a line, but they do not intersect. To make the structure K-dense, a point *z* must be added such that $\{z, x, u\}$ is a cut and $\{z, y, v\}$ is a line. This is local property of *X*. If all such local structures of *X* do have a point *z* each, then (*X*, *co*) is N-dense.

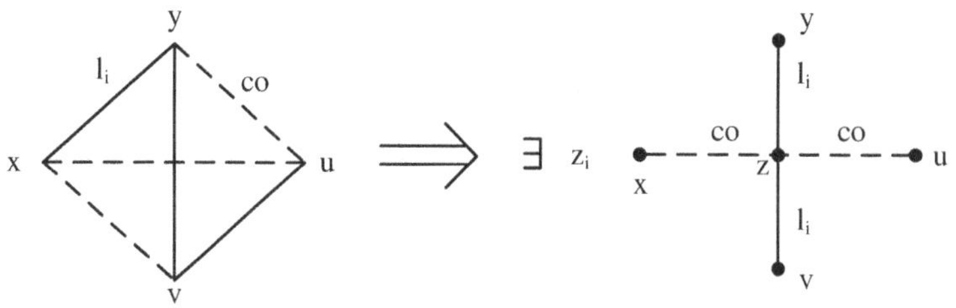

Fig. 16.3 N-dense: definition

Definition 16.5 N-dense

$N-\text{dense}(X, co) :\Leftrightarrow \forall x, y, u, v \in X:$

$((x\ li\ y) \wedge (y\ li\ v) \wedge (v\ li\ u) \wedge (x\ co\ u) \wedge (x\ co\ v) \wedge (y\ co\ u))$

$\rightarrow (\exists z \in X : (x\ co\ z) \wedge (z\ co\ u) \wedge (y\ li\ z) \wedge (v\ li\ z))$

This definition is as shown in Fig. 16.3.

$$N-\text{dense}(X, co). \tag{16.12}$$

(X, co) is not only globally K-dense but also locally N-dense. K-dense in fact implies N-dense. When all cuts of X are finite subsets of X, N-dense is equivalent to K-dense.

If all lines that go through x go also through y, then y is a cluster point of x, denoted by $x\ Cl\ y$. Cl is reflective as well as transitive. Let

$$x\ Cl\ y :\Leftrightarrow x, y \in X \wedge Li(x) \subseteq Li(y),$$
$$Cl(a) = \{y | \exists x \in a : x\ Cl\ y\},$$

$Cl(a)$ is the set of all cluster points in a. In terms of topology, $Cl(a)$ is the closure of a, i.e., the smallest close set that contains a. (X, Cl) is called fundamental topology. It becomes T_0 topology, if P and G are defined as below.

Definition 16.6 $P := Cl - Id,\ G := P \cup P^{-1}$

The relation $x\ P\ y$ denotes that signal x must start or end at a point on a line of y.

$$P^2 = \varnothing, \tag{16.13}$$

$$G^* = X \times X. \tag{16.14}$$

If any two lines of X have two crossing points, then there must be a splitting point between the two crossing points, since otherwise the two segments between the two crossing points would degenerate to just one point. But X cannot be simplified further. That is to say, $x\ P\ y \rightarrow\ \nexists z : y\ P\ z$ (such z is a crossing point). Or in other words, $dom(P) \cap cod(P) = \varnothing$.

Similarly, it is true that $dom(P) \cup cod(P) = X$.

Note that *cod*(*P*) is the set of all points that is a crossing point, and *dom*(*P*) is the set of all points that are not a crossing point. For occurrence nets, all T-elements are crossing points and all S-elements are not crossing points. Thus, for

$S := dom(P)$ and $T := cod(P)$,

$(S, T; P)$ is an indirect (by (16.13)) and connected (by (16.14)) net. So, *P* is the indirect mapping obtained from flow *F* of a direct net. Two direct nets may be obtained from (X, co), i.e., $(S, T; F)$ and $(S, T; F^{-1})$. *S* and *T* are as given above from *P*, and since *co* is a natural unordered relation, the whole order relation on *X* is decided by the order between two points. Thus, there are just two possible order relations on *X*. The directions of these two orders are opposite. These two structures are occurrence nets with the following properties.

$$\forall s \in S : | {}^{\cdot}s | = | s^{\cdot} | = 1$$

$$\wedge \forall t \in T : | {}^{\cdot}t | > 1 \wedge | t^{\cdot} | > 1 \qquad \text{by (16.13)}$$

$$\wedge \forall s_1, s_2 \in S : ({}^{\cdot}s_1 = {}^{\cdot}s_2 \wedge s_1{}^{\cdot} = s_2{}^{\cdot}) \rightarrow s_1 = s_2 \qquad \text{by (16.14).}$$

Since $P^2 = \varnothing$, if $x \ P \ y$, then *x* and *y* are neighbor points. $G = P \cup P^{-1}$ is a neighboring relation. Let $Vic = \{y | x \ G \ y\}$ be the set of neighbors of *x*. $x \notin Vic(x)$ by definition of *P*.

$$co^2 \subseteq co \text{ is true in } Vic(x) \text{ for all } x \text{ in } X. \qquad (16.15)$$

$$\overline{co}^2 \subseteq co \wedge \overline{co}^2 \neq \varnothing \text{ in } Vic(x) \text{ for all } x \text{ in } X. \qquad (16.16)$$

There are two neighbor points on every *x* line (*x* line is a line of which *x* is a point), one before *x* and one after *x*. All points before *x* are pairwise concurrent, and so are all points after *x*. A point before *x* and a point after *x* are ordered (they are in relation $\bar{co}$). Equation (16.15) is the transitivity of *co* in *Vic*(*x*). So all neighbors of *x* are classified into two *co* equivalent sets: one before *x* and one after *x*. (X, co) does not tell which of these two sets is before *x* and which is after *x*. But it needs one point to be fixed as before or after *x*, the positions of all others are fixed. Equation (16.15) tells that points in *Vic*(*x*) are locally orientable: there are exactly two possible directions to choose.

Cl' is the corresponding relation of *Cl*:

$$x \ Cl' \ y :\Leftrightarrow Co(x) \subseteq Co(y).$$

Cl' is transitive and reflective. The difference between Cl' and *Cl* is: $Cl \subseteq li$, $Cl' \subseteq co$.

Similar to *P* and *G*, *D* and *H* are defined by

Definition 16.7 $D := Cl' - Id$, $H := D \cup D^{-1}$.

$$D^2 = \varnothing, \tag{16.17}$$

$$D^2 = P^2, \tag{16.18}$$

$$H^* = X \times X. \tag{16.19}$$

It is easy to prove

$$x\ D\ y \rightarrow (\forall c : cut(c) \wedge x \in c \rightarrow y \in c) \wedge x \neq y.$$

Thus, D is a strict "implies" relation inside every cut. Since $cod(D) \subseteq dom(P)$, $dom(P) = S$, if $x\ D\ y$, then x must be a point for signal interacting, not a state element. So, "implies" is not a correct saying. The right way is "x is the detail of y." Figure 16.4 shows that x and y are in the same cut.

As shown in the figure, x is an interacting point. When it is hard to conclude what is happening in $Vic(x)$, y is true. That is why y is the detail of x. $H^* = X \times X$ tells that every point of X is either itself a detail, or detail of some other point. So, every t in T has an S-point as its accompany (recall the four-season system and accompany elements of seasons).

The last three axioms are about continuity (no gap, no jump). To keep it simple, these axioms are given with $(X, <)$.

Equation (16.20) is cone intersect property (CIP). The set of all points smaller or equal to x is called front cone, and the set of all points greater or equal to x is called posterior cone. CIP means that if x and y are not ordered, then x and the front cone of y intersect, x and the posterior cone of y as well intersect.

$$\forall x, y \in X : x\ \overline{li}\ y \rightarrow \exists u, v : u < x < v \wedge u < y < v. \tag{16.20}$$

The relation among x, y, u, and v are as shown in Fig. 16.5, in which (b) is the same co as (a), but (16.20) is not true for u and v. It is difficult to propose (16.20) in terms (X, co).

The last two axioms can be derived from strict partial order $(X, <)$ that satisfy (16.1) to (16.20). They are worthy to be given explicitly.

If the front cone of x plus y is the front cone of y, then there is a jump between x and y, as shown in Fig. 16.6.

Axiom (16.15) does not allow jump. There is no point between x and y in Fig. 16.6, y is the direct successor of x. Such relation between x and y is denoted by $x < \cdot\, y$,

$$< \cdot = < - <^2.$$

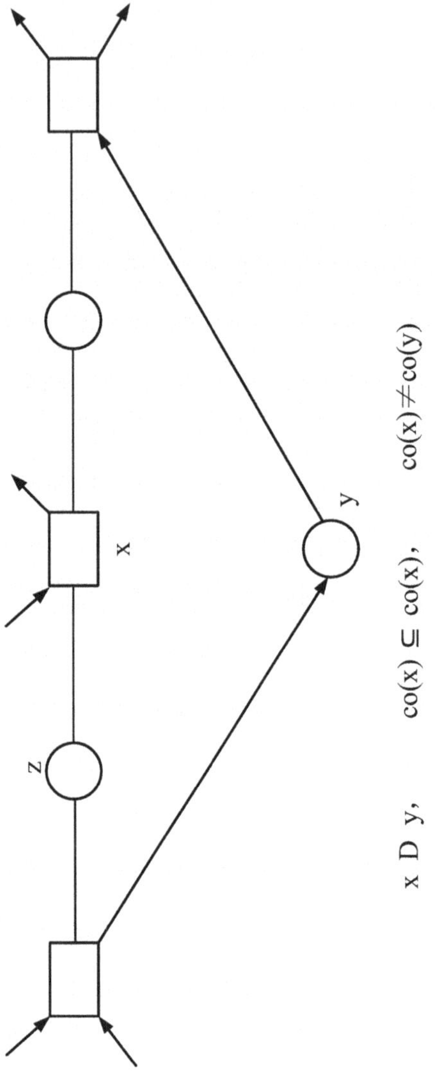

Fig. 16.4 *x* is the detail of *y*

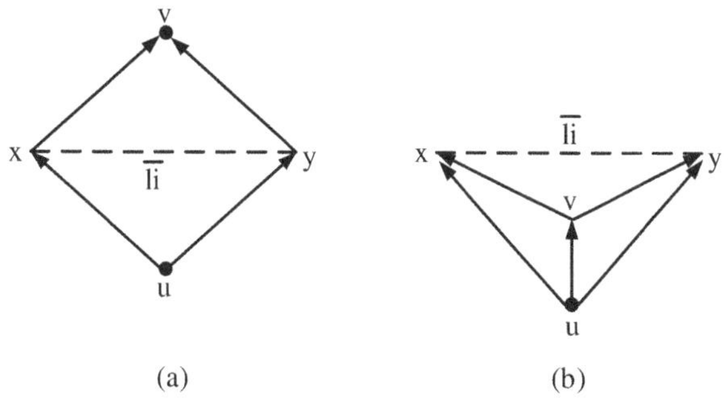

Fig. 16.5 (**a**) CIP property (**b**) $x\ \overline{li}\ y$, but not CIP

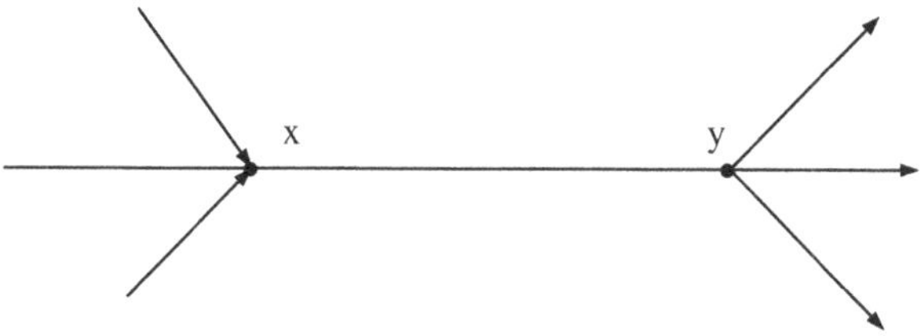

Fig. 16.6 Jump

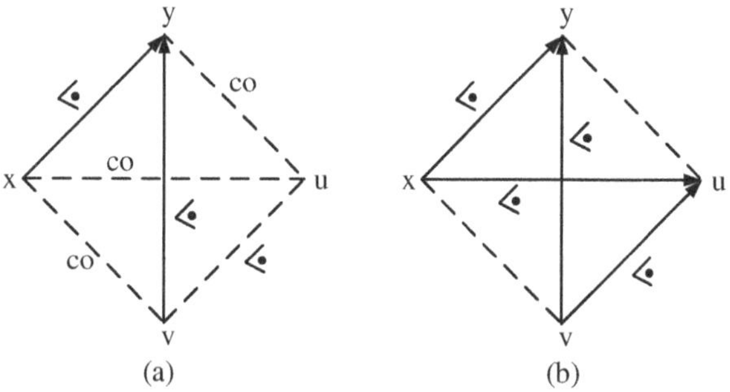

Fig. 16.7 (**a**) Gap of type G1, (**b**) Gap of type G2

If strict partial order $(X, <)$ satisfies $\leq\, = \ <\cdot^*$, then $(X, <)$ is a combinatorial order. For combinatorial order $<$, if $x < y$, then y can be reached through a finite number of direct successors.

If $(X, <)$ has an N-shaped structure as given at the time N-dense was defined, but point z required by N-dense does not exist, then $(X, <)$ contains a gap of type G1. The gaps shown in Fig. 16.7 are of type G1 in (a) and type G2 in (b).

To remove point z from Fig. 16.4 that explains $x\ D\ y$, obtained is a gap of type G1. If a point is deleted from X, obtained is a gap of type G2.

$$(X, <)\text{ is a strict combinatorial partial order with } K - \text{dense property, no jump, no gap of type G1.} \tag{16.21}$$

$$(X, <) \text{ is a strict combinatorial partial order with } K\text{ – dense property, no jump, no gap of type G2.} \quad (16.22)$$

If (16.21) is true, then $(X, <)$ is G1D continuous. If (16.22) is true, then $(X, <)$ is G2D continuous.

Though the above 22 axioms contain much repetition, they are not complete yet. It is not a complete description of concurrency. These axioms aim at important properties of intransitive concurrency, especially to describe transitive structures and properties with intransitive concurrency. I hope to describe all implementable signal structures, discrete (digit type) or continuous (simulation type).

Epilogue

Application is the mere purpose of Petri nets, but it is not applicable everywhere. It is suitable for the description and analysis of concurrent and distributed systems. Besides, flow of resources (materials, signals, data or information, etc.) is among its main characters.

There have existed many research papers in the literature, and many new elements (figures) have been added in order to promote the power of nets. But in fact, the power of nets is equivalent to Turing machine. So, new elements may be added, but not to promote modeling power. Rather, it is to make application easier.

Data types have been added to nets, and C-nets have been proposed and used for business process management in this book. The author welcomes criticism from readers.

C. Yuan, *Principle of Petri Nets*, https://doi.org/10.1007/978-981-97-7336-7

Appendix 1

Preface written by C. A. Petri for the "Petri Nets"

Status Report on Net Theory—Foreword

C. A. Petri

Twenty-nine years ago, net theory of communication was initiated by my doctoral thesis entitled "Communication With Automata." At the time of this writing, the plan which was described in that thesis is just carried out; the project approaches completion.

From its very start, net theory was based on physics; it was, in fact, a physical theory proposed in the language of computer science. Theoretical computer science, at the time, consisted of theories of automata and of formal languages (classes of symbol strings). It was shown that the conceptual framework of computer science (of 1960) was not suitable to describe a physical system. One important item missing in computer science was the notion of concurrency, the symmetric relation between two distinct world-points (space-time points in the sense of relativity theory) which describes them as unconnected by a causal chain: separated in space, but not reachable from each other by a light signal because of the bounded velocity of light. It was exceedingly difficult to persuade scientists of 1960 that concurrency had anything to do with computer science, and that its non-transitivity which is so obvious in relativity was part of the very essence of signaling.

Today, every beginner knows at least of the practical importance of concurrency, for example, in parallel processing. To make this basic concept of concurrency visible to the eye, I invented and later improved a graphical notation for combinatorial physical processes and systems, along with a game which could be played with little pieces, or "tokens," which mirrored elementary physical symmetries in such a way that the playing of the game was a simulation of a physical process. Please keep

C. Yuan, *Principle of Petri Nets*, https://doi.org/10.1007/978-981-97-7336-7

in mind that the graphical notation and the rules of the game are not net theory, but only illustrate some theorems of net theory.

The ambitious plan of 1960 was to formulate all "natural laws" which govern processes of communication in a language and conceptual framework which included both physics and computer science. To this end, computer science was enriched by the notion of concurrency; today, we know of a well-established duality theorem which asserts, among other things, that concurrency is the precise dual of choice (e.g., the choice of a program path by executing an if-statement). Today, we also know that net theory can pay its debt to physics back: just as space and time cannot be separated in a transformation of motion, in order to comply to Lorentz invariance—so also space, time, and statespace cannot be separated in a transformation of process (the process associated with a particle is the history of its life, namely the history of the position it occupied in statespace and in space, together with the transitions from one position to another).

In order to apply net theory with success, it is by no means necessary to study physics, or to remember the physical interpretation of net theory. Rather, a user of net theory can forget these and can just rely on the fact that every net which we can specify explicitly (draw on paper) can be connected by a short (≤ 4) chain of net morphisms to the physical real world; your net is, in a very precise sense, physically implementable. The four morphisms denote:

1. An injection. You don't want to describe the universe, but a (small) part of it. That part is—unlike the universe—not a system which is closed with respect to the flow of matter, energy, and information.
2. A refinement. You don't want to describe your system in all physical details, the elementary physical interactions, but very much coarser (factors of 10^{30} are typical for hardware).
3. A breaking of physical symmetries. You want to have a definite direction (from past to future) for the execution of processes, whereas the "perfect net" of the physical universe is time reversal-invariant.
4. An abstraction from what, in your purposeful activity, belongs together. You need a concept which ties, for example, the switching events or program steps which belong to the execution of a computer transaction or of a commercial transaction between people together to a pragmatic unit. These ties are not just physical ones; they are a necessity for your mind since you want to conceive of a large distributed physical (technical) process as a whole as something of which no physical part can be omitted without destroying the idea of a complete, or balanced, transaction.

March 23, 1989

Bibliography

1. Best, E., Devillers, R.: Concurrent behavior: sequences, processes and programming languages. Studien der GMD No. 99 (1985)
2. Best, E., Randell, B.: A formal model of atomicity in asynchronous systems. Acta Infom. **16**, 93–124 (1981)
3. Brauer, W. (ed): Net Theory and Applications, vol 84. Springer LNCS (1980)
4. Castellano, L.: BETA-processes of C/E_Systems. Workshop on petri nets, Espoo (1985). In: Rzenberg, G. (ed.) To appear in: "advances in Petri nets 1985". Springer Verlag
5. Commoner, F.: Deadlocks in Petri nets. Report, Applied Data Inc., CA-7206-2311 (1972)
6. Commoner, F., Holt, A.W., Even, S., Pnueli, A.: Marked directed graphs. JCSS. **5**, 511–523 (1971)
7. Devillers, R.: The semantics of capacities in P/T_nets: a first Look. Workshop on Petri nets, Espoo (1985)
8. Fernandez, C., Nielesen, M., Thiagarajan, P.S.: A note on observable occurrence nets. In: Rozenberg, G. (ed.) Advances in Petri Nets 1984, pp. 122–138. Springer Verlag (1985)
9. Ferandez, C., Thiagarajan, P.S.: D-continuous causal nets: a model of nosequential processes. TCS. **28**, 171–196 (1984)
10. Genrich, H.J., Lautenbach, K., Thiagarajian, P.S.: Elements of General Net Theory. In [4], pp. 21–163
11. Genrich, H.J., Stankiewicz-Wiechno, E.: A Dictionary of Some Basic Notions of Net Theory. In: [4], pp. 519–535
12. Goltz, U., Chong-Yi, Y.: Synchronic structure. In: Rozenberg, G. (ed.) Advances in Petri Nets 1985. Springer Verlag
13. Nielsen, M., Plotkin, G., Winskel, G.: Petri nets, event structures and domains I. TCS. **13**, 85–108 (1981)
14. Jantzen, M., Valk, R.: Formal Properties of Place/Transition Nets. In: 4, pp. 165–212
15. Peterson, J.L.: Petri Net Theory and Modelling of System. Prentice Hall, Hoboken (1981)
16. Petri, C.A.: Nosequential Processes. GMD-ISF Report 77.5 (1977)
17. Petri, C.A.: Concurrency as a basis of systems thinking. GMD-ISF Report 78-06 (September 1978). In: Proc. 5th Scandinavian Logic Symposium, AalBorg (1979)
18. Petri, C.A.: Concurrency. In: [3]. pp. 251–260
19. Petri, C.A.: State transition structures in physics and in computation. Int J Theor Phys. **21**(12), 979–992 (1982)
20. Resig, W.: Petri Nets: an Introduction. Springer EATCS Monographs in Theoretical Computer Science (1985)
21. Resisg, W.: On the Semantics of Petri nets. Bericht No. 100, Fachbereich Informatik, Universit at Hamburg (1984)

C. Yuan, *Principle of Petri Nets*, https://doi.org/10.1007/978-981-97-7336-7

22. Voss, K., Genrich, H.J., Rozenberg, G. (ed.): Concurrency and Nets, Springer-Verlag (1986)
23. Petri, C.A.: Nets, Time and Space. Theoretical Computer Sience, vol. 153. no. 1–2, pp. 3–48 (1996)
24. Wil van der Aalst, Kees van Hee, Workflow Management Models, Methods and Systems, 1st ed., MIT Press (2002)
25. van der Aalst, W.M.P.: Verification of workflow nets. In: Application and Theory of Petri nets 1997, volume 1248 of Lecture notes in computer science, pp. 407–426. Springer-Verlag, Berlin (1997)
26. van der Aalst, W.M.P.: The application of petri nets to workflow management. J. Circuits Syst. Comp. **8**(1), 21–66 (1998)
27. Prior, C.: Workflow and Process Management, Workflow Management Coalition Handbook 2002 (2002)
28. Plesums, C.: Introduction to Workflow, Workflow Management Coalition Handbook 2002 (2002)
29. Sadiq, W., Orlowska, M.E.: Analyzing process models using graph reduction techniques. Inform. Syst. **25**(2), 117–134 (2000)
30. Work Group 1, WfMC specification, interface 1: process definition interchange organizational model (1998). http://www.wfmc.org
31. Bider, I., Khomyakov M.: Is it possible to make workflow management systems flexible? Dynamical systems approach to business processes. Proceedings of Six International Workshop on Grupware, pp. 138–141. CRIWG2000, IEEE Computer Society Press (2000)
32. van der Aalst, W.M.P., Stoffele, M., Wamelink, J.W.F.: Case handling in construction. Autom. Construct. **12**(3), 303–320 (2003)
33. van der Aalst, W.M.P.: Three good reasons for using a petri-net-based workflow management system. In: Navathe, S., Wakayama, T. (eds.) Proceedings of the International Working Conference on Information and Process Integration in Enterprises (IPIC'96), pp. 179–201, Cambridge (1996)
34. Mani Chandy, K., Misra, J.: Parallel Program Design—A Foundation. Addison-Wesley Publishing Company
35. Zhou Guo-fu, Y., Peng, Y.C.-Y., Wan-ling, Q.: UniNet description of program. J. Syst. Simul. **8**, 85–88 (2003)
36. Chong-Yi, Y.: S_invariants in cyber net systems. J. Comput. Sci. Technol. **10**(3), 239–252 (1995)
37. Jensen, K.: Colored Petri Nets. Springer-Verlag, Berlin (1997)
38. Petri, C.A.: Kommunikation mit Automaten. PhD thesis, Institut fur Instrumentelle Mathematik Bonn, Germany (1962). In German
39. Lecture Notes in Computer Science, 84 (1979)
40. Lecture note in Computer Science, 188 (1984)
41. Lecture note in Computer Science, 222 (1985)
42. Lecture note in Computer Science, 254, 255 (1986)
43. Chongyi, Y.: Principles of Petri Nets. Publishing House of Electronics Industry (1998)
44. Chongyi, Y.: Principles and Applications of Petri Nets. Publishing House of Electronics Industry (2005)
45. Zhehui, W.: Introduction to Petri Nets. Machine Press, China (2006). Yuan, C.-Y., Zhao, W., Zhang, S.-K., Huang, Y.: A three layer model for business process—Process logic, case semantics and workflow management. J. Comp. Sci. Technol. 22(3), 410–425 (2007)
46. Chongyi, Y.: Assignment: operation on a physical object. J. Front. Comp. Sci. Technol. **2**(5), 487–499 (2008)
47. Chongyi, Y., Yu, H., Wen, Z.: Program: expressions of operations on physical objects. J. Front. Comp. Sci. Technol. **3**(2), 144–153 (2009)
48. Chongyi, Y., Wen, Z., Xin, G., Huang, Y.: Definitions and specifications of O-expressions. J. Front. Comp. Sci. Technol. **4**(1), 20–28 (2010)

49. Chongyi, Y., Huang, Y., Wen, Z., Shuzhi, H.: O-expression: a petri net representation. J. Front. Comp. Sci. Technol. **4**(11), 961–976 (2010)
50. Chongyi, Y., Wen, Z., Yu, H.: A way to verify software. Proceedings of the 2010 world congress
51. Yuan, C., Huang, Y., Zhao, W., Li, X.: A study on fairness of place/transition systems—to make fairness fairer. Trans. Inst. Meas. Control. **33**(1), 55–58 (2011)., ISSN 0142-3312

The manufacturer's authorised representative in the EU is Springer Nature Customer Service Centre GmbH, Europaplatz 3, 69115 Heidelberg, Germany. If you have any concerns regarding our products, please contact ProductSafety@springernature.com

Printed and bound by CPI Group (UK) Ltd, Croydon, CR0 4YY
01/10/2026
02225934-0003